Painted Walls of Mexico

NUMBER THREE

The Elma Dill Russell Spencer Foundation Series

PAINTED
WALLS
OF
MEXICO

From Prehistoric Times until Today

Text by Emily Edwards

Photographs by Manuel Álvarez Bravo

Foreword by Jean Charlot

UNIVERSITY OF TEXAS PRESS
AUSTIN & LONDON

Typesetting by Service Typographers, Inc., Indianapolis, Indiana
Printing by the Meriden Gravure Company,
Meriden, Connecticut
Binding by Universal Bookbindery, Inc., San Antonio, Texas

To Bodil Christensen

This book tells the story of Mexican murals equally well in words and with pictures. Though it is an objective report, documented and exhaustive, no reader could be misled into believing that it is yet another thesis, constructed by some conscientious and gifted post graduate intent on a Ph.D.

Indeed not! Both authors—writer and photographer —were vitally involved in the esthetic drama whose roots reached back to the nineteen-twenties, when the mural renaissance was acquiring bulk and style. Only a handful of painters shared with a handful of friends the load of these lean years. The hand that held the brush moved over the damp fresco mortar to the rhythm of an obbligato of jeers and catcalls. Perched high on the mural scaffold, his back turned to this blatantly critical world, the painter himself hardly knew where, if ever, he would gain support and understanding.

Those who shared this moment cannot forget its mood. As I read the text and ponder the plates, I share again with both authors the throbbing drama. Memories pull at the leash of scholarly apparatus that the very form of the book demands. Achieving their goal of objectivity, the authors add to it a bonus. No reader could remain immune to the veiled fever that they felt, and that he feels in turn, and that communicates better than any statistics the quality of the exciting subject matter.

Emily Edwards, with enthusiasm, marshals such voluminous and complex data that one less familiar with the story would falter under the load. Manuel Álvarez Bravo is impelled by the same fervor. If one should pick the most impersonal of visual media, documentary photography would be the choice. Yet no artist who did not experience the excitement of the mural revolution, even if master of an equally exacting technique, could match the beauty of these pictures. That is perhaps because Alvarez Bravo, unconsciously, has blended into one the portrait of Mexico and his self-portrait. Thus, thanks to the common outlook of the authors, an all-pervasive *mexicanidad* informs both the text and the plates of this book, raising it to a more coherent level than would a recital of facts only.

Mexican art is one in three. As we follow its transformations through two milleniums, its organic wholeness appears to suffer violence, sliced as it is into three broad segments, Pre-Hispanic, Colonial, and Modern. The three appear at odds, even at war with each other. How could the theogonical drama that spills human blood down the steep steps of pagan pyramids ever dovetail into the Murillo-esque graces of the Seven Archangels holding lilies? In turn, how could these eighteenth-century *santos* be kin to the loud frescoes painted in the twenties of our century, that flaunt red banners and brandish clenched fists?

Yet the three styles are but masks that the one individual, Mexico, puts on at wish, or discards. Deeply embedded in soil and race, underlying themes bridge unscathed from one era into the next. Typical is the persistence of the theme of death. Skulls are piled up on Aztec temple racks. The Catholic hermit hugs a skull to his breast as a reminder of bodily corruption. About 1900 Guadalupe Posada, no muralist himself but an unpolluted mirror for *mexicanidad*, portrayed skulls decked in the accoutrements of the living: clerical skulls topped with a biretta, feminine skulls under beflowered hats, military skulls with waxed mustache and plumed shako. In the forties, when Pablo O'Higgins and Leopoldo Méndez decorated a newly built maternity hospital, their first care was to paint on its walls a female skeleton some thirty feet tall!

Mural painting presupposes in its maker a certain amount of selflessness. The painted wall is only a fragment of an architectural complex. Communication remains its essence, and the message must be stated in terms clear to the man in the street, the devout in his church, or the unionized worker in the meeting hall. By definition a mural is not intended to cater to the specialized art lover. Walls are not a proper surface for a naked display of self, a dialogue between the id and the ego. Some of the finest moments in the history of art remain antimural in essence. Such are, in our century, the esoterical probings of analytical cubism and, later on, the outpourings of abstract expressionism. The mural painter, as he plies his craft, soon learns to use a healthy dose of humility.

It so happened that in any century when walls beckoned to Mexican artists they themselves were preconditioned to the task. This mural vocation was never a matter of ignorance but of choice. Mexican art is not ignorant of foreign arts, but rather cautious in regard to their lure. At times Mexicans work with the grain. In the seventeenth century imported Zurbarans of the morose kind could hardly be distinguished from the local product. Eighteenth-century artists gratefully acknowledged the lessons of Spain. The Royal Academy of the Fine Arts of San Carlos of New Spain, founded in Mexico City, modeled itself and its teachings on the Royal Academy of San Fernando of Madrid. In our century Paris replaced Madrid for the Mexican artist. A Montparnasse exile for more than a decade, Rivera, together with Gino Severini, took part in the elusive hunt for a fourth dimension that crossed over the borderline of the metaphysical into higher mathematics. At the same time, Siqueiros, stranded in Italy, tried his hand at *pittura metafisica* along the lines stated by Carlo Carra. Europe could have spoiled for those artists a native taste for mural painting. Paris prided itself on its sophistication. Master painters conquered peak after peak in their quest for the esoteric. The nonartist, the bourgeois, was soon left behind, quite out of breath.

Paris shunned all forms of didacticism and shied away from even the mildest of storytelling. Nineteenth-century Romanticism seemed gross, with its accent on experiences shared by all men—passion and pain and death. The position of the elite was well stated by Jean Cocteau in a self-satisfied dictum: the relation between the molding of a chair and the corner of a table holds for us a drama equal to that of the cornered lion devouring the burnoused Arab hunter.

At that very time, Mexican artists, now including Rivera and Siqueiros, who had returned to the *patria,* felt themselves compelled to work against the grain of the Parisian trend. Murals dictated their attitude, and their style in turn was adapted to the many who looked at the murals, not the least among them the masons who, day after day, in close communion with the painters, troweled the walls for the frescoes.

From the local point of view it would be true to say that the rest of the world was out of step with Mexico. What was being spread on public walls came close to what the seventeenth century had called *peinture d'histoire.* Mexicans painted history in the making, its actors, heroes and villains alike, still alive or freshly dead. Their aims were didactic, and communication with the nonartist was a must. To this end they stressed anew the old-fashioned themes that Paris had discarded—passion and pain and death. It was of course a sincere reflection of the highly dynamic moment and milieu. Naturally, outside Mexico the work was branded as insufferably unfashionable. A visitor who was also a well-known art critic, with the forlorn hope of deflecting us toward saner ways, suggested that all Mexican muralists should subscribe to Parisian vanguard magazines!

That was in the twenties. Fashions change. Social conditions change. In the thirties, Mother Spain became involved in a civil war that, for turmoil and bloodletting, came close to matching the ways of its errant child, Mexico. Spanish Picasso reacted as the Mexicans had. He painted *Guernica,* a mural. In it, anguished mothers hug to their breasts murdered infants. The bull has gored the horse. Its gashed carcass collapses over the dead hero, a broken sword still clenched in his fist. American and European art lovers, who knew that Picasso could do no wrong, were led to reassess the esthetic potential of historical painting. Seen in the new light, the Mexican murals seemed less obtuse, and the ways of their makers less provincial. Already, fifteen years before *Guernica,* the Mexicans had forcefully stated the artist's right to deal in intense human drama, and his duty to master didactic requirements. As usual, the muralists were too busy at work to notice the change of wind in the international critical atmosphere, and too involved in fresh problems to tip their hat to Picasso.

The uniqueness of Mexican art comes from its refusal to merge unquestioningly in the international picture of the moment, of any moment. As we have seen, it goes at times with the grain, at other times against the grain. It does so for reasons that always are its own. This stubborn attitude in the face of outside pressures is what saves Mexican art as an entity, a self that takes many forms and yet always remains itself. If one would pluck a parallel from the many to be found in the history of art, I would choose the case of Peter Breughel. Still in his twenties, he left his Lowlands and toured Italy. The Renaissance was at its height, with already a touch of overripeness. From all Europe artists flocked to Rome, and to Florence, and to Parma. Breughel was but one among that flock of young artists. Perhaps we remember him today as the one true master among them, because, far from deflecting his style toward Italian grandeur as did the many, he realized instead, face to face with the *Last Judgment,* that his task was inverse. It was to remain true to race and to country. Breughel returned to his Northern *patria* more consciously Flemish than when he had left it. Perhaps Rivera, in history, would never have been as Mexican as he is, had he not experienced years of exile in that Rome of his day, Paris, and had he not reacted in the end as Breughel did before him.

JEAN CHARLOT

PREFACE

Diego Rivera instigated the making of this book. He had seen murals that were painted both before and after the Conquest of Mexico and had admired decorations on the walls of popular gathering places: he was convinced that the people of Mexico have always painted their walls. This work was undertaken to illustrate his belief.

That was long ago, when relatively few paintings of remote antiquity had as yet been unearthed, when Mexico's mural renaissance was still young. To photograph known murals and to make a descriptive catalogue of their sites did not then seem to be an impossible task. Through succeeding years this record has been augmented, concurrently with the constant dramatic emergence of fresh murals from all periods; the authors, striving to catch up with the times, have never found a stopping place. The reader is invited to share in the adventure of discovery of both old and new wall paintings in this rich field of Mexican art so recently come into its own.

The photographs in this book, taken from murals that span more than two thousand years of cultural life in Mexico, form an autographic history of the successive peoples whose civilizations have flourished here. The genius of the people is tied to the land, and their art from all ages is Mexican art. The visual material objectively presented here makes its own comment as art. The text gives the locations and descriptions of the painted walls, and indicates the links of time and circumstance that connect them.

Our record of mural painting from the successive periods, though not exhaustive, does follow the main stream of this Mexican tradition, with indication of its confluent currents—a stream that continues to flow through time from deep springs. The story of Mexico's painted walls is told for the interested reader, rather than the specialist. The pursuit of this subject has been exciting—because of art which is found exactly where it was painted, which expresses the sense of place and of rapport between people and place, and which reveals the knowledge and beliefs that have ruled the artists and their times. The forgotten, buried cultures come alive again through art created to influence forgotten gods; later ages are revealed through art undertaken to influence men; and the long tradition is pictured here—from the magical singing walls of Teotihuacan* to the modern walls that sometimes shout their messages for the present time.

In every instance the photograph has been taken from the original painting on the wall—an effort which in itself was no small undertaking. When the record was begun very little had been written about Mexican murals and this little not recently enough to be a safe guide. Many excursions were made to search for paintings. Sometimes a long trip taken to photograph recorded murals led to the disappointing discovery that the paintings had all but disappeared. Experience of the murals has been supplemented by reading whatever relates to this art. For such an extensive field, both in area and in time, a great number of sources have necessarily been consulted. So this book, in order to suggest the milieu of wall paintings, makes a resumé or synthesis of research by scholars in different periods of Mexican culture. Any errors, however, are our own.

Until archeology began to extract Mexico's past from the earth that had swallowed it all knowledge of pre-Conquest civilizations had to be acquired from the chronicles of learned friars, who set down oral legends in which history and mythology mingle. After the first fierce destruction of codices and temples by the Conquerors the monks had realized that these legends were all that remained of Mexico's history. The few codices that escaped destruction, or were painted by Indian artists after the Conquest, suggest the kind of painting that flourished just before the Spaniards arrived. Knowledge of the art of Early Mexico is being enriched by paintings found or excavated in ruins of ancient cities, some of which had been forgotten long before Europeans first reached these shores. Most especially, in Teotihuacan, the immense pyramid city of the Valley of Mexico, archeological paintings recovered from the earlier Classic Horizon establish that this was an elaborately painted city.

* A note here on the spelling of Nahuatl proper names in this book might be helpful. It seems appropriate to spell these words so as to indicate Nahuatl pronunciation. According to Mexican scholars Nahuatl *always* stresses the penultimate syllable; since no exceptions occur, no accents are necessary. For this reason the accents imposed on some spellings by Spanish influence, to which modern readers have become accustomed, do not appear in this account.

Our photographs are from relatively few well-known sites—samples, as it were, of an art that once existed in great abundance. Mexico's scholars are gradually making the connection between chronicles and sites, and the vigorous new science of Mexican anthropology is nourished by intensive research. Admittedly, much dating in prehistory is tentative. Division into cultural horizons offers a convenient solution, but these do not coincide exactly in the various regions. The use of radioactive carbon in dating has resulted in a revision of chronology, with a tendency to move earliest monuments backward in relation to the Christian Era. In the establishment of distribution and continuity of archeological mural art, some sites in which paintings no longer exist are included; but ancient art continues to be found. All archeological zones can be visited.

The earth stirs—it is like watching a sleeping giant in the act of waking as the earth relinquishes hidden human treasure from its prehistoric past. Art builds a bridge between the spirit of man and his environment, and its expression is all that is bequeathed to us by the remote past. The painted walls uncovered here bear revelations from the mysterious peoples of Early Mexico.

Four and a half turbulent centuries have passed over Mexico since Spaniards first approached the mainland of Mesoamerica, or Middle America, to discover "Mexican magnificence." During this time, through conquest, colonial rule, revolts, invasions, and revolution, mural art has never ceased to be a cultural solvent in Mexico. The successive styles, as wave after wave of alien influence has been absorbed into Mexican visual expression, are recorded here, illustrated in wall paintings made in the service of the Church and, also, for other needs of the community, as public painting has continued to be a form of communication for Mexicans in different walks of life.

A creative current has flowed strongly on public walls in the wake of the Mexican Revolution of 1910. Assertion of a national art was inherent in the Revolution and, also, in the initiation of the mural decoration of public buildings by José Vasconcelos, as Minister of Education, in 1920. Further inspiration came in 1921 through eloquent appeals to young artists of the Americas to create their own modern art, appeals published in Barcelona by David Alfaro Siqueiros, a young veteran of the Mexican Revolution. He proclaimed that modern art must be expressed as public art: monumental, heroic, human—related to the Machine Age and, also, to great art of the past, including native American art; an art revolutionary both in form and in content.

The ensuing mural movement surged from different emotional springs: Diego Rivera's loving rediscovery of his native land and of its cultural heritage; José Clemente Orozco's need for mural art to create "a new world"; Siqueiros' concept of art as revolution; Jean Charlot's identification of his art with the plastic expression of Mexico; and as many other motivations as there were participants. For the few muralists who created the Mexican Mural Renaissance, as for the many artists who later entered its current, to paint on walls has proved to be an irrevocable commitment, holding them for life.

The complex Mexican Revolution has been continued on these public walls. Officially sponsored, the steady flow of mural art in public places testifies to the general delight of the Mexican people in visual expression, as well as to their interest in following the many Mexican visions of the past, the present, and the future unfolded on these walls.

This book is made in homage to Mexico's cultural tradition. The highly interesting quality of Mexican art and scholarship has greatly rewarded our pursuit of the long course of mural expression in this land. Photographer and writer, like the muralists themselves, were caught into the creative stream—enchanted, bewitched by an authentic art that integrates the land and the people.

ACKNOWLEDGMENTS

"Painted Walls of Mexico" is essentially a work of collaboration—not only between photographer and writer, but between the authors and many persons who have aided in gathering and presenting this illustration and description of Mexico's long mural tradition.

The original plan, followed through the years, was made with the assistance of muralist Pablo O'Higgins, who also accompanied the authors on their first photographic explorations for murals of all eras, thus helping them to get started.

Bodil Christensen, dedicated student of the native arts and traditions of Mexico, has given steadfast guidance to this work as it progressed, freely sharing her selective library, which has magically disclosed sorely needed information, and her alert awareness of new mural developments. First explorations for Colonial and Popular murals were made in the company of Miss Christensen and her late sister, Helga Larsen, by bus and on horseback through the state of Morelos. More recently various mural sites from all periods have been visited with Miss Christensen.

Lawrence W. Fontaine took the authors by automobile over almost impassable roads, in the states of México, Tlaxcala, and Puebla, to search for murals and to photograph them.

Author-archeologist Doris Heyden contributed most special help in locating murals, in completing a chronology of mural photographs, and in reviewing data from different periods.

Some needed photographs have been generously given by Jean Charlot from records of his original research. For a few sites, where it was not feasible for the authors to make their own photographs, prints have been supplied from files of the National Institute of Anthropology and History (INAH) and from newspaper files. The authors are indebted to the Fondo Editorial de la Plástica Mexicana for the use of some photographs made by Manuel Álvarez Bravo for this great publishing house of Mexican art, which now generously shares them for reproduction in this volume. The great mass of mural photographs included here, however, have been made specifically for this book. Many of these could not now be taken; this is especially true of the perishable paintings of the people, "Arte Popular," of which perhaps not one represented here now survives.

Mexican officials charged with the preservation of National Monuments have courteously provided us through the years with *permisos* to photograph the murals, a special permit being required for each site. The director of promotion, Ing. Joaquin Cortina, has granted the University of Texas Press license to publish the photographs of murals from Pre-Conquest and Colonial monuments, all objects of Mexico's cultural heritage being under official supervision and control.

Generous assistance has been given the authors by specialists in different areas of Mexican art and archeology. Dr. Sylvanus G. Morley, late director of the Chichén Itzá project for the Carnegie Institution of Washington, facilitated progress by helping us secure photographic details of Mayan murals that have since disappeared. Part One was named "Early Mexico" for the authors by Mexico's late brilliant artist-archeologist, author Miguel Covarrubias. Studies of archeological murals by Dr. Alfonso Caso, distinguished Mexican anthropologist, which explore the beliefs and values of the great periods of native civilizations, are the principal sources for interpretation of the wall paintings in Central and Southern Mexico. Salvador Toscano, late historian of Pre-Colombian Art, in 1944 made a most helpful summary of the known murals of Early Mexico. Dr. Ignacio Bernal is responsible for information about recent mural discoveries in Teotihuacan, and he has supplied photographs of these for reproduction. Manuel Toussaint, late noted historian of Mexico's Colonial Art, while director of the Department of Colonial Monuments had investigated much mural art from the sixteenth century; his writings greatly facilitated our search for wall paintings from this period for Part Two. The work by Robert Ricard has been an authority for the distribution of the mendicant orders and their monasteries during the sixteenth century. George Kubler throws much light on the architectural and communal development of Colonial monasteries and churches. Elizabeth Wilder Weismann has assisted with precise information about Colonial murals.

Part Three, Academic Art, rests almost exclusively on writings by muralist Jean Charlot, based on his original research on the art of the nineteenth century.

In Part Four, the most original section of this book, Manuel Álvarez Bravo focuses attention for the first time on the mural art of the people of Mexico, an art that presumably has never failed of expression throughout Mexico's eventful history. Although Popular paintings are fast disappearing from the cities of Mexico, information about wall paintings in remote towns, contributed by artist Dorothy Loeb, indicates that some semi-Popular mural art still survives from the past century. New paintings appear sporadically throughout Mexico.

For Part Five of this work, in which this record is brought to the art of today, various muralists, writing eloquently of their art and of their time, have been original sources of information and understanding. We are most greatly indebted to Jean Charlot for his carefully recorded experience as a participant in the rebirth of mural painting in Mexico, and for his research on the preceding period, which in 1963 he reported in *The Mexican Mural Renaissance: 1920–1925*. Jean Charlot, however, had previously loaned to the writer of this account the manuscript of an earlier version, his original research forming the basis for Part Five of this book. Some data for recent sites have been obtained from the Plenns' mural guide.

The making of this book has been both an adventure and a discipline. The adventure of discovery began for the writer on a Texas ranch, when she was awakened in the middle of the night by artist Lucy Maverick, to be shown by lantern light the first photographs of modern Mexican murals to come out of Mexico—intercepted briefly on the way to New York for publication.

During several seasons early in the mural movement Diego Rivera most generously conducted classes in the analysis of great works of art for interested fellow artists, among whom this writer was privileged to be included. The quality of his imparted knowledge has contributed, certainly, to the general excellence of mural work done in Mexico during the contemporary period. The writer is indebted to Rivera for any special understanding of this art.

A list of those who have contributed to the writing of this book would be endless. The initial research in Mexico's mural tradition was sponsored by Narciso Bassols as Minister of Education. Among the friendly critics who have given the writer courage to proceed, Sibyl Browne, Jean and Zohmah Charlot, Carolyn Zeleny, A. Hyatt Mayor, and most especially Charles Ramsdell come instantly to mind.

Various versions of the text have been typed and retyped, notably by nieces Floy Fontaine Jordan and Frances Waller Syfan, and by friends Helga Larsen and Florence Whipple Dies.

The manuscript of *Painted Walls of Mexico*, after having been laid aside for some years, was introduced to the University of Texas Press by Lois Wood Burkhalter; since this time it has been rewritten in its entirety and with reference to more recent developments. Mr. and Mrs. John Fielding Maher have made grants to assist in this work.

Mrs. Richard French Spencer, by including this volume in the Elma Dill Russell Spencer Foundation Series of the University of Texas Press, has assured its excellent production. The Press has coped patiently with this amateur writer in bringing the voluminous subject matter into orderly coherence within one volume.

A warm "thank you" goes to each of these cooperators, as well as to the many others, including members of our families, who can remember various special services that they have performed to help make this book possible.

E.E.
M.A.B.

CONTENTS

PLATES

(color plates in italics)

* On the maps the mural sites are numbered in accordance with the order in which they are discussed, and numbered, in the text. On pages opposite these maps they are listed in two ways: in the order of appearance in the text (numbered in series as they appear on the map) and in alphabetical order (with series, or map, number in parentheses).

Painted Walls of Mexico

Art is food for the nervous system and
as essential to human life as bread.

Artists are those who feel and express the
spirit of their times. Each region in the
world and each epoch has its own style of art.

DIEGO RIVERA (1930)

PART ONE: EARLY MEXICO

PART ONE: *Early Mexico,** 1700 B.C.-A.D. 1521

---

* Pre-Classic or Formative Horizon (1700–200 B.C.)
  Classic Horizon (200 B.C.–A.D. 900)
  Post-Classic Horizon (A.D. 900–1521)

The Beginnings of Mural Art in Mexico

The most intimate records of life in Early Mexico are painted on walls. Vestiges of mural art on some of the earliest monuments are known to us, and fragmentary painting from succeeding periods survive in many places, conserving for us knowledge of the beliefs and sensibilities—"the spiritual residue"—of the peoples whose patterns of culture were developed in this land.

Rock paintings of undetermined antiquity decorate an occasional cave or rock shelter in the canyons of rugged Western Mexico. In the far northwest, notably in Lower California, are found rock paintings that relate to others in adjacent areas of the United States, but not to the painted walls of tombs and temples left in Mexico by the city builders of the southern regions known as Mesoamerica. In these regions some paintings have been found on canyon walls, but they often refer to late periods of the city cultures, not to remote beginnings. The rock paintings, as they are usually superimposed, probably were intended to make the sites sacred for magic. The canyons have deepened through the centuries, until now painted caves and cliffs rise high above the beds of streams, and are difficult of access; they can be seen more easily from far than near. Sources of the great mural traditions of Early Mexico are being sought in paintings on rocks, in caves, and on structures made by man.

Mural paintings have been found in some of the earliest cities of Mesoamerica—the name given in Mexican archeology to the regions of related cultures which comprise the high central plateau of Mexico, the adjoining coastal plains, all of Mexico to south and east, and much of Central America. This volcanic land is formed by the great mountain ranges of North America, which converge in Central Mexico to rise as snow-capped peaks; southward the land mass lowers and breaks into the two highlands of Southern and Southeastern Mexico, the southeastern area being geographically and ethnically one with adjacent Guatemala and Honduras. Protected by water on all sides but the north, where a vast arid region flanked by mountain ranges makes a formidable barrier, and a short stretch on the south, where the land tapers off to the Isthmus of Panama, Mesoamerica permitted its early inhabitants to evolve their various cultures over a long period of time in relative peace and independence.

Throughout Mesoamerica the same basic culture, developed through astronomical calculations to regulate the growing of food crops, was general, and earliest monuments in the three highland regions show similar beginnings. These were theocratic societies ruled by priestly orders, with elaborate ceremonial centers built in populous areas. Cultural horizons, or stages of development, in all three regions were more or less contemporary, and influences of these evolving civilizations, one upon another, are being traced by acheologists in the field.

Of the great numbers of archeological sites known to exist throughout Mesoamerica, relatively few have been explored. Wherever monuments have been uncovered they have apparently been painted inside and out, and we can expect to continue to find traces of interesting murals as new sites are explored. Fragmentary bits of color clinging to plaster and to sculptured form indicate the magnificence of the polychrome decoration which everywhere has characterized this colorful land and establish the existence here of a continuous mural tradition. Fortunately, wall paintings have been found in enough sites to show the character of this art under various cultures.

Mural painting begins in the Pre-Classic, or Formative, Horizon, from which period few monuments are known, the Pyramid of Cuicuilco and the innermost structure of the Great Pyramid of Cholula being the chief ones.

In each of the three sections of the country the Formative Horizon of Mesoamerican cultures was followed by a Classic Horizon of great vitality, which began approximately with the Christian Era. A range of several centuries, including the time of Christ, has been accepted as the period for the emergence of the remarkable cultures evidenced in monuments from the Classic Horizon of Mesoamerica. So great was this cultural flowering during succeeding centuries that outside influence and knowledge were assumed to have been added to native accomplishments. The archeologist today painstakingly guards links that bind these two horizons, deciphered and undeciphered symbols holding many clues. The study of painted symbols and hieroglyphs indicates that wall painting was also a widely practiced system of writing.

Most interesting wall paintings survive from the Classic Horizon in the various divisions of Mesoamerica:

In Central Mexico murals have been excavated in a number of sites of the great pyramid city of Teotihuacan in the Valley of Mexico—paintings that survive from successive Classic Periods of Teotihuacan civilization.

In Southern Mexico, Monte Albán, built on a small mountain in the highland near Oaxaca City, contains tombs with murals from different periods of this ancient ceremonial center of the Zapotec people.

In Southeastern Mexico the remarkable paintings discovered in Bonampak in the Valley of the Usumacinta River have thrown new light on the Classic Horizon of Mayan civilization.

The ninth century witnessed a sudden end to the sacred city of Teotihuacan; a Post-Classic or Renaissance Horizon was developed upon ruins of this culture by the Toltec Nation in their city of Tollan, just over the northern rim of the Valley of Mexico. Gradually, through infiltration or conquest, the new culture of the Post-Classic Horizon was extended beyond Central Mexico to Northern and Western and to Southern and Southeastern Mexico. This horizon marks an apparent shift from the long period of theocratic rule throughout all of Mesoamerica to domination of the sedentary peoples of this land by tribes of migrating warriors, who continued to come in waves from beyond the northern fringes of Central Mexico. The newcomers brought to Mesoamerica new weapons and new gods; they contributed also great vitality, and they created new forms of art. The militarist Toltec culture is recorded in murals found in areas of Central, Southern, and Southeastern Mexico, the southeastern area including the Peninsula of Yucatán.

Recorded history in Mexico begins with dispersal of the Toltecs from Tollan in A.D. 1250. Migrations of hunting tribes from the north, the Chichimecs, culminated with those of the Aztecs, whom the Spanish—in 1519—found dominant in much of Mesoamerica. Scarcely anything so perishable as painted plaster has survived from the time of the destructive Spanish Conquest; the painted walls of this record had at that time been long lost in hidden or buried temples and in tombs. From these paintings rescued from the past we can judge of the wealth of mural material that has existed throughout this land.

Wall painting relates closely to other arts of Early Mexico—ceramics, sculpture, and architecture—of which great quantities have been recovered, and most especially to codices of which few have survived; mural art acquires interpretation from these sources. Styles of Mesoamerican art are classified as Mexican or Aztec for Central and Southern Mexico, and as Mayan for the arts of Southeastern Mexico and Central America. Although interrelations have existed among the various cultures, a very real difference of intention is found between the creative arts in these regions, "Mexican" or "Aztec" denoting an ample, severe, geometric art, with architecture expressed in horizontal forms and painting dedicated to religious uses, "Mayan" meaning an elaborate, concentrated, and natural form of expression, charactererized by architecture of aspiring vertical forms and by painting concerned with events from human life.

The record of known paintings from Early Mexico made here is not complete but, rather, suggestive of this rich tradition of mural art. The brief outline of history is offered to anchor these mural sites in place and time and style.

The photographs—true text of this book—have been taken in every instance from original paintings on walls in the various sites. Wall painting is a most perishable art. Despite the great care used in excavating and supervising ruins, the first paintings to be discovered have gradually been destroyed by the elements, the jungle, the populace, and the collectors. A few of the paintings represented here have disappeared since being photographed. Many wall paintings from Early Mexico now exist in copies only, which, however valuable for archeological study, do not give direct experience of the quality of this art.

Realizing the irreplaceable value of these wall paintings, officials of the National Institute of Anthropology and History in 1961 established a Department for Conservation of Pre-Hispanic and Colonial Murals, so that paintings can be located, preserved, and restored under expert direction. Among the responsibilities of the new department are careful investigation and analysis of techniques employed. Without this analysis, it has been general practice to consider all paintings on plaster as fresco painting.

A "fresco" is a painting made by applying water color

to a surface of fine lime-and-sand plaster while still wet, when the color integrates with the surface of the plaster as it sets, thus producing great durability. There are variations of this medium, such as color applied to moist limestone, called "accidental" fresco, and color mixed with plaster for use on exterior walls. The drawings for these old paintings were first incised with a thorn or painted with a fine brush in red; they were then filled in with colors by cooperating painters, and reoutlined in red or black by the master artist. Often, while still damp, the surface was burnished with a smooth rounded stone until it shone with the luster of enamel. It is a matter of conjecture as to whether this burnishing was done after the paint was applied, as practiced by masons in Mexico today, or before painting, as practiced by Greek mural painters, so that the burnished surface retained its moisture for weeks to allow painting in true fresco. Investigation by the new Mural Department may solve this question.

Sometimes pigment mixed with thick limewater has been spread over a previously dried surface. Also, "tempera," color mixed with an agglutinant, was often applied after the plaster was dry. Speculations about adhesive substances used have included juices of nopal or of orchid, and human blood. Through some chemical miracle true frescoes, and some judged not so true, have been found firm and brilliant in color after having been buried for more than a thousand years.

The pigments used are similar in many ruins, backgrounds being painted solidly in earth-red and figures being painted with a variety of rich earth tones juxtaposed with blue, like turquoise, or green of copper oxide, or with white, and all outlined in red or in black that turns to purple. Animal, mineral, and vegetable sources of colors were recorded at the time of the Conquest by Sahagún.

Painstaking observation of the rhythms of nature from temple observatories made possible the development of agriculture and the invention of remarkable calendars by priests of Mesoamerica; astronomical knowledge also inspired in them respect for the ordering principle and imposed upon their creations a framework of law derived from nature. For these worshipers of the sun, solar orientation was of first consideration and conditioned all plans of ceremonial centers. In Central and Southern Mexico the principal temples face west with a deviation of seventeen degrees to north, an angle which records the point of the sun's setting on those days when the sun passes directly over the zenith and at midday casts no shadow. In Southeastern Mexico the Mayas placed their temples to face the sunset on the days when days and nights are equal, which is to say the true west of the equinox.

Architectural details became elaborately geometric and formal. The sculptured idol, fashioned to embody an idea, tended to be solid and immobile like the architecture. Mural painting, incorporated with architecture, took form from it, and it was accommodated to the wall within the geometric law that governed the whole. But something new entered with painted form, for it moves within its frame to quicken consciousness, through elaborate detail it defines thought, and it frees the imagination to wander in regions to which it alludes.

Early Mexican painting belongs to an esthetic almost entirely different from Old World conceptions of beauty. Although wall paintings vary in design, from squat, angular forms of gods and priests loaded with hieroglyphic symbols and repeated in friezes, as seen in Teotihuacan, to figures taken from life and made to exist in a painted environment, as found in Bonampak, it is believed that no painting is primarily decorative or representative, but that each form and color and relationship, fulfilling the office of a written language and functioning as an instrument of magic, is surcharged with meaning. Priests ruled every aspect of culture in the theocratic systems under which Mesoamerican civilizations developed. In conducting human affairs they negotiated for control of destiny through rituals and sorceries with deities identified with heavenly bodies or with elements of the earth; painted forms became magic symbols to regulate the attributes and influences of the gods. Precise form and execution distinguish these painted walls, and hieratic rules of number and measure control form for its evocation of wonder, awe, terror. And always there is style—the unconscious, instinctive rhythm of the people.

It would be difficult to exaggerate the prevalence and great brilliance of the painted walls of Early Mexico. Pyramids, temples, palaces, tombs—all were enriched with designs in color. Wherever people congregated, monuments were built for communal pageantry in service of priests and gods, and everywhere wall decorations were an intrinsic part of this service. Some walls, gleaming white or red with burnished plaster, were settings for elaborate costumes of priests or warriors—as reflected in paintings. Exterior decoration, of which practically nothing has survived, was especially rich in temple courts—centers of ceremonial life for people of the surrounding country. Fortunately, fragments of elaborately painted interiors of tombs and temple-palaces, probably reserved for initiates, survive and continue to be unearthed.

TOLTEC
A.D. 900-1200
NORTHERN LIMIT

AZTEC:1521
NORTHERN LIMIT

NOT SUBJECT TO AZTECS

TOLTEC
NORTHERN LIMIT

AZTEC:1521
NORTHERN LIMIT

HUASTEC

OTOMI

TOTONAC

NAHUA

TARASCAN

OLMEC

MIXTEC

ZAPOTEC

NAHUA

YUCATAN
MAYA

MAYA

MAP I.   EARLY MEXICO: Pre-Spanish Culture

MURAL SITES (in order of appearance in text)

Central Mexico

1. Cuicuilco
2. Cholula
3. Teotihuacan
4. Tajín
5. Tollan
6. Ixtapantongo
7. Huapalcalco
8. Tamuín
9. Tizatlan
10. Ecatepec
11. Malinalco
12. Tenayuca

Southern Mexico

13. Yagul
14. Xaaga
15. Monte Albán
16. Colotlipa
17. Acatlan
18. Yucuñudahuí
19. Teloloapan
20. Xochicalco
21. Mitla
22. Zaachila

Southeastern Mexico

23. Palenque
24. Chinikihá
25. Yaxchilán
26. Bonampak
27. Chichén Itzá
28. Chacmultún
29. Tzulá
30. Tulum

MURAL SITES (in alphabetical order)

Acatlan (17)
Bonampak (26)
Chacmultún (28)
Chichén Itzá (27)
Chinikihá (24)
Cholula (2)
Colotlipa (16)
Cuicuilco (1)
Ecatepec (10)
Huapalcalco (7)
Ixtapantongo (6)
Malinalco (11)
Mitla (21)
Monte Albán (15)
Palenque (23)
Tajín (4)
Tamuín (8)
Teloloapan (19)
Tenayuca (12)
Teotihuacan (3)
Tizatlan (9)
Tollan (5)
Tulum (30)
Tzulá (29)
Xaaga (14)
Xochicalco (26)
Yagul (13)
Yaxchilán (25)
Yucuñudahuí (18)
Zaachila (22)

The decoration of a wall makes distinctive demands on an artist, and it is of special interest that knowledge of this ancient tradition, affirming the profound native roots of Mexico's mural expression, re-enters human experience in the living stream of art.

Distribution of cultural groups in Mexico today remains essentially what it was at the time of the Spanish Conquest of Mexico in 1521: Nahuatl or Mexicano is still the language native to the Central Highland; Huastec, Otomi, and Tarascan are still living languages to the north of this area; Mixtec, Zapotec, and Mayan are still spoken throughout Southern and Southeastern Mexico; numerous idioms are spoken in isolated areas. The indigenous cultures still survive in sufficient degree to color with great variety the life and art of the people of Mexico.

Central Mexico

Pre-Classic or Formative Horizon, 1700–200 B.C.

VALLEY OF MEXICO

Cuicuilco, "House of the Ancients," near Tlalpan, D.F. (Archeological Zone; Site 1).

The Valley of Mexico is a bowl enclosed by an irregular, jagged rim of volcanic mountains, with the companion snow-capped volcanoes, Iztaccihuatl and Popocatepetl, forming the eastern edge. Eruptions had left no outlet for water from the high valley, so that, at the dawn of the Pre-Classic Horizon, when small groups of primitive farmers arrived in the Valley of Mexico they found it a paradise of lakes surrounded by forests. This valley has been more thoroughly excavated and studied than any other area of Mexico.

According to a summary of the Pre-Classic cultures of the Valley made by Roman Piña Chan, the earliest settlements, dating as far back as 1700 B.C., were located west of the lakes on land higher than the areas lying to the east, and so were in less danger of inundation. However, about 200 B.C. the volcano Xitli erupted into the southwestern area to form the Pedregal, the lava flow south of Mexico City, and more settlements were then made in the east.

Pyramid of Cuicuilco. In the path of the lava was the Pyramid of Cuicuilco, possibly the earliest monument extant in Mesoamerica, which now rises through the Pedregal near the suburban town of Tlalpan. This is a circular or slightly oval mound built of adobe blocks and river stone in four receding tiers; it was faced with uncut stone. Two ramps or stairways lead to the broad summit, where a temple was erected of logs with thatched roof upon its polished red surface. A mural decoration found on an altar, built of stone and clay, showed symbols drawn in color directly on the stone and enclosed by a painted frame (Noguera: 1939). This is the earliest wall painting reported so far in Mesoamerica. The Pyramid of Cuicuilco tells us that theocratic rule had developed in Central Mexico and that the people had learned to work together under the direction of priestly leaders by the year 450 B.C.

Intensive study of various artifacts, especially of ceramics, used as funeral offerings, and found in successive strata of the earliest settlements in the Valley of Mexico, has established that a second cultural group had arrived here about 1000 B.C. Their artifacts connect them with the lowland culture of the Jaguar People (1500 B.C.–A.D. 300), called also Archeological Olmecs and sometimes confused with the Historic Olmecs of the Gulf Coast. The Jaguar People have left in the Valley of Morelos and in Puebla related works, the earliest manifestations of this culture; their art is found also in such widely separated regions as Oaxaca, Veracruz, Michoacan, Guatemala, and Honduras. The junction of the two different cultures in the Valley of Mexico during the Pre-Classic Horizon has been preserved for modern scientific study through their cult of the dead.

The Rain God Tlaloc derives from the jaguar, that symbolizes this culture. New knowledge and greater prosperity had followed the arrival of the Jaguar People in the Valley of Mexico; the first pyramidal bases for temples built here became prototypes for the great pyramids of the New World. The God of Fire, represented by a figure formed as a hunchback carrying a brazier on his back and with face deeply wrinkled—already a very old god—has been found in Cuicuilco. Many figures of this god have been excavated in Teotihuacan. All of earth's forces that relate to man were deified by the people of this valley and represented in man's image. "Reasoning in terms of sympathetic magic they created fetishes and idols" (Piña Chan: p. 61). They created new forms of art and great monuments that symbolize the splendor with which their gods were adored.

VALLEY OF PUEBLA

Cholula, "Place of Springs," Puebla (Archeological Zone; Site 2)

East of the Valley of Mexico the long Valley of Puebla lies between snow-capped volcanoes: Malinche is to the north; Citlatepetl, the great Peak of Orizaba, rises steeply from the Gulf Coast to the east; Iztaccihuatl and Popocatepetl stand guard to the west. This valley forms the southeastern edge of the high Central Plateau of Mexico. Here Cholula came into existence with the earliest cities of Mesoamerica, and it has never been a dead city.

Cholula is built around a pyramid—reputed to have been raised by giants—which grew through Pre-Classic, and Classic Horizons into the largest artificial mound in America—the largest in area in the world. It was in use from the late Pre-Classic or Formative Horizon until A.D. 1200, when the Toltecs conquered Cholula and overthrew its theocratic rulers. The city persisted, however, under the new rule as a center of religious pilgrimage for a large area. At the time of the Spanish Conquest, Cortés reported it as a huge metropolis in which he counted "four hundred towers"; but at that time the Great Pyramid overlooking the flat valley was already a ruin, which Motolinía described in his sixteenth-century chronicle:

. . . today there is so much of this structure to see that, if it did not show that it is made of stones and clay and in places of cut-stone and mortar and of adobe, no one would believe but that it is a small hill. Upon it are many rabbits and snakes and some parts are converted into cornfields.

The valley surrounding Cholula is dotted today with numerous churches (reputedly, one for each day of the year), and the immense pyramid is surmounted by a shrine to the Virgin built of its stones during the eighteenth century. A busy town fills the center of this very old city of Cholula, which is still a focus of pilgrimage.

The Great Pyramid of Cholula. The Codex of Cholula records of the Great Pyramid:

Here began the precious and small generation of man . . . All those who lived and even the great men were then lost by drowning everywhere . . .

. . . When they came together again, they said, if floods should overtake us one day, we will climb up . . . There were those who said, all together we will climb to the sky up to the region of the winds, an act which occurred in 587 . . . Finally the Toltecs arrived at the Tlahchiualtepetl [Artificial hill].

When scientifically explored by means of tunnels cut through it, the Great Pyramid of Cholula was discovered to be composed of four superimposed pyramids, all oriented to face west with a deviation of seventeen degrees to north. The labyrinth of tunnels clearly discloses walls and stairways of these and of other structures, for the Pyramid as it grew had swallowed neighboring temples.

Inner Pyramid: The oldest paintings on plaster so far found intact in Mexico are those painted upon the innermost or earliest of the four pyramids. This square, truncated, stepped mound—formed of seven recessions or stories—was built upon a nucleus of adobe late in the Formative Horizon. Upright cornices of cut stone that finish successive sloping walls were added later and indicate transition to Classic culture. The painted decoration is upon the stone cornices, whose construction is closely related to sculptured cornices found in Teotihuacan. According to Ignacio Marquina, under whose direction the paintings were excavated, the painted cornices are upon part of the front of the Pyramid, on all of the north side and part of the east, and on all four sides of the two highest divisions that rise from a wider step or platform. Especially in the two cornices which crown the Pyramid, it can be seen that the four-foot-high constructions are parallel, one being a short distance above and behind the other. Each cornice is formed of a continuous panel about twenty-one inches in height framed above and below by similar double projections, and all surfaces are plastered and painted.

The single motif repeated in the recessed panels of the cornices to form identical friezes—a figure more than ten feet long—is interpreted by Dr. Alfonso Caso as a locust, or a mythological insect, showing a certain relation to the Butterfly God adored in the region of the Papaloapan River. This insect figure (Plate 1), consists of a large, red, human skull drawn front-view in black, with eyes and teeth of white or gray—large enough to fill the height of the panel—with black horizontal wings painted to either side of the skull, red antennae that reach up over the heavy frame above it, fangs below, and a long insect body, drawn in red, that extends to the left side in the panel. One unit closely follows another in these painted insect friezes. Among many figures now uncovered, only two vary in the color of skulls and antennae, yellow replacing red.

The supervisor of the Archeological Zone of Cholula

1. Insect Frieze (detail). Inner Pyramid, Cholula, Puebla.

conducts visitors through lighted tunnels to see these paintings. In a small Regional Museum across the road from the entrance into the Pyramid, copies of the insects are on display; also a scale model of the Great Pyramid of Cholula shows this original structure with its painted friezes placed within the final mound.

Temple Walls: Upon adjoining outer walls of a temple buried within the Great Pyramid, large frescoed glyphs painted in black and white on a yellow ground were uncovered in 1931. The symbols, about three feet in height, are formed of canes and knots in different combinations. Other large decorations on temple walls within this site include friezes made of checkered black-and-white rectangles.

A painting of a large animal was uncovered on a smooth plastered panel at floor level on a wall deep in another tunnel of the Great Pyramid of Cholula. This figure, twenty-seven inches high and five feet long, is painted solid yellow and may represent a cougar (puma). One paw reaches up and out to a red-and-black shield, the head seems averted, and the slim body ends in a curving tail. Narrow bands of brilliant red follow the outlines of the body and frame the panel. This painted animal is unlike any other known from Early Mexico.

Mound, Cholula. Painted surfaces have been detected and await excavation in a small mound across the road from the Great Pyramid and immediately north of the Regional Museum of Cholula. As it is constructed entirely of adobe, this ruin is judged to antedate the Pyramid, and its painting could belong to a very early period of Cholula.

The pyramid builders of Cholula are related to the builders of Teotihuacan.

Classic Horizon, 200 B.C.–A.D. 900

VALLEY OF MEXICO

Teotihuacan, "Place Where the Gods Reside," (Archeological Zone; Site 3)

Northwest of the towering white masses of Iztaccihuatl and Popocatepetl in the Valley of Mexico lies the great city of Teotihuacan, which had been burned and destroyed more than six hundred years before the Spanish Conquest. Its name, designating it as the home of the gods, and the legends of giant builders and of gods who met here and died to create the Fifth Sun and the Moon are the only known references to the extensive city that lies buried under pueblos and cornfields northeast of what was formerly Lake Texcoco in the high, mountain-rimmed Valley of Mexico. In this sacred city, placed where all roads converge, a civilization apparently grew in peace and spread, through commerce, over large areas during approximately a thousand years.

The ceremonial center of Teotihuacan is dominated by the Pyramids of the Sun and the Moon, which are approached from a broad avenue, Camino de los Muertos, or "Way of the Dead," of more than a mile in length. The immense Pyramid of the Sun, like the Pyramid of Cholula, faces west with a deviation of seventeen degrees to north. Constructed during the two first periods of Teotihuacan to flank the Way of the Dead, the Pyramid of the Sun, through its orientation, established the axis of the city. The body of this pyramid is discovered to contain an older structure; the final monument, belonging to the Second Period of Teotihuacan, must have involved the cooperative labor of a great many workers over a very long span of time. The smaller Pyramid of the Moon, as part of the same grand plan, faces down the long avenue from the northern terminus. Further excavation of this monument may show that its construction antedates that of the Pyramid of the Sun.

Extensive exploration of Teotihuacan has revealed the design of a beautiful city built along the great avenue—with temples and palaces covered with red or white stucco and with polychrome decorations of cut stone or of painted plaster—with plazas, roadways, and complexes of temples and living quarters extending over surrounding areas. Excavation often reveals structures superimposed during successive periods of the city. Temple interiors dating from the Third and Fourth Periods of the city have been elaborately painted. Because this city was built upon a foundation of stone and not, as in some parts of the Valley of Mexico, upon deep mud, it can be excavated.

The earth of Teotihuacan is enchanted—within it

the essence of a great culture still lingers. Scientific excavation has gradually uncovered fragmentary frescoes with magic images of gods and priests, men and spirits, symbolic birds, snakes, and animals—paintings which record the knowledge and the beliefs of the unknown people whose culture flowered in this city. Interpreted in the light of religious concepts current in the Valley of Mexico at the time of the Spanish Conquest, the painted walls of Teotihuacan are expressions of some of those beliefs. The paintings affirm Teotihuacan as a city of mystery and magic—truly a "home of the gods."

Fragments of paintings have been found on walls in various sites of Teotihuacan, and some of these were the first archeological murals to be excavated in Mexico. The sites are recorded here in order of discovery.

Temple of Agriculture or Temple of the Frescoes. The first fresco was excavated in Teotihuacan in 1884 by Leopoldo Batres (who later restored the Pyramid of the Sun) in a ruin on the west side of the Way of the Dead and near to where it ends in the small plaza of the Pyramid of the Moon. This painting of a conventionalized bird, shown front-view with outstretched wings and enclosed by angular designs, was interpreted as an owl. It is known to us from a copy which shows a green bird with small eyes and a dark fringed beard, the head being encircled by symbols like flower petals and crowned by five small upright feathers. Upon each wing is superimposed a red fret, or squared spiral. Possibly the bird represented is the sacred quetzal.

A second painting, uncovered soon afterwards on a similar panel, contains small human figures. This panel, of which also only a copy has been preserved, is painted across its lower third with two wide bands to represent water—the lower of very dark green and the upper, jade green—both bound by undulating parallel lines of blue and yellow. The water is filled with red-and-yellow ovals shaded to suggest a third dimension. Above the water and to the sides of the panel stand two similar monumental figures or temples before which incense is being burned, the black smoke making symmetrical patterns that resemble huge insects or, as Seler described them, "demons of darkness descending from heaven." Over the central part of the panel eleven squatty figures are placed upon the background as if upon a map, a form of composition used often in Early Mexico to indicate space. As in a market scene, several figures at the highest level seem to exchange the oval objects noted in the water. Toward the forms, at the sides, lower figures hold objects—vases, rubber balls, feathers, seeds, and a bird; so these were interpreted as priests making offerings to the God of Agriculture, the site being called the Temple of Agriculture. The figures, painted pink or yellow, sit or stand in a variety of postures, their costumes varying from breechcloths to a long, black, flowing robe; one man wears a black suit with short trousers and carries a folded cloth on his shoulder. Several figures wear masks of fish or birds as headdresses, and others have caps or long hair; speech scrolls—a characteristic of Teotihuacan paintings—are placed before some mouths. These two small painted panels (about three feet square) are from the Third Period of Teotihuacan.

Within this complex of four superimposed temples, on the long wall of a vestibule built during the Second Period, later excavation uncovered three large panels about seven feet in height, the central one being longer than the other two. Although separated by adobe partitions, the panels are related in design by horizontal bands of a water design, which suggests that originally this was one continuous painting. Superimposed on the center of each panel is another painting, some details of which were described in 1913, soon after discovery, by Eduard Seler:

They represent garlands of water-plants with shield-like leaves surrounded by a pronged circle and covered by a large headdress of green feathers. On the other wall there are yellow and dark colored whirls and in the midst of them, on a dark ground, figures of marine shells and red and yellow-colored buttons, probably buds of water-plants. On the lower border the figure of a turtle may be detected among the same sea-shells and yellow flower buds.

Green feathers, whirls, turtles, and marine shells reappear in paintings found in other sites of Teotihuacan.

Because the thin coat of color is in tempera (pigment mixed with an agglutinant), the surface is disintegrating and details are indistinguishable, the panels appearing as brilliant mosaics of color. These paintings are now protected by glass behind metal doors. They can be seen only with special permission.

Frescoed bands decorate the pyramidal base and stairway of the first or innermost temple of this site. Bands of green rings, for jade, are painted upon red between undulating lines, for water—a motif interpreted as precious liquid or blood, which recurs often in Teotihuacan. These paintings from the earliest period are unskilled in execution.

Teopancaxco, "In the House of the Gods." Frescoes were uncovered in 1894 in San Sebastián near the railroad station of San Juan Teotihuacan. As the paintings were found in a ruin under the house of a potter named

Barrios, the site is also called Casa del Alfarero or Casa de Barrios.

Teopancaxco paintings are on the lowest levels of the walls of three adjoining rooms that have been solidly plastered and decorated. The original low walls have been raised and roofed to protect the paintings, a procedure followed in later excavations where paintings exist on similar lower sections of walls. Elaborately dressed figures stand in friezes forty inches in height. What exists now is fragmentary and faded, but early copies have many details. Seler (1913) described a painting that still shows faintly:

In the middle of the south wall of the inner chamber a disc is seen in an upright position on a kind of altar . . . To this symbol there are advancing from both sides figures of men. Their heads are overlapped by the fantastic head of a snake, whose body is remarkable for a star-shaped design. On the cheek we note a disk colored green, exactly similar to the disk of jadeite which the earth goddess *Coatlicue* has inserted in her cheek.

All of the figures have before their mouths a very large and broad spiral scroll adorned with flowers which means adorned-speech or song. They hold in the left hand a *copalxiquipilli* or incense bag, a well-known priestly attribute, and with the right they pour a liquid to the ground. This liquid has a border of scum, it is finely dotted, and it may be that it originally exhibited a blue coloring, but it is fringed with flowers like the sign of adorned-speech or song, and from this fact it must be inferred that this liquid is not meant as pure water.

These singing priests wearing on their cheeks the *tlaxapochtla* of the goddess of the moon and the earth, pouring out pulque as an offering on the ground, most likely are to be considered as the adepts and followers of the same deity of the moon and of the earth and for the same reason I am inclined to interpret the disk mentioned above not as a solar disk but as an image or symbol of the moon.

Also from Teopancaxco is a frescoed figure of a warrior preserved in the Museum of Teotihuacan, showing a richly attired warrior carrying a shield and a quiver of darts. He wears a huge headdress adorned with feathers, and from his mouth come two speech scrolls extending up and down.

Antonio Peñafiel, excavator of the murals, wrote of Teopancaxco in 1900:

The floors are well polished like all of those discovered in Teotihuacan . . . The colors of these priestly hieroglyphic figures are the following: red ochre, which forms the general background of all frescoes, rose color, the green of arsenide of copper, light yellow and ochre, black turning to violet,

2. Priest of Tlaloc, Rain God (detail of wall). Tepantitla, Teotihuacan.

and white. There are to be seen on some fragments found in the same place other colors but the foregoing are the principal ones.

Subterranean or Superimposed Buildings. Within a complex ruin excavated in 1917, on the west side of the Way of the Dead and far south of the Temple of the Frescoes, large painted decorations can be seen upon a stairway that approaches an altar. As in the Temple of the Frescoes, borders here are formed of green rings on a red base. Complicated designs of squared spirals in various colors fill long recessed panels. The rich color and bold design of this temple decoration suggest the magnificence of the painted city of Teotihuacan.

Tlamimilolpa, "On or Above the Ruins." During 1934–1935, in cornfields east of the Pyramid of the Sun and near the Church of San Francisco Mazapan, the lower walls of a great aggregation of buildings were excavated by the Swedish archeologist Sigvald Linné, who reported (1942): "Probably more than 300 rooms connected and with plazas—like a small village . . ." Several of the rooms and a court showed traces of wall paintings, all done in red and blue on a surface of fine white plaster. A section of decoration in one room was saved and copied—a complicated symmetrical design of straight and curved lines repeated exactly on all walls. In another room fragments existed "of a freer character not so severely geometric . . . a certain dash and elegance of touch nevertheless revealed that a master had here been at work."

Dr. Linné's book, with the report of these few murals found in living quarters, had scarcely been published when the ruin of the Temple of Tepantitla was discovered nearby, with the most interesting, elaborate, and best-preserved frescoes that had been discovered in Teotihuacan up to that time.

Tepantitla, "Place of Walls." Tepantitla was accidentally discovered within a small mound when a frescoed wall was plowed into and partly destroyed. In this fresco, under a strong pattern of opposed diagonals, are painted two similar, front-view images of the masked god Tlaloc—God of Rain and the oldest god in Mexico, who under different names appears in all early Mesoamerican cultures. The people of Teotihuacan most especially were worshipers of Tlaloc: god of rain, vegetation, the mountains, and lightning, of drought and of hail.

Dr. Caso has observed of Tlaloc that he is one of the easiest gods to be recognized for his characteristic mask, which in front view makes the god appear to wear spectacles and a mustache. These large figures of Tlaloc are painted in different tones of earth red; in left hands they hold darts or bolts of lightning; instead of right hands they have claws.

At a lower level of this site two large ochre-colored animals painted in spaces to either side of a doorway face it as if to enter. The figures are faint; large oblong symbols can be seen diagonally crossing the bodies.

Room I: The upper temple contains various paintings. In a half-destroyed enclosure, which must have been an inner sanctuary, seven singing priests walk in procession at floor level upon three adjoining walls, as if they had entered at the central doorway and were approaching an altar opposite it. The two-foot-high figures (Plate 2) are doubled in height by elaborate serpent masks adorned with quetzal feathers, placed as headdresses, and by high double song scrolls. Dr. Alfonso Caso, in his fascinating study of the paintings of Tepantitla (1942), describes the religious ritual:

. . . they take from bags they carry in their hands seeds of all kinds of plants, or maybe jade beads, which they throw to the earth. These are the Tlaloques, that is to say the ministers of the god of rain, the clouds, who cast to the earth liquid drops, as precious as jade, that will turn into food for man; for this purpose the priestly Tlaloques go in procession singing hymns of abundance. Animals, flowers and plants, rich ornaments and humble objects of pottery appear represented within the symbol of speech adorned with flowers, indicating song; these are the ministers of the god, those who make everything grow and bear fruit.

Room II: In the adjoining room, to the right side of the connecting doorway, fragments of the upper part of a frescoed wall have been lifted into place and reconstructed with immense knowledge and skill, so that the composition of the whole wall is apparent. A large masked and plumed figure of the Rain God dominates this upper wall. Open hands of the god pour water to the earth, and on either side small figures of Tlaloques attend him. Great waves decorated with shells and turtles rise and fall at his feet. A quetzal with outstretched wings and raised tail feathers forms his headdress, from which grow two trees, one with butterflies and the other spiders. A similar large figure of Tlaloc is indicated on the corresponding wall to the left of the doorway.

This second room is notable chiefly for numerous small figures that cover all lower panels of the walls. Dr. Caso interprets the section under the large figure of Tlaloc described above as representing Tlalocan, the heaven of Tlaloc (earthly paradise) situated in clouds upon mountaintops between the warriors' heaven of

3. Tlalocan, Heaven of Tlaloc (two details of panel). Tepantitla, Teotihuacan.

the firmament and Michtlan, the heaven of common death beneath the earth (Plate 3).

Sahagún, an early Franciscan chronicler, described Tlalocan: "The earthly Paradise where they believe there is no end of pleasure and refreshment, free for a spell from torment."

Torquemada described it more fully (1613):

Here there is imagined to be great pleasure and happiness where there would be no sorrow; and here there would never lack ears of green corn, squash and flowering plants, chilis, or small green peppers, tomatoes and beans, which are the vegetables they usually eat. In this place they imagine that there live gods called Tlaloques . . . and that these appear to the priests and attendants of the idols who wear long hair. They said that to this place of false Paradise went those who died of lightning or drowning, the lepers and those with sores, the gouty and the dropsical. And dying of these incurable diseases they were not burned but placed in special tombs, and placed with them were branches or sprouts of rush on the cheeks and over the face,

4. Singing Figures (detail of second panel). Tepantitla, Teotihuacan.

and the forehead was anointed with *Texutli*, which is the blue color they used, and on the head were put certain superstitious papers and in the hand a rod, because they said that as the place was fresh and pleasant this would become green again and put out leaves.

When the dead revived they were greeted by this exhortation: "Awaken! now the sky turns red, now comes the dawn of day, now the birds of yellow plumage begin to sing and the golondrinas color of fire, now butterflies go flying." Dr. Caso (1936) has observed a connection between an individual's social class and the fate of his soul:

For the early Mexicans the fate of souls after death was determined not by conduct but by the social class to which the deceased had belonged, and, above all, by the kind of death he had had. It was believed that this was the manner in which the gods showed the predilection that they had for their servitors, whom they nominated and selected, giving them a kind of death in accord with the attributes of the divinity.

In the center of the panel picturing Tlalocan rises a mountain, from which gushes a stream that divides into two rivers, flowing in opposite directions along the base of the wall. The river to the right side (the best preserved) flows past planted fields, painted below it, and trees, corn, and flowering shrubs, above. It contains fish, and ends in a small lake at the extreme right of the panel, where an island is painted with a huge frog upon it. In the pool in the central mountain small figures swim and dive, and beside the water's edge one figure wrings a cloth from which drops of water can be seen falling. Along the bank of the river men rest under trees or smell flowers, and one is about to eat a stalk of corn, "leaves and all." Scattered over the dark-red background of the panel, many groups of little men engage in varied activities, but all of them are playing, and all are singing, as a symbol before each mouth indicates. Just above the lake, at the river's end, one figure stands apart. While he raises a leafy branch above his head, five speech scrolls come from his mouth as he sings or orates, and huge blue tears fall from his eyes. He is the recent arrival in this heaven. The branch in his hand is the rod that was buried with him and which now in the land of abundance has put out leaves (Plate 3). Similar branches are carried by all figures in this gay paradise where men of various colors sing and play together. One group plays ball, another chases a butterfly, four men carry a singing companion by arms and legs, tumblers clasp hands between legs to form a chain, a man carries a child on his shoulders. The merriment that reigns is evident.

Dr. Caso (1942) describes Tlalocan, "Mansion of Tlaloc," as "the place of delight, of eternal fertility and abundance . . ." Contrasting this painting with representations of the gods and their attributes, he remarks, "but this painting of Teotihuacan, full of happiness and reality, represents for us a certain human good which is of universal longing. Through its slender and almost ethereal figures it is expressing the illusion and the desire to arrive through death at a place of delight and rest."

The small figures (about five inches high) are outlined in the same deep red of the background and filled in with gold ochre, earth pink, and blue, the head or limbs of a figure often being painted a color different from the body. A few front-view faces are represented and an occasional figure has long hair or a hat. Breechcloths are worn. No women are shown.

Left of the doorway, under the second large figure of Tlaloc, a continuing decoration of the lower panel of the wall, or dado, is less well preserved than its companion panel of Tlalocan. Small singing figures (Plate

6. Hand from Tlaloc Talus (upper left), and Hands from Panel of Hands (three details)
Central Room, Palace, Tetitla, Teotihuacan.

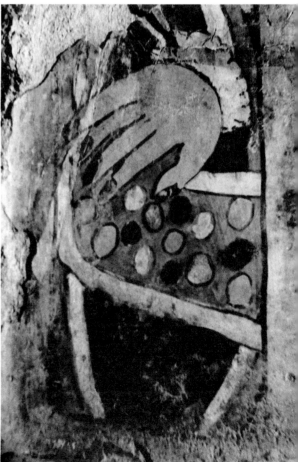

7. Jaguar-Priest. South Room, Palace, Tetitla, Teotihuacan.

4), dressed in tunics and wearing hats and sandals, carry heavy rods as if hastening to a ballgame. Other figures wear breechcloths, like the figures in Tlalocan, and one of these sits upon a pyramidal structure in the center of this panel.

A border framing the entire wall is formed of two large intertwined snakes, one decorated with starfish, the other, with turtles. A second border, enclosing the doorway, repeats units of flowering plants alternated with masks of Tlaloc.

On the opposite side of the room, the lower panel is filled with busy sprites, interpreted as *curanderos,* or "healers." This panel (now indistinct) when first copied showed a variety of cures being prepared and practiced—figures gathering medicinal herbs, catching insects, taking pills, massaging, singing, and dancing for magical cures. Two figures, sitting before an urn and mixing a potion, can still be seen.

Angular flowering forms painted in pale green and shades of rose decorate a passageway leading from Room II to a large open court. Indistinct figures of eagles—a new symbol—show in an enclosure to one side of this court. To the other side is the wall with the two figures of Tlaloc first mentioned, through which this site was discovered.

Tetitla, "Place Full of Stones." In 1945 most extraordinary paintings were uncovered in Tetitla, a ruin southeast of the Pyramid of the Sun, near the entrance to the

Archeological Zone of Teotihuacan, and a short distance behind the stables belonging to the owner of the land.

Patio I: The area uncovered at this time is Patio I, which is enclosed on two sides by temple or palace rooms that show decorations within and without.

Vestibule: Tetitla is another temple or palace dedicated to the Rain God. Frescoed lower panels have been excavated in a series of rooms built on two sides of the small square court. Steps descend into this court from three sides, but along the fourth, or west, side it is faced by a narrow portico with a central doorway and an opening at either end. To the sides of the doorway projecting panels are decorated, each with two front-view figures of Tlaloc (Plate 5, color, p. 24), forming a frieze of four identical figures. Each masked god wears a headdress of another and similar pea-green mask crowned with green plumes, all outlined in a slightly darker blue; from a circular collar hang squared ornaments. Yellow hands with red nails outstretch to either side of the god to pour collections of objects to the earth—heads, hands, jars, shells—fashioned as if made of clay and often falling upside-down (like the symbols in the song scrolls of the Tlaloques in Tepantitla). This flow of blessings is bordered by a scalloped symbol of water that suggests a rosary.

There is also a fifth figure of Tlaloc, for which a strange arrangement is made: a figure of the Rain God, similar to the four on the long wall, is painted on the left end wall of the portico in the space between the corner and the opening; but as only one hand with its flow of blessings can be accommodated, the other creating hand, with its symbols, is painted in the corresponding space at the other end of the portico (Plate 6).

Center Room: The central doorway of the vestibule opens into a room at one end of which is a long frieze of creative hands combined with disks and other symbols (Plate 6); one large hand reaching up alternates with two smaller hands reaching down. All hands are painted yellow with bright red nails and are partly encircled by a ruffled white cuff. At either end of the wall a small hand drops varicolored grains of corn onto a *comal*, or flat pottery dish used for cooking tortillas. One is reminded of Trini the diviner in Steinbeck's "Forgotten Village." Divination was an important priestly function in Early Mexico.

South Room: In the room that is reached from the left end of the portico the figure of a kneeling Jaguar-Priest fills a panel of the dado (Plate 7). This fantastic figure faces a doorway to an inner sanctuary, one knee resting beside a yellow path marked with divine footprints; painted between two blue streams, this path leads to an elaborate temple. The figure of the Jaguar-Priest (Plate 8), garbed in jaguar mask, tail, and claws, holds in his right hand a small round shield adorned with feathers and raises with his left hand an ornate rattle decorated with green and yellow plumes. The blue-painted body of the priest is covered with a red mesh design, netted, also, over arms, legs, tail, head, and ears; the lidded eye of his mask is yellow; a long tuft of green plumage and two symbols like pennants stream from above his head; bands of green feathers fringe his body; a large spotted symbol of speech, edged in blue and green, rises from his mouth, and an apron of blessings falls from the upraised hand. Villagra Caleti wrote in 1951: "This scene refers to the ceremony performed by priests to petition water of Tlaloc, god of Rain. Sahagún says that they approach the temple decked with 'a sort of net, shaking a rattle and that in this they passed all the day'."

The composition of the panel of the Jaguar-Priest is dominated by parallel notched lines of blue and green placed diagonally at regular intervals across a pink background. From these lines hang dark-red points like fern fronds—interpreted as rain.

There is precise geometry in this design. The entire panel, with its frame of repeated symbols, occupies one-third of the width of the room. The width of the inner panel is two and one-half times its height, and its center is marked by the upraised hand. Exact proportions

8. Jaguar-Priest. (detail). South Room, Palace, Tetitla, Teotihuacan.

9. Parrot with symbols. Court, Palace, Tetitla, Teotihuacan.

10. Jaguar Devouring Hearts. Temple, Second Patio, Tetitla, Teotihuacan.

and shapes included also the missing companion panel on the other side of the doorway, which is now in the Bliss Collection in the United States.

Symmetry and repetition, number and measure, distinguish almost all mural paintings found in Teotihuacan, but the paintings of the Jaguar-Priest show asymmetry or side-balance. Here geometry is an instrument of magic.

Fragments remaining on lower walls of this room indicate that similar figures of the Jaguar-Priest were repeated on all, but that these priests were directed toward the center of the unbroken wall opposite the guarded doorway, where their paths met at what may have been a centrally placed temple and the principal decoration of the room.

North Room: A narrow room leading from the right or north end of the portico is decorated also with figures of kneeling Jaguar-Priests, similar to the one depicted but not so precise; an adjoining room retains feet of more kneeling priests laced here with green instead of

red. Attributes of temple and of jaguar are of the Rain God Tlaloc.

South Temple: Facing the south side of the court, a chamber is decorated with a second frieze of creative hands. In repeated units, two hands embrace a row of five green rings from which depend green bars, with a ruffled design of water flowing from the hands. Here red hands with bright-red nails are painted on a dark-red ground.

The two other sides of this court had not been excavated at this time except where they meet in a doorway; here a beautiful parrot (Plate 9) and glyphs can be seen.

Plastered fragments with small painted figures found in this site are gradually being reconstructed by the artist-archeologist Agustín Villagra Caleti.

Patio II: Twenty years later, under the direction of Laurette Sejourné (1963), the area adjoining the Palace of Tetitla was explored for more frescoes. As no architecture could be found here from the last period of Teotihuacan, this level was penetrated and a second

5. Tlaloc Talus, Figure. Vestibule, Palace, Tetitla, Teotihuacan.

Courtesy Dr. Ignacio Bernal and Instituto Nacional de Antropología e Historia.

11. Sacred Quetzal. Second Patio, Tetitla, Teotihuacan.

stucco floor was located. However, this floor appeared too soon to admit of wall space between, so it was removed, and excavation in a selected place reached a third stucco another meter down. Here the adventure became greatly rewarding, as various paintings appeared on these lower walls, thirteen different motifs being repeated, with other designs, proving this to be a mural site of great importance from an earlier period.

An orange-colored Jaguar Devouring Hearts (Plate 10), the first painting to appear, is unusually strong in character and color for Teotihuacan frescoes. The most conspicuous figure found here was the sacred Quetzal (Plate 11), painted front view, suspended in the act of alighting with wings and legs to sides. Placed centrally and alone on a background of brilliant red and framed in black, this great bird dominates the patio. Another motif is of a singing god partly enclosed by a symbol of water (Plate 12). A section of the upper wall, carefully reconstructed from fragments found in the debris, shows entwined snakes with a bird's head like the Quetzal.

Atetelco, "Stone wall near the water." A short distance beyond Tetitla a group of temples has been uncovered within a small area known as Atetelco. Although walls

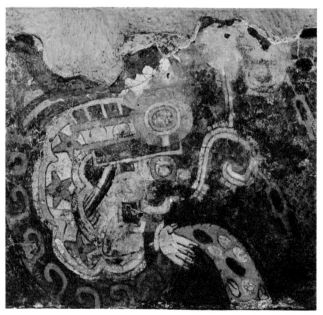

Courtesy Dr. Ignacio Bernal.

12. Water Song. Second Patio, Tetitla, Teotihuacan.

13. Jaguars and Coyotes (details). Portico II, Temple. Atetelco, Teotihuacan.

14. Priest of Tlaloc. Portico III, Temple, Atetelco, Teotihuacan.

of all the temples show that they have been decorated, murals have been found intact in only the temple complex of the "white patio." In this painted temple of Atetelco similar porticos face three sides of a small quadrangular court, central steps between squared pillars descending from each portico to the court. A central doorway in each portico gives entrance to an inner chamber or shrine. Paintings have been recovered intact upon the sloping dados of all three porticos, in two of which the figures are approximately the same.

Porticos I and II: Upon the rear panels of Porticos I and II pairs of plumed animals, painted one behind the other, face the central doorways (Plate 13); another similar pair on each end panel faces the court. The two animals differ—a coyote, with lines drawn for fur and bushy tail, alternates with a jaguar covered over with a red netting, like that worn by the Jaguar-Priest of Tetitla. Each animal has a singing scroll and each devours a bleeding heart. In the first, or south, portico the

figures are enclosed by a single snake, decorated with circles and bordered with feathers, whereas a border of two entwined snakes with dissimilar markings frames the animal frescoes of the central, or eastern, portico, the two snakes sharing one animal head and tail. Jaguar claws superimpose on the twisted snakes.

Portico III: The dado of the third portico is decorated with plumed figures of a priest of Tlaloc facing the central doorway (Plate 14). He carries a shield with darts tipped by balls of cotton; his mask is a bird's beak and rounded eye; great masses of feathers flow from his headdress and shoulders; a hand grasps a staff from which sprinkle large drops; from his mouth extend two long, thin song scrolls. His footwear is elaborate, but bare divine footprints wander over the earth-red background of these panels. A wall, formed of rows of precious symbols and interrupted by steps placed centrally, frames the priestly figures, and the entire dado is further enclosed by a border formed of repeated units of a

15. Dancing Figure. Doorway, Temple, Atetelco, Teotihuacan.

front-view head of Tlaloc, adorned with a collar of jade and a headdress of plumes falling to either side.

Upper Walls: Numerous frescoed fragments of upper walls of the three porticos were found in rubble that filled the court. By separating similar details of designs, tracing these, and piecing together the tracings, patterns of entire wall decorations have been most skilfully reconstructed by Agustín Villagra Caleti (1951). The main body of each wall is discovered to have been covered over with a design of large meshes, netted of feathered cord decorated with precious symbols.

In the central Portico II the entire wall is framed by entwined snakes—similar to those enclosing the animals of the dados below, but larger; masks of the Rain God, Tlaloc, and jaguar claws are superimposed alternately upon the twists of these serpents. Feathered heads of four serpents symmetrically frame the doorway; elaborate song scrolls, from which depend large raindrops, fill all spaces. Within each large mesh of the wall design, a small, stylized figure of a priest painted in profile faces the doorway. He wears a headdress of feathers, with a bird's beak at front and a nose mask of jaguar teeth attached; a shield with darts is in one hand and a rattle in the other; a large conch lies across his breast. From the jaguar mask and from both ends of the shell come speech scrolls, with drops falling from all scrolls. Like the priest of the third portico, this figure wears decorative footgear.

The upper wall of Portico I as reconstructed is quite similar to that of Portico II. In Portico III, however, the meshes are not loosely netted as in the others but are tied with rosettes. Small figures with double speech scrolls fill openings as in Portico II, but the enclosing border is a temple similar to the enclosing border of the priests in the frieze below. The wall is fringed by feathers, with oval designs superimposed; a scalelike surface, as of a snake, lies between.

Doorway: On doorjambs of a corner entrance to the court are painted two figures with elaborate speech scrolls and twisted feet (Plate 15)—they may be singing and dancing.

Paintings in this court are in three tones of red: pure, rich earth-red, red opaqued with lime, and red diluted to pink over the white plaster. The reason for the red color is given in the song of Tlaloc, collected by Sahagún and translated by Eduard Seler: "My god (or my priest) has painted himself dark red with blood [of the victim]." In Early Mexico human blood was offered as nourishment to the gods.

The remarkable friezes of rapacious jaguars and coyotes painted in the Temple of Atetelco suggest a more violent form of religion than do the kneeling jaguar-priests in Tetitla or the singing priests in Tepantitla. These companion jaguars and coyotes relate closely to bas-reliefs of similar animals that decorate the temple-pyramid in Tula or Tollan—great city of the Toltecs just north of the Valley of Mexico; also they suggest the frieze of the Temple of the Tigers in Chicén Itzá, a city in Yucatán conquered by the Toltec nation. It has been suggested that these paintings from a late period of Teotihuacan could indicate intrusion by a military order into the sacred city, before its destruction in the ninth century of our era, and that the Toltecs could have been these invaders. However, the latest discoveries in Tetitla (Plate 10) confuse this issue.

The frieze of serpents with superimposed jaguar claws and masks of Tlaloc finds a very early analogy in the Temple of Quetzalcoatl, from the second period of Teotihuacan, uncovered from within a later structure. This small, very early pyramidal temple is built of successive sculptured friezes formed of undulations of a serpent; heads of Tlaloc, God of Rain, and of a serpent identified as Quetzalcoatl, "Plumed Serpent," God of Culture, superimpose alternately upon the serpent friezes; these two forms possibly express different aspects of the same god. Tlaloc in mask of jaguar-serpent appears upon artifacts from the very early culture of the "Jaguar People," for whom Tlaloc was the principal god. In Mesoamerican religious tradition the jaguar is associated with Tlaloc, one of whose guises is that of the "Earth God," who possesses "the heart of the land." The serpent's feathers represent vegetation.

Zacuala. "*Hidden Place.*" Near Tetitla and Atetelco and two kilometers southwest of the Pyramid of the Sun, extensive excavation, carried on since 1955 under auspices of the Mexican government, has uncovered large complexes of buildings.

Un Palacio en la Ciudad de los Dioses, a study of a palace in the City of the Gods, the important mural site of Zacuala, was written by Laurette Séjourné, under whose direction the site was explored. This book is profusely illustrated with colored photographs and copies of restored paintings found in this site. Around two patios, one of which is raised, excavation has uncovered the lower walls of a series of passages and rooms with painted plaster still intact on many walls.

Various symbols of the gods of Central Mexico are painted in polychrome upon red walls in Zacuala. As interpreted by L. Séjourné, these are: Tlaloc, God of the Rain of Fire; Sky Eagle, "speaking of the fertile union of sky and earth" with the split tongue of a serpent; the handbag of the Serpent that conducts Quetzalcoatl to Tlapallan, Land of the Sun; a figure sowing a current of flowers; Xipe, the Flayed One; Xochipilli, Lord of Flowers, with the head of a quetzal bird; the Young Sun, as an eagle; Tiger Warrior, a figure in tiger mask, tail, etc.; undulations of Quetzalcoatl as Feathered Serpent, decorated with flowers and feathers; a head of this god; also, Quetzalcoatl Rojo, shown front-face in red mask with headdress of green feathers and a large ornate collar. Quetzalcoatl is interpreted as combining various symbols in one image: man, tiger (primitive instincts), bird (the celestial), serpent (the terrestrial).

Here are found, also, friezes of entwined symbols, like snakes, adorned with water or speech symbols or eyes, and enclosed between bands; a star symbol of the morning; eyes enclosed by turquoise and by a halo; and drops of blood for sacrifice. A figure holding a flower and carrying a laden basket on his back is interpreted as Yacatecutli, God of Wandering Merchants. Flesh and basket are painted yellow; costume, ornaments, headdress, and song scroll are blue-green. All is fragmentary and indistinct.

Laurette Séjourné, in her *Un Palacio en la Ciudad de los Dioses,* questions that Teotihuacan was destroyed by fire or by any outside force, or that there was interruption between the culture of Teotihuacan and that of the Aztec nation seven hundred years after Teotihuacan was abandoned. She suggests that the priesthood, guardians of this civilization, had left, for mystic reasons, and had carried their knowledge and beliefs to other regions. The frescoes are "holy writings" interpreting "mystic death and resurrection." She believes Teotihuacan to have belonged to the Nahua language group. This is an exciting and controversial book.

In Zacuala no paintings duplicate figures of the gods exactly as they are found on other walls of Teotihuacan, since these gods are variously interpreted. Little by little Teotihuacan iconography is bringing to life this former "City of the Gods," which now certainly validates its title, since it is peopled only by gods and their priests.

Yahuala. In the area called Yahuala, Construction 3 is a site which was at first named Templo de las Mariposas, as decorations on the temple's base were thought to resemble butterflies. In two friezes a bird, which more resembles a parrot than a quetzal, is represented.

Ceremonial Center. While this record of Teotihuacan frescoes continued to grow with new discoveries, murals were being excavated in areas somewhat removed from the Ceremonial Center of Teotihuacan, indicating the immense size of the buried city, but not touching the mural potential of its great center. After some preliminary exploration in this area, the National Institute of Anthropology and History, or INAH, began in 1960 to realize the dream of comprehensive discovery and consolidation of the monumental ruins in the ceremonial area, which extends the entire length of the Road of the Dead from the Pyramid of the Moon at the northern extremity to the Ciudadela at the south.

The first discoveries and reconstructions, made at this time in the Plaza of the Moon with brilliant use of scientific methods, were so impressive that in 1962 the

Photo R. Moya. Courtesy Instituto Nacional de Antropología e Historia

16. Quetzalpapalotl Blows Conch. Excavation by Jorge Acosta and Eduardo Matos, Zone 2, Teotihuacan.

Mexican government appropriated a large sum to INAH so that the ambitious plan of restoration could proceed without delay. Gradually, mounds of earth that for centuries have marked this area are being transformed into stepped temple pedestals faced with stone. These impressive structures surround the Plaza of the Pyramid of the Moon and border the Road of the Dead, affirming the grandeur of this city in its last period. Behind the pyramidal temples extend ruins of elaborate palaces, where exploration of a few selected sites in depth has uncovered superimposed structures. Indications are everywhere that the walls of Teotihuacan have been painted both inside and out during different periods. Most especially, frescoes have been recovered from the next to last period of Teotihuacan civilization. For the work of discovery and reconstruction the Cere-

monial Center is divided into zones that begin with the Plaza of the Moon, each zone being under the direction of a different archeologist. The murals are identified according to the zone where they are found.

Dr. Ignacio Bernal, in his interesting report of the initial work of consolidating Teotihuacan monuments (1963), mentions a few sites in which frescoes had been uncovered at that time. In all exploratory work frescoes continue to be unearthed, but no special effort is being made to mine the rich treasure of mural art that lies buried in Teotihuacan. This work is but begun.

El Palacio de Quetzalpapalotl, Zone 2: Frescoes were first discovered in a palace complex behind the temple in the southwest corner of the Plaza of the Moon, and near the Temple of Agriculture, where the first frescoes had been excavated in 1884. Extensive exploration of this site by Jorge Acosta, assisted by Eduardo Matos, disclosed at different levels a series of patios and temple rooms which have been more completely restored than in other sites. This is called the Palace of Quetzalpapalotl, "Bird-butterfly," from bas reliefs of birds that decorate stone pillars around an open court. A frescoed dado in this court is a decorative frieze of the stepped spiral, a design later associated with the Toltec god Quetzalcoatl. In an adjoining temple, named Caracoles Emplumados, "Shells with Feathers," from sculptured decorations found here, very many frescoed motifs were found, among which green birds with yellow bills and feet are painted in profile, four in a row on the walls that flank the stairway. All motifs had been outlined in black and afterwards filled in with color.

The large West Patio of the Palace of Quetzalpapalotl is enclosed by rooms, and murals have been found in those on the north side. A procession of jaguars blow conchs through mouthpieces (Plate 16), the shells decorated with plumes, speech scrolls extending, and water dripping. In another room a Teotihuacan personage in a feather headdress is painted in different tones of red. Jaguars covered with nets, as in Tetitla and Atetelco, appear here also (Plate 17).

Montículo 1, Zone 4: In the first mound of Zone 4 of the Ceremonial Center, adjoining Zone 2 on the west side of the Road of the Dead, Hector Gálvez found a small room from the next to last period. In it painted decoration, preserved on the lowest section of all walls, also covers one upper wall and parts of two others. This fresco indicates an original continuous frieze around the room, a frieze formed of currents of water which are represented by heavy lines that rise in peaks at regular intervals, with undulations of a great serpent showing here and there. Animals and birds, or fish, appear in the frieze in a variety of relationships. In one incident, water filled with symbols flows from the mouth of a seated jaguar facing a seated bird or fish. Between lines of the frieze, water flows in one direction from the mouth of a jaguar and in the other from the mouth of a strange bird-fish (it has teeth). An upright jaguar, decorated with spots formed as three-petal flowers, holds the head of the bird-fish between its teeth (Plate 18). In another episode, animals strongly drawn in black confront each other with teeth and claws. This realism, so distinct from other known Teotihuacan paintings, is considered to presage painting in the last period.

Zone 3: In Zone 3, just across the Road of the Dead from Zone 4, was found a polychrome painting of a

Photo R. Moya. Courtesy Instituto Nacional de Antropología e Historia

17. Jaguar. Excavation by Jorge Acosta and Edurado Matos, Zone 2, Teotihuacan.

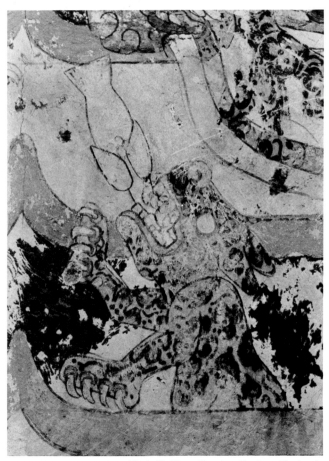

Photo R. Moya. Courtesy Instituto Nacional de Antropología e Historia

18. Jaguar Devours Bird. Montículo 1, Zone 4, Teotihuacan.

huge jaguar which is unlike all known Teotihuacan paintings in scale. Unfortunately, it is largely deteriorated, and shows only faintly. A procession of squat figures with a variety of headdresses and glyphs has been especially noted in this zone.

Palacio en Plaza del Sol, Zone 5: Zone 5 adjoins Zone 3 on the east side of the Road of the Dead. Various frescoes have been found from the next to last period of Teotihuacan in a palace at the northeast corner of the Platform of the Pyramid of the Sun. The upper palace from the last period had been completely destroyed.

In collaboration with the Department of Restoration and Cataloguing of the Heritage of Art (INAH) a laboratory has been organized for the preservation and restoration of the numerous frescoes that are being uncovered in Teotihuacan. Wherever it is possible to protect paintings on walls such protection is being provided, with the use of different techniques as required. Frescoes that cannot be protected where they are found are most carefully removed with the plaster and placed on sheets of aluminum, often being saved completely. Dr. Bernal expects with time to gain a real museum of Teotihuacan painting. "It is needless to insist on the importance that all of these frescoes have for our knowledge of Teotihuacan life, religion, and art" (1963, p. 35).

With the destruction of this city at the end of the eighth century the Classic Horizon of Central Mexico came to an end.

Papantla, Veracruz.

Tajín, "Thunder Bolt" (Archeological Zone; Site 4). Where mountains descend from the Central Plateau to the eastern Coastal Plain, near the semitropical town of Papantla, a complex of ruins attributed to Totonac culture indicate that here, also, fresco painting has flourished.

The ceremonial centers of Tajín were abandoned A.D. 1200, after a period of political chaos subsequent to the dispersal of the Toltec nation from their city of Tollan in the highland of Central Mexico.

Tajín Chico: This is an area near the Pyramid of Tajín, where a large number of mounds have been located and are being excavated under the direction of José García Payón. Fragments of painted plaster found in one mound are guarded in the Museum of Jalapa, one small priestly figure in a feathered headdress being very well preserved. This figure, exquisitely painted in different tones of red and green, indicates the possibility of finding here painted walls of exceptional quality.

García Payón considers that the people of Tajín were a branch of Teotihuacan culture.

Post-Classic Horizon, A.D. 900–1521

Tollan (Tula), "Place of Reeds," Hidalgo (Archeological Zone; Site 5)

When Teotihuacan was first being explored it was assumed to have been the original Tollan of the Toltecs. More recent study of ruins near Tula, Hidalgo—situated in a fertile valley just north of the Valley of Mexico—identifies this extensive city as Tollan of Toltec legend. The Toltecs, a combination of Nahuatl-speaking tribes from the north and of the civilized sedentary people conquered by them in Central Mexico, became heirs to what remained of Teotihuacan civilization. Their culture was called Nahua, and the Nahuatl language is still spoken in the Central Highland.

Toltec means "Citizen of Tollan" or "Metropolitan" and, by implication, "artist and master builder." Tollan, the legendary city of Quetzalcoatl, "Plumed-Serpent," here a great priest and chief of the Toltecs, was the scene of a religious reformation that failed, for from this place he was expelled. The priest Quetzalcoatl, identified after death with the planet Venus, became the Culture God of the Toltec nation in conflict with the Tribal God, Tezcatlipoca, God of Sorcery and of Darkness, including human sacrifice. Torn by tribal and ideological warfare, Tollan lasted only three centuries (it was destroyed in 1156); but Toltecs in successive migrations—east, west, north, south, and southeast—imposed their mythology and their art forms upon various peoples and, as mercenaries or conquerors, extended the militaristic Post-Classic Horizon of Early Mexican cultures. Quetzalcoatl became the symbol of Toltec civilization.

Quetzalcoatl under different names is identified in legends of Mesoamerica as the ancient, beneficent god, Creator of all Mankind. As the Feathered Serpent he is sculptured upon the earliest of Teotihuacan monuments. In Central Mexico, Quetzalcoatl appears under a variety of names in accordance with his functions. Dr. Caso, in *The Aztecs: People of the Sun*, explains the diverse concepts of Quetzalcoatl as "god of wind, of life, of the morning; the planet Venus, god of twins and of monsters;" and for each attribute he had a different name. Identified with Venus as both the morning and the evening star, Quetzalcoatl represents life and also death, the latter aspect being symbolized as his twin brother, Xolotl. Therefore, as Tlahuizcalpantecutli, Quetzalcoatl appears with two faces, one alive and the other a skull. Such identification has been the basis for many myths.

Scientific exploration of Tula was initiated in 1940

by the National Institute of Anthropology and History under the direction of Jorge R. Acosta. In contrast to the open cities of Cholula and Teotihuacan, Tollan was built in a defensive position protected by a river with high banks and by mountains. This city had been most thoroughly destroyed. Relatively few monuments have been excavated in Tula and no mural paintings have been uncovered, but in different parts of Mexico where wall paintings have survived from the Post-Classic Horizon, these relate to Toltec culture. Also, it is arresting to find in Tula reliefs of the paired jaguar and coyote painted in the friezes of Atetelco in Teotihuacan. Paired animals recur on the Temple of the Tigers in Chichén Itzá, later conquered by Toltecs. Wherever the Toltecs migrated new art forms, found also in Tula, record their arrival.

Vigorous new art created by the Toltec civilization finds expression in various sculptured forms from the Pyramid of Quetzalcoatl in Tula. There are indications that the walls of an immense loggia extending across the front of this pyramid-temple had been plastered and painted; however, color now exists only on a section of a frieze in painted relief which decorates the wall bench of the loggia: a procession of nineteen squat figures of priests or warriors, each carrying a shield and darts in one hand and a staff in the other, are shown against a bright red background, the varied costumes, headdresses, and ornaments being painted in vivid blue and yellow, accented with white; red-orange is used for flesh, and all is outlined with black. Whereas in Teotihuacan practically all figures are painted singing, in Tula a speech scroll is placed before only one figure. A cornice of snakes painted alternately red and blue tops the frieze.

Ixtapantongo, or Colorines, México (Archeological Zone; Site 6)

Barranca del Diablo, "Devil's Canyon." Toltec paintings, although not found in Tula, have been discovered upon the walls of Barranca del Diablo, or "Devil's Canyon," west of the snow-capped Peak of Toluca, near Valle de Bravo, and very close to the hydroelectric plant of Ixtapantongo. It is also near the town of Colorines, by which name the site is also known. This is the southwestern fringe of Central Mexico.

Various rock paintings *(pinturas rupestres)* are known to exist along stream beds in Western Mexico, and the Toltec paintings in Devil's Canyon have been superimposed on others of more primitive character; also, remains of paintings made after the Toltecs mark this as a site chosen by successive peoples for religious and magical ceremonies. After perhaps a thousand years of erosion, a long series of groups of figures painted on irregular and cavelike surfaces rise high upon the Canyon's walls. The stone had been prepared with a very strong agglutinant so that here and there the color still adheres. According to Villagra Caleti the colors used are yellow, green, red, black, and gray—all surely of mineral origin. Every part is indistinct.

Villagra Caleti copied the best-preserved section of the paintings and identified as gods the figures placed at high levels and as ceremonies of human sacrifice what is painted below. These rock paintings are the first murals found that were surely made by Pioneer Toltecs.

The highest figure is of a god almost identical in costume with the colossal sculptured figures that once surmounted the Pyramid of Quetzalcoatl in Tollan. Villagra believes that this painted figure is of the War God of the Toltecs, whereas the Atlas-like pillars represent warriors. A legend tells of the miraculous birth of Huitzilopochtli, Aztec God of War, in Tollan of the Toltecs.

Below the God of War is a figure with attributes of Xuitecutli, the Fire God, wearing a blue bird in his headdress with two protruding reeds. He carries an *atlatl,* or "throwing stick," and arrows—characteristic arms of the Toltec warrior.

To the right, facing this figure, is a warrior who carries, as if it were a banner, a painted symbol of the sun—similar to one found in the Temple of the Tigers in Chichén Itzá, that was painted after the Toltec conquest of Northern Yucatán. Next comes Quetzalcoatl (a figure badly destroyed) with a serpent and the Venus symbols that distinguish this god.

In a row below these gods, Xipe-Totec—the flayed one in "golden robes"—God of Jewelers; Mayahuel, Goddess of the Maguey Plant; and Pantecatl, the Pulque God, form a festive trio. Adjoining these, a warrior with but one leg is interpreted by Villagra as Tezcatlipoca, the Toltec God of Night and Magic and Human Sacrifice.

Figures in the lower section are smaller: a dancer in eagle costume carries a gourd cup; two seated figures beat a drum placed between them, the one best preserved wears a coyote mask and is interpreted as Huehuecoyotl, God of Dance and Song. Three men have names painted beside them, names consisting of calendar signs for the day of birth.

On the lowest level of this painted group appear human sacrifices preceded by a tree with skulls and banners—the tree called *colorín*. (As noted above, a town named Colorines lies nearby.) A priest painted black stands beside a sacrificed woman's body, while of three priests seated in a row announcing the sacrifice, two blow trumpets and the one in the center, a conch. Other figures present arrows before a sacrificial scene. Villagra thinks that this level represents a ceremony honoring the gods above.

Happenings in this world have entered into Toltec paintings.

Huapalcalco, "House of Wood," Hidalgo (Archeological Zone; Site 7)

The Sierra Madre Oriental, as it steps in great ridges from the high central plateau to the Gulf coastal plain, has left a pass through the fertile Valley of Tulancingo "Little Tollan," and from earliest times traffic has moved through here between highland and lowland and along valleys to north and south. This is the Camino de las Conchas, so called because sea shells appear along with similar artifacts in the archeological regions whose roads converge in Huapalcalco, the archeological zone of this valley. Roads lead from here southwest and up to Cholula and to Teotihuacan, east and down to El Tajín, north through La Huasteca (country of the Huastecs) to Tamuín, and due west up to Tula. Excavation in Huapalcalco shows ties with all of these regions, suggesting that whoever controlled this crossroads of the Sierra could dominate the peoples whose merchants must pass this way. It is not surprising that this valley was strongly allied with the militant Toltecs of Tollan.

As different complexes of ruins in Huapalcalco are scientifically explored, fragmentary mural paintings have appeared from distinct cultural horizons. Excavation in one group of pyramidal mounds shows these to have been faced with stone, plastered, painted red, and polished. The sloping walls were topped by a continuous, open, vertical panel, framed above and below with tile to form a cornice around the temple; stairs rose on the west side to temple rooms placed on the pyramidal base to overlook the valley. Paintings found on one wide cornice show friezes from two periods superimposed, the upper one a design of rectangular *grecas* between bands done in black and white, the under painting a decoration of red circles on white. In another site a geometric, undulating drawing in red was uncovered. Superimposed during successive reconstructions, fragments of the walls of temple rooms show that these have been painted in black, red, white, and yellow. One painted fragment presented an interlaced geometric pattern done in blue, green, red ochre, pale rose, yellow ochre, and black, such as have been found in Teotihuacan and El Tajín from the Classic Horizon.

Some vestiges of murals may antedate those in Teotihuacan to show transition from the Pre-Classic or Formative to the Classic Horizon. One group records contact with Tula and with the cultures of the Gulf coast and with a late period of Cholula and conquest and destruction by the Aztecs. The conquerors then built their own temples and took possession of this fertile, temperate valley from where they controlled the only pass between the coast and the Valley of Mexico.

People with varied arts and beliefs had moved through the Valley of Tulancingo from earliest times, and it must have served as a center for the developing cultures of Mesoamerica. The archeological zone of Huapalcalco is newly opened for study by the Instituto Nacional de Anthopología e Historia (INAH) through scientific exploration by Cesar Lizardi Ramos and Florencia Müller Jacobs.

Tamuín, San Luis Potosí (Archeological Zone; Site 8)

At the northern limit of Mesoamerica (the area of related cultures) the ruins of Tamuín are situated on a tributary of the Pánuco River as it flows north from the mountains of Hidalgo on its way to the Gulf of Mexico. The archeological zone, lying across the river and several miles downstream from the present town of Tamuín, can be visited conveniently only in the dry season.

In 1946 Wilfrido Du Solier excavated the plaza of a pyramid which is being eaten away at the rear by the encroaching river. He found paintings in one of three temples: ". . . the first Huastec frescoes known to Mexican archeology, which refer to the god Quetzalcoatl to whom, apparently, were dedicated the monuments of Tamuín, probably the capital city of the Huastecs" (1946). The walls of two altars, and of a low bench or platform that connects them, have been solidly painted with friezes of figures bordered above and below by designs like Greek frets done in one or more colors. Du Solier published a copy of twelve figures in procession, from the first altar, which is shaped like a truncated cone. The reproduction is of a frieze thirteen inches high and fifteen feet long, enclosed by a band of green and by a red fret seven inches wide. The figures are painted in red on gray plaster. Du Solier (1946) says of this frieze:

A distinctive style of interpreting hands, feet, eyes, and in general a purely regional ethnic character of the figures leads us to accept in a categorical manner that it is the product of Huastec artists inspired by their own ideas; it depicts, most probably, people seen in the region, whether the figures represent priests of the time of the artist or contemporary gods.

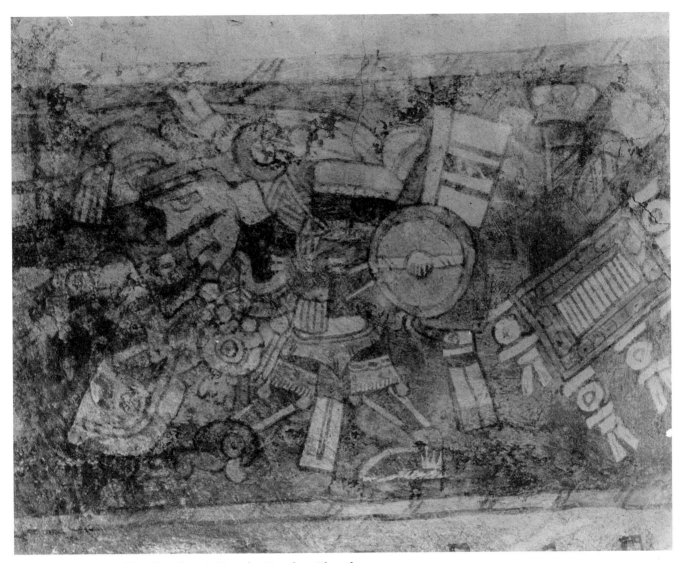

19. Tezcatlipoca (detail). Altar A, Temple, Tizatlan, Tlaxcala.

The few figures remaining on this altar show most unusual character drawing—like very sophisticated caricature. Similar paintings upon the long bench and the second altar are less well preserved. Du Solier reports that much pictorial material exists in this area. The Huastecan language is related to Mayan.

Tizatlan, "Place of Chalk," Tlaxcala (Site 9)

Near the city of Tlaxcala the village of Tizatlan clusters about a hill, which at some distant time had been augmented into a pyramid overlooking the Valley of Tlaxcala. The ruins of a small temple, uncovered in 1927 on the flat summit of the hill, contain two low, oblong altars, built side by side and painted with very fine designs.

Palacio de Xicotencatl. At the time of the Spanish Conquest this hill was important as the site of the Palace of Xicotencatl, one of the four Tlaxcalan chiefs who were effective allies of the Conquerors against the Aztecs. There is a legend that in a dream a villager of Tizatlan saw Xicotencatl with royal treasure, and that in digging for this he uncovered the temple ruin. The paintings on these altars, left by predecessors of the Tlaxcalans in this valley, proved to be real treasure. The altars are built of adobe covered on top with a layer of archeological brick, such as have been found elsewhere only in Tula and in the region of Tabasco. Both altars are plastered over with a thick mortar which is painted on fronts and sides; the color is judged to have been applied after this was dry.

In 1927 Dr. Caso published a detailed illustrated study of the paintings found in the ruins of Tizatlan (pp.

20. Skull (detail). Frieze, Altar A, Temple, Tizatlan, Tlaxcala.

139–172), in which he identifies the figures. The following notes are based on his study and on visits made by the author to these altars.

The front of each altar is divided equally by a canal that leads from a basin in the upper surface, the two side panels being painted with related subjects.

West Altar, A: On the west altar two figures are pictured battling; the one in the right panel, identified as Tezcatlipoca, is very similar to the painting of this god in the Borgia Codex (Plate 19). This God of Darkness and Magic and of the Night Sky is characterized by a face painted in alternate bands of black and yellow and by the replacement of one foot by a smoking mirror. In his right hand he holds an *atlatl*, or "spear-thrower," and in his left he carries a shield, a banner, and two darts; an ornament rising from his shoulder ends in three quetzal feathers; at his temple he wears a second smoking mirror. Various other symbols adorn Tezatlipoca, whose body is painted black and red.

The figure on the left side of the canal is identified as the God of the Planet Venus, Tlahuizcalpantecutli,

one of the many representations of Quetzalcoatl, conceived here as the evening star. His head is like a human skull; his yellow hair, symbol of light, is decorated with bloody stone knives and stiff black-and-white feathers. "The body of this god is painted white with red stripes, like other stellar deities, and hunting tribes, and victims condemned to sacrifice." A turquoise spear-thrower terminating in a flower is in one hand; the other holds two banners, a shield, and darts.

This figure symbolizes light and life, the battle being between light and darkness—between life and magic, including human sacrifice.

A symbol of the fire-serpent, a Xiucoatl, weapon of the Sun God, Huitzilopochtli, is painted behind the second warrior. This is the symbol of the new fire with which the Sun God defeats his sister the Moon and, born anew each day of Mother Earth, puts to flight his brothers the Stars.

The two sides of this altar are covered by a frieze in which recurs a series consisting of a skull (Plate 20), a heart, a hand, and a round symbol. A narrow yellow band is placed above and below the paintings. "Black lines show that it is a cord, a *mecatl*, symbol of fasting and sacrifice." The units of this frieze are painted deep pink and decorated with bands of blue and yellow; each unit squares so as to expose very little of the red background; the hearts at lower corners transform into faces. These figures are found in codices, ". . . especially you can see them in skirts of the goddess of the Earth."

East Altar, B: The divided front surface of the east altar also shows two related paintings: placed in the center of each side is an oblong vessel of water surrounded on three sides by symbols that may be clouds. In the one on the left (Plate 21) swims a nude and jewelled woman, identified as Mayahuel, the Goddess of the Maguey Plant, whom Sahagún says was an Olmec woman who invented the method of extracting pulque. She is accompanied by a strange fish, which, with shells, is repeated as the central figure in the vessel on the right. To the sides of the unit with the nude woman are painted very lively figures of a jaguar and an eagle: the jaguar, disguise of Tezcatlipoca, signifies the Night; the eagle is the symbol of the Sun. A shell and a head with characteristics of Tlaloc, the Rain God, are placed to the sides of the other vessel.

The upper parts of both panels are filled by groups of three old bearded gods with painted faces, the central ones kneeling and the others inclined towards them. Dr. Caso interprets these as night gods.

The two sides of the east altar, alike but not equal, are covered by a double band of hieroglyphs, thirteen

21. Mayahuel (detail). Altar B. Temple, Tizatlan, Tlaxcala.

in each row, in which, as in a checker-board, an unalterable figure alternates with variable figures; the figure repeated throughout is a scorpion, and the others —heart, hand, skull, square shield, sacrificial thorn, and circle—are all emblems of sacrifice (Plate 22).

A narrow band of colored squares, red, blue, white, yellow, and black, recur in this regular order beneath the frieze on both sides of the altar; each being decorated with a cross and four points. According to Sahagún, red corresponds to the north, blue to the west, white to the south, and yellow to the east, given in counterclockwise order; the black square represents the central region, or better still the region below, or the dark. Under this band, between two lines of yellow cord, a stepped spiral is painted black and white, and

the whole is fringed with stylized eagle feathers. Dr. Caso (1927) believes that the decoration of the whole of Altar *B* is like a mantle covering the altar, edged with *Xicalcoliuhqui* (stepped spiral) and fringed with eagle feathers. He adds that Sahagún, speaking of the Toltecs, tells us that their costume was a mantle painted with blue scorpions, the color which actually predominates in the scorpions of these paintings. Dr. Caso concludes that the Altars of Tizatlan served for auto-sacrifice. The paintings of Tizatlan he judges to be from Mixtec-Puebla culture, the same development of Toltec culture which produced the Borgia Group of Codices, "the most beautiful of all." Tizatlan is not far distant from Cholula. It may have been a colony of this great religious center, which after A.D. 1200 was under Toltec rule.

22. Frieze. Altar B, Temple, Tizatlan, Tlaxcala.

Ecatepec, "Hill of Wind," near San Cristóbal, México (Site 10)

Cave Mural (destroyed). North of Mexico City and just south of the town of San Cristóbal Ecatepec a small cave found in a hill was decorated with a most interesting but partially destroyed painting of Quetzalcoatl. The discoverer of the fresco, Wilfrido Du Solier, published in 1939 a copy of the painting and his interpretations of it.

The copy shows a circular temple like those dedicated to Ehecatl-Quetzalcoatl, described by Salvador Toscano (1944) "the god of wind, of hurricanes, and he who sinuously sweeps the fields before the rains arrive." Within this painted temple stands the priest Quetzalcoatl, who at death became the planet Venus: Tlahuizcalpantecutli-Quetzalcoatl, "Lord of the House of Dawn." Quetzalcoatl appears here in his dual capacity as both the evening and the morning star, one side of the double figure being a skeleton with a skull, and the other, a bird with a red beak: commemorating, according to Du Solier, "the death of the priest Quetzalcoatl and the creation of the Venus star." Twelve rings painted in a row form a border below the temple.

Malinalco, "Place of Dry Grass," México (Archeological Zone; Site 11)

Malinalco, an ancient city of the Matlatzinca in the mountains south of Toluca, was in process of being subjugated and rebuilt by the Aztecs shortly before arrival of the Spanish in the sixteenth century. During extensive excavation of the ruins of Malinalco by José Garciá Payón, from 1935 to 1939, a fresco was discovered under an adobe wall, which had been built over

it as if to hide the painting. What remained of the painting was saved by applying Duco over the surface to hold the color in place. A copy made by Miguel Angel Fernández shows one complete figure of a warrior and two partially preserved similar figures walking in procession armed with shields and with darts poised for throwing. Through symbols adorning these figures García Payón identifies this mural (1946) as representing the souls of warriors converted into stellar gods in the Mansion of the Sun above the Earth, "the divine land of war."

The warrior that is whole wears a blue-black mask and a headdress formed of a number of different symbols. All three figures have arms and legs painted white and striped lengthwise with orange-red; stiff bowknots are tied on arms and legs; rich turquoise ornaments are attached to girdles. These warrior-gods walk upon a wide celestial band formed of eagle feathers and jaguar skins to represent the northern sky. Among the Aztecs the military organizations of Eagle Knights and Jaguar Knights were both Knights of the Sun. García Payón says of them (1946, p. 154):

Metaphorically, they shared the courage of the most valiant of birds and the bravest and fiercest of animals, and so in the Mansion of the Sun were combined the eagle of the newcomers with the jaguar of the ancient cultures.

García Payón believes that the temple in which the painting was discovered was a symbolical representation of the House of the Sun upon this earth where valiant Eagle and Jaguar Knights have died in battle.

Tenayuca, "Place of Walls," D. F. (Archeological Zone; Site 12)

The Pyramid of Tenayuca situated a short distance northwest of Mexico City is distinguished by a large number of modeled and painted serpents placed along the platforms at its base on the north and south sides. A tomb or altar in the plaza before the Pyramid is decorated with paintings in fresco.

The interior of the rectangular altar measures 1.05 m. by .47 m. Upon the mortar with which it is lined is painted a frieze formed of alternating crossbones and skulls; a yellow stripe with black diagonal lines to represent rope is placed below; lower still are blue forked figures placed at regular intervals.

Dr. Caso, in his study of the hieroglyphs of Tenayuca (1928), finds the paintings in this altar similar to the designs painted on the sides of Altar *A* in the ruins of Tizatlan, Tlaxcala, described above. A difference is that the crossbones found in Tenayuca are replaced in Tizatlan with cut hands and hearts. Dr. Caso interprets both altars to represent the skirt of the goddess of the earth, these altars corresponding to the west, "the region of the death of the Sun, according to the mythological concepts of the ancient Nahuas." He adds:

The Pyramid of the Sun is a temple to the Sun, perhaps to the death of the Sun. The Xuihcoatl (Fire-Serpents) . . .

placed on the two sides of the temple are the carriers of the Sun, the dragons of fire that carry him on his course, and the altar of skulls represents the tomb of the god: the Earth, the place where the Sun falls headlong (Tzontemoc) and dies to light the world of the dead.

The altar of Tenayuca is kept locked but it can be opened by the guard upon request.

Southern Mexico

Southern Mexico is the land of Zapotec and Mixtec peoples, whose distinctive cultures have coexisted here since the dawn of Mesoamerican civilization. Of the Zapotecs it was related by Friar Burgoa (1674):

I have found no reference with semblance of truth, of the first arrival of this nation, nor of the origin of their lords, from which it may be deduced they are very ancient . . . To boast of bravery they claim to be sons of jaguars and other wild beasts; if they were great chiefs of ancient lineage, they considered themselves descendants of old and shady trees; those who were proud of being untamable and stubborn said they were born of rocks and cliffs.

And by Thomas Athol Joyce (1920):

The Zapotecs have no legends of immigration, "issued from trees, caves, and rocks in the locality." The Mixtecs have similar myths but also immigration legends (possibly akin to Toltec or Chichimeca) . . . .

The ruins most closely resembling those of Teotihuacan are those of Monte Albán.

The transition to Southern Mexico is made by swift descent from Central Mexico's highest regions to semitropical valleys. The Sierra Madre Oriental and the Sierra Madre Occidental here become one, and the merged range, Sierra Madre del Sur, breaks into choppy mountains and valleys, difficult of passage. The Southern Highland follows the Pacific coastline east, rises to formidable heights in Oaxaca, then drops and narrows to the Isthmus of Tehuantepec.

Alta Mixteca, or "Mixtec Highland," is the name given to the northwestern part of the Southern Highland; Zapotec culture is concentrated in the southeastern region of Oaxaca; from Veracruz to the Pacific Ocean, Zapotec and Mixtec cultures were dominant.

However, through the centuries these warring nations had successively occupied certain sites.

Numerous archeological sites are known to exist in Southern Mexico; however, little excavation has been done so far in this region. Because we are concerned here with conflicting contemporary civilizations, where some sites over a long period of time more than once changed hands, we cannot classify paintings from Zapotec and Mixtec cultures regionally, as has been done with other cultures. Therefore, these paintings are presented, not by geographical region, but according to the cultures that produced them. The sites of greatest interest are Monte Albán, where Zapotec paintings from all three cultural horizons have been found in tombs, and Mitla, where Mixtec paintings from the Toltec Horizon were discovered. Both sites are near Oaxaca City. Some paintings on living rock have been found in caves and tombs, and some on mortar in ruins, throughout the Southern Highland; of these a few are noted here. Although polychrome pottery was made by the Mixtecs, and the most beautiful codices are from this culture, so far no comparable wall paintings have been found from the late period. Exciting excavations have been made recently in Tehuacan, Puebla, which is south of the towering mass of Mexico's highest volcano, Citlatepetl, or Peak of Orizaba, and on the road that leads from the Gulf Coast to the Central Highland. Here have been found textiles, corn, and beans that are dated as far back as 5000 B.C., greatly antedating all other evidences of settled populations in Mexico. This discovery further confuses the chronology of Early Mexico, in which archeologists do not always agree, and we can expect cultural horizons to be receded in time in the rapidly evolving new science of Mexican anthropology. The paintings that have been found in Southern Mexico are dated from the different horizons, indicating that mural art has been here for a very long period of time.

Rock Paintings

In an area east of Oaxaca City, exist *pinturas rupestres,* "rock paintings," but no one knows whether Zapotecs or Mixtecs painted them or from what period they derive.

Yagul, Oaxaca (Site 13)

The site El Caballito Blanco, "Little White Horse," is a cave near Yagul. It can be noted from the highway to Milta, being marked by a red painting of glyphs on a rock that has fallen in front of it. The painting that gives it its name is on the rear wall of the cave. Those who first saw the white figure thought that it resembled a horse, but it has been judged to represent an insect, especially one that runs on top of water with long legs to the sides. It seems to have antennas, but no one knows what it is. Above and below the figure are painted *grecas,* or bands of frets.

Xaaga, Oaxaca (Site 14)

Xaaga is a site near Mitla, Oaxaca, where a rock painting of red hands is considered to be from the same unknown period as that of El Caballito Blanco. These could be Pre-Classic.

Zapotec Paintings

The mural site of greatest interest in Southern Mexico is Monte Albán, where Zapotec paintings from the different horizons have been found in sealed tombs. These paintings rarely survive for long after being exposed to changing conditions of the atmosphere, and descriptions are of their appearance when first discovered.

Pre-Classic Horizon

Monte Albán, Oaxaca (Archeological Zone; Site 15)

Monte Albán, ancient religious and burial center of the Zapotec nation, covers the top and terraces the sides of a small mountain that overlooks the Valley of Oaxaca. During extensive excavation, carried on seasonably since 1924 under the direction of Dr. Alfonso Caso, there has emerged a sacred city with large plazas surrounded by pyramidal structures built over tombs. Archeological material of unprecedented variety and richness has been found in Monte Albán. Pre-Classic culture of the Jaguar People is represented in sculptured relief on huge stone slabs which adorn walls

found within a later temple, whereas ceramics and articles of gold and precious stones—the famed "jewels of Monte Albán" discovered in Tomb 7—indicate that this burial center had been used recurrently until the time of the Spanish Conquest. The Zapotec Classic Horizon of Monte Albán was succeeded by a period related to the Post-Classic Horizon.

Although fragments of color discovered on ruins of temples show that Monte Albán had been a painted city, it is only in tombs that murals have been conserved. To date nearly two hundred tombs have been explored; the walls of a number of these have been decorated with polychrome paintings. Different periods of culture in Monte Albán are represented in murals, which, when discovered, were preserved well enough to show the styles of art that have flourished in this shrine of Southern Mexico.

Tomb 72. According to Dr. Caso, Tomb 72, though sacked long ago and greatly deteriorated, with its roof fallen in, shows from its structure and large dimensions that it belongs to a very early period when the culture of Monte Albán was still in the Pre-Classic or Formative, Horizon, corresponding to the earliest period of Teotihuacan.

On a wall of this tomb were found vestiges of a wide band of color framing a decoration, like an architectural panel of Teotihuacan. The enclosed design included the glyph of a god, repeated three times, shown with different numbers or day-signs, and a bag—"the Zapotec hieroglyph for the end of an inscription" (Caso, 1938).

Classic Horizon

Monte Albán, Oaxaca

Tomb 103. The entrance and the three interior walls of Tomb 103 have been entirely covered with paintings, but now only side walls show preserved art work—a few imperfect glyphs of serpents and birds. A frieze around the cornice is formed of red spirals on a green ground, and the same design appears on the door lintel. Dr. Caso found paint applied directly to stone and to clay mortar, so that it has not endured. This is the most important tomb on the Mount; it has its own funeral pyramid built over it.

Tomb 104. "The most beautiful in architecture of all of those discovered and the one that has paintings best preserved" (Alfonso Caso: 1938).

This is a small tomb with five niches. A single large figure of a god or priest, accompanied by a symbol and two glyphs is painted upon each side wall facing toward an immense head on the rear wall. Both figures

Courtesy Instituto Nacional de Antropología e Historia

23. Corn God and Glyphs. Tomb 104, Monte Albán, Oaxaca.

are painted with heavy bodies and legs in dark red; each carries in one hand an immense bag and extends the other hand in the gesture of sowing seed. They wear very short skirts, one of yellow and the other a jaguar skin, held by blue girdles, the front ends of which form banded aprons with huge red-and-blue buckles at the side; the sandals are ornamented, and around the gods' necks are hung strings of jade or turquoise beads with pendant pearls. Earplugs and large headdresses complete the costumes. The head and headdress of each figure occupies a space equal to that required for the body and its adornments, the whole being about five feet in height. But great differences are obvious:

The figure on the south or left wall—of grotesque physiognomy—is interpreted as Xipe-Totec, "Our Lord the Flayed," God of Spring and patron of jewelers. His complicated headdress is formed of white paper and two tufts of quetzal feathers. Everything about Xipe-Totec is more exaggerated than in the other god; his eye is reversed, a crescent of white showing above the dark, giving a curious expression. "The eye transforms into a half-moon" (Caso, 1938). Before Xipe a *papagayo* (a yellow parrot with red and blue feathers) is painted above a niche, and two large glyphs of serpents or birds fill the remaining section of this wall.

The more conventional figure on the righthand wall represents the Corn God. He wears behind, attached to his belt, six jaguar tails and a large fan decorated with quetzal feathers. His headdress, from which extends another tuft of feathers, is the serpentine mask with upturned nose characteristic of this god. This mask is repeated above the niche in front of him, and two large masks or glyphs fill the space beyond (Plate 23).

The key painting of this tomb is in the center of the far wall—a great red head with eyebrows and lips painted blue; a nose ornament and a collar of jade with pendant pearls adorn it. The headdress is formed of a single knot caught in the center by a red bead. Large symbols extend symmetrically from the head and fill the end wall, except where interrupted by three niches (one below the head in the center and one in each corner) decorated with spots of vermilion. This head no longer exists. Large painted symbols decorate the door jambs of this tomb.

Dr. Caso records that the paintings are done on a coat of stucco and that it is clearly obvious that first the figures were drawn with red paint and afterwards filled in with solid colors: red, blue, yellow, black and gray, leaving the color of the stucco for those spaces that needed to be white; that finally the figures were outlined with black, sometimes correcting the first red outline. The background of the painting was filled in rapidly with a brush in uneven strokes of the same red as the figures, only paler, made of the same paint diluted. All the colors seem to be from mineral earths. In Dr. Caso's opinion "There is undoubted resemblance between these paintings and others from Teotihuacan culture, such as the priests painted in Casa de Barrios and on some vases that have come from Teotihuacan" (1938).

Tomb 105. Tomb 105 is a large cruciform tomb partly hewn from living rock with a flat roof formed of long stone slabs. An antechamber, entered by descending high steps, leads through a low opening into the tomb, which is about six feet in height. This chamber is elaborately painted with nine pairs of gods and goddesses.

Dr. Caso has observed of it: "It must be noted that the infernal gods of the ancient Mexicans, those who had charge of the different regions in the place of the dead, were precisely nine and, according to the Codex Vaticano A or Codex Rios, each god has his companion, as is seen represented in this tomb" (1938).

Many of the figures are very well preserved. The finest and also the least well preserved are two pairs of deities, represented as facing one another on the thickness of the doorway, accompanied by glyphs for names. On the south wall the god is old and bearded; he wears a turquoise mask on his breast, and a huge headdress made of jaguar skin upon his head. A beautiful jaguar head drawn in front of him with the number two below indicates his name. His lovely goddess faces him. She wears a very ornate headdress with a turquoise earplug against her very fair hair. Her name is represented by a deer head and the number one. Corresponding figures on the north side of the doorway were less well preserved but retained beautiful details and color, a few details being still visible when the site was visited in 1934.

Two large niches divide Tomb 105 to form the arms of a cross. From this point to the doorway on both sides, two pairs of gods and goddesses face the doorway as if to leave the tomb. Upon far walls of the deep niches and the adjoining wall spaces, a god and goddess painted on each side face toward the rear wall of the tomb, where another pair is facing a large framed skull, the glyph of Death, painted between them. Friezes around the tomb, above and below the figures, are formed of large units. Those above, interpreted as symbols of the throat or jaws of heaven, include repeated eyes hanging down as stars, symbols of celestial night.

Squared symbols, limited on top and bottom by bands of yellow and blue, form friezes along the base of the wall, and the gods and goddesses walk along the upper margins as if in haste.

The figures of Tomb 105 are smaller than the two in Tomb 104 (described above). These figures were superimposed upon older decorations, which on the farther walls of the tomb show through and confuse the design. Near the entrance the eight figures were almost intact and the finished beauty of the paintings could be appreciated. Alternating gods and goddesses walk in procession, a god leading on the right side, a goddess on the left. The gods' costumes are similar to those worn by the gods in Tomb 104: short skirts, girdles with large buckles, decorative fans attached to belts, sandals, earplugs, and large headdresses—only here the ornaments hang from wide collars instead of from strings of beads. On the right side two gods carry bags in one hand and with the other throw seeds to the earth; those on the left hold staffs, one carrying a bag and the other, a round shield.

Goddesses are also elaborately dressed: each wears a decorated skirt with a girdle tied to hang in front, and a short triangular cape, or *quetzquémitl*, extends over the skirt. Three of the four goddesses cross hands over their white capes; it is as if these were transparent. Double anklets of beads show above bare feet, and all goddesses wear necklaces and earplugs. Their varied headdresses are as large as those of the gods. The goddesses have seemingly old faces, but golden hair.

Name glyphs and speech scrolls with each figure combine to make the whole figure form approximately a square, the head and headdress and speech symbol filling one-half of the space. The background of the figures is light red, a darker red being used for flesh and adornments, with blue, yellow, and black distributed throughout.

This tomb was found well sealed. The description given above presents the condition in which these finest paintings of Monte Albán were discovered, much deterioration having since occurred. The nine pairs of gods seem to be evidence that this painting is from a period when the Highland culture had become dominant, but the absence of ceramics makes secure dating impossible.

POST-CLASSIC HORIZON

Monte Albán, Oaxaca.

Tomb 113. On door jambs of Tomb 113 were found columns of glyphs, and the figure of a man carrying a lance and a bag; also, there were meanders and friezes, but all were very destroyed.

Tomb 125. Tomb 125 has been most interestingly described by Salvador Toscano (1944):

The paintings on the front of the small Tomb 125 are poorly conserved but these are the most surprising of the Zapotec picture writings. The lintel of the entrance is decorated with processional figures of tigers, with turrets and bodies of interlaced snakes; but the special interest of the paintings lies in the door jamb where the painter made, with more care and greater richness of color, a complex scene in which priestly figures and tigers can still be identified.

Other tombs. Fragmentary murals were found in other tombs of Monte Albán: Numbers 10, 50, 52, 110, but these were less clear than the ones described above.

Mixtec Paintings

The skilled Mixtec nation made elaborate polychrome pottery, examples of which are extant; this culture produced also the greatest number and most beautiful of the codices that have survived from Pre-Conquest Mexico. Temples pictured in these codices are integrally painted. Nothing commensurate with this art has been uncovered on walls in this region, but there are some indications that mural art was prevalent in different Mixtec areas over a long period of time. It is hoped that paintings will be uncovered in tombs left by these people.

ROCK PAINTINGS

A few rock paintings found in the rugged Alta Mixteca can be assumed to be from the Mixtecs, whose culture has been dominant throughout this area. However, it is not known when rock paintings were made.

Colotlipa, Guerrero (Site 16)

East of Chilpancingo, in the Alta Mixteca of the state of Guerrero, rock paintings, on which nothing has been published, were found by Robert Weitlaner, on the inner walls of a cave. The cave is near Colotlipa, a village south of Chilapa. Unfortunately, notes on this discovery are not available, but this writer remembers a report that the paintings were of two jaguars and that they were rather finely drawn.

Acatlan, Guerrero (Site 17)

In the same general direction as Colotlipa, a little north of Chilapa near Acatlan, rock paintings were first reported in the spring of 1948 by E. Cornejo C. The site was visited by Bodil Christensen, who photographed

24. Eagle Sun and Xolotl (detail). Wall Frieze, Mitla, Oaxaca.

a figure and described the site in a letter to the author:

The frescoes are outside a cave painted on the rock itself ten meters above where you stand. The color is still pretty good, strange to say, as sun and rain must have beaten against the paintings for more than 400 years. As far as I can make out, one represents a seated figure of life size; the legs are crossed and something is held in the hands. The colors are red and green and a little yellow. It would be very hard to trace the figure because on a scaffold you would be too close, and there is no possibility of getting to the level of the paintings at a little distance, as they are situated halfway up the mountain side. Maybe it would be possible—only difficult.

Miss Christensen's photograph shows, indistinctly, a front-view figure seated cross-legged with profiled head facing to its right. Painted in the deep red of iron oxide, the figure is outlined and ornamented with beads and earplugs in the light green of copper oxide. Touches of yellow show faintly near the head. Another painting, a large dark head in profile, shows nearby on the slightly sheltered surface of the mountain. Miss Christensen remembers the paintings as looking like a Mixtec codex.

Classic Horizon

Yucuñudahuí, "Hill of the Mist," Oaxaca (Site 18)

In the Alta Mixteca, east of the region where the rock paintings have been seen but far west of Monte Albán, Dr. Caso reported in 1938 the finding of a painting on a tomb on a hill near Tilantongo called Yucuñudahuí.

This is a site occupied by Mixtecs in an early period; ceramics found here indicate contact with both Teotihuacan and Monte Albán.

Tomb I. A painting was found upon a stone slab that covered the entrance to Tomb I here. Dr. Caso described human figures combined with glyphs painted in brilliant red, and all enclosed by a frame. Only the lower parts of two standing figures remained, painted to either side of a square containing a head, which he considered to resemble the Zapotec God of Rain, Cosijo. Numerals were placed under each unit of the decoration. The little painting that remained on walls of the tomb showed figures and numerals in the same brilliant red; one of two seated figures had crossed legs. These paintings were from late in the Classic Horizon; they have entirely disintegrated.

Unclassified

Teloloapan, "In the River of Rocks," Guerrero (Site 19)

Teloloapan, an almost unexplored early city, lies west of Iguala in the Alta Mixteca. In Mexicapan, a *barrio* of Teloloapan, a frescoed ruin uncovered in 1931 was reported to Miss Christensen in 1940 by E. Cornejo C. Through exposure the geometric decoration had soon deteriorated, but what remained at that time showed that the building had been decorated elaborately with brilliant colors and bold designs.

Xochicalco, "In the House of Flowers," Morelos (Site 20)

Situated southwest of the City of Cuernavaca, where the foothills of the Nevada de Toluca cut down into the Valley of Morelos, Xochicalco is a very early fortified town built upon a terraced hill, with artificially made subterranean passages and chambers extending into a large part of the hill. According to Eduardo Noguera (1945), traces of paintings, like hieroglyphs, exist on the plastered walls within the hill, but because the designs are not well preserved and the passages are without light, no particular study has been given them. The fortresslike character of this large temple city suggests that Xochicalco formed a link between the theocratic period and the militaristic period that followed it, the culture of this region having been strongly influenced by Toltecs who appeared here in the eleventh century. The Mixtecs at the time of the Spanish Conquest were notable for painting and for their knowledge of hieroglyphic writing; perhaps interesting painted material may still be found at this site.

In the center of Xochicalco is built the great Temple of Quetzalcoatl, encircled with immense sculptured serpents in high relief. Within convolutions of the serpents priestly figures are seated, front-view, with legs crossed and heads in profile, and hands raised in subtle gesture. In posture these seated figures are similar to the seated figure painted on the mountain side near Acatlan, Guerrero, described above. This suggests that in Xochicalco there was a confluence of cultures, the serpent being from Highland culture and the seated figures being reminiscent of certain Mayan figures.

POST-CLASSIC HORIZON

Mitla (from Michtlan, Nahuatl), "Entrance to the Land of Rest," Oaxaca (Archeological Zone; Site 21)

Mitla, built by Zapotecs from A.D. 1000 to 1300 in a valley between low-lying mountains twenty miles east of Monte Albán, after they had abandoned that city, was the last important Zapotec sanctuary. Subsequently it was occupied by the Mixtec nation. Constructed over subterranean chambers of tombs hewn from living rock, the wonderful palaces of Mitla have never been overgrown. The walls of these Zapotec buildings are faced inside and out with elaborate stone mosaics, fashioned into a great many variations of the stepped spiral, showing that the Post-Classic Horizon initiated by the Toltecs had come to the Zapotecs. The paintings found in Mitla, however, belong to Mixtec-Puebla, or Toltec, culture and are closely related to the Pre-Conquest codices of the Mixtecs, of which relatively many have survived.

Palace Courts. Frescoes originally existed in recessed panels placed high above doorways on all walls of two adjoining courts, the panels being twelve inches high and from twelve to eighteen feet long. The plastered surfaces were filled with stylized figures of gods enclosed by borders painted above and below. Everything was painted in red outline on a background of the same

earth red—like negative painting found on pottery in this region. The first copies of the frescoes of Mitla, made by a German architect named Mülenpdorft, were reproduced in 1890 by Antonio Peñafiel. Careful copies of these frescoes made by Eduard Seler were published, with his interpretation, in Berlin in 1895, and in Washington in 1904.

According to Seler (1904), the west side represented "the starry sky of night and the related gods," and the east side, "the Bird god, the eagle of the clear and radiant sky: the Sun." The photograph of two figures reproduced in this book (Plate 24) represents the Eagle, symbol of the sun, and Xolotl, "the dog that conducts the sun to hell":

The figure of Xolotl, the twin brother of Quetzalcoatl, is characterized by the physiognomy of an animal. He is adorned with Quetzalcoatl's conical cap of jaguar skin and his necklace of shells. The torn ears of a dog appear here almost in the shape of feather tufts. (Seler: 1904)

Bands of double rings, like those found in Teotihuacan, can be seen in the photograph painted above and below the figures. This painting is almost gone.

Small Court. In a small court excavated in another area of Mitla a wall retains a few details of a long frieze. Among these a small figure, apparently flying and holding a torch, and flowering forms can be seen faintly.

In 1927 Dr. Caso published a description of glyphs painted in fresco on the walls of a tomb in Mitla (La Tumba de Sevilla No. 2).

Zaachila, "Place of Salt," Oaxaca (Site 22)

Situated south of Monte Albán, Zaachila had been a most important Zapotec center of government. However, according to John Paddock, a tomb found here decorated with painted reliefs is from Mixtec culture of the late period just before the Spanish Conquest.

Southeastern Mexico

The land of the Mayas rises east from the Isthmus of Tehuantepec to form the Southeastern Highland, which is occupied by the Mexican state of Chiapas and by Guatemala and Honduras; from here the land mass extends north as the large, flat Peninsula of Yucatán. Great rivers flow from the Highland through tropical forests to the Gulf of Mexico. In the Highland and

along the Valley of the Usumacinta River cities of the Southern Mayan Empire flourished during the Classic Horizon of Mesoamerica, the river serving as a trade route between Guatemala and the Gulf Coast. Known also as the Old Mayan Empire, this civilization extended over the Southeastern Highland as far as Copán; also, it entered the Peninsula of Yucatán to form the

Northern Mayan Empire. The Mayas were the only navigators of Mesoamerica and their influence was strong throughout the Gulf coastal region.

About A.D. 900 the Mayas were caught into the great upheaval which destroyed theocratic rule throughout Mesoamerica. Ceremonial cities of the Southern Empire were permanently abandoned at the end of the Classic Horizon, whereas some centers in Yucatán were restored under Toltec rule; for this reason the Northern Empire was called also the New Mayan Empire. Populations of both regions are still predominantly Mayan.

Classic Horizon

USUMACINTA RIVER BASIN

After more than a thousand years of disuse, a few ruins in cities of the Usumacinta River Basin retain evidence that these buildings have been elaborately painted.

Palenque, "Palisades," Chiapas (Archeological Zone; Site 23)

Palenque, an important Mayan religious center in the Usumacinta Valley until the end of the eighth century, was the first of the ruined cities of Mesoamerica to be explored officially—it is here that American archeology was born. Captain Antonio Del Rio's report of his exploration of the ruins of Palenque in 1786, when finally published in London in 1822, prompted subsequent expeditions. John Stephens, an American explorer and archeologist, and his collaborator, Frederick Catherwood, an English artist-architect, visited Palenque in 1840. In reporting the ruins and the marvelous reliefs in stucco found there, they noted also fragmentary remains of fresco painting. Catherwood (1844) wrote of the principal building, El Palacio:

Every part appears to have been elaborately decorated with sculpture in stone, stuccoes, and paintings. In several of the apartments, which have the usual triangular arch, I noticed that the walls had been painted several times, as traces of earlier subjects were discernible where the outer coat of paint had been destroyed. The paintings were of the same nature as the frescoes of Italy—water colors applied to cement.

The colors noted by Stephens in El Palacio are red, yellow, blue, black, and white, but today little painted plaster remains in this ruin except some hieroglyphs painted in black upon an inner wall.

Painting, the most perishable art, does not now distinguish Palenque, but continuing exploration of monuments here has disclosed a fresco stratum. Upon walls of the Hidden Chamber, recently discovered deep within the Temple of the Inscriptions, large, brilliantly colored figures in low relief are partially obscured by a lime deposit.

Chinikihá, Chiapas (Site 24)

By 1903 several Mayan cities in the Usumacinta River Basin had been explored for the Peabody Museum by Teobert Maler, an Austrian who, as a boy, went to Mexico with Maximilian and remained to become an enthusiastic explorer of the region of the Mayas. He made tracings and drawings of paintings he found. In Chinikihá Maler discovered a building that had been decorated inside and out in "fiery red" with scrolled designs. He also found here a row of hieroglyphs painted in small white squares, only a few of which were intact: "One of the little pictures shows two charming faces in profile, one placed over the other, surrounded by some explanatory signs" (Maler, 1903).

Yaxchilán, "City of Green Stone," Chiapas (Site 25)

Of the paintings in Yaxchilán, Maler wrote (1903):

The hall . . . was formerly very richly decorated in color, including the entrances, the niches, and the surfaces of the vaulted ceiling. Unfortunately, the stucco which afforded a smooth surface for the paintings had mostly fallen off, but the remains display a magnificent design made up of leaves, scroll work, and flowers, interwoven here and there with the forms of human beings and animals. Among the colors are dark red, white, etc. Green is not as frequent as blue. The whole effect of the colors must have been cheerful and agreeable. It is a pity that so interesting an example of Maya mural painting is only preserved in such small fragments that, even with the most earnest desire to do so, it is quite impossible to reproduce it in comprehensible form.

In 1946 Dr. Sylvanus G. Morley reported that scrolls and figures painted in red and blue could still be seen upon walls of a shrine in the back chamber of Structure 33 in Yaxchilán.

Bonampak, "Painted Walls" (Maya), Chiapas (Archeological Zone; Site 26)

Although some paintings found in Yucatán had previously given an idea of Mayan painting from a later period, a panel from Uaxactún, Guatemala, reproduced by the Carnegie Institution, of Washington, and the paintings described above by Maler were about all that was known of mural painting from the Southern Mayan Empire until the spring of 1946, when, in the deepest jungles of the Usumacinta Basin, Bonampak was discovered.

In Bonampak a temple has been found with all walls of its three rooms completely covered with frescoes of astonishing power and beauty. The Lacandon Indians of the vicinity (a remnant of the original Mayan population) have known and guarded this temple. One of them led the discoverer of the frescoes, Giles Healy, to it, but in subsequent exploration of the paintings the Indians most carefully took no part. For the Lacandones the Temple of Bonampak is a living temple.

The murals of Bonampak have been visited under conditions of hardship and danger in the jungle. The ruins were first explored officially in the spring of 1947 by archeologists from the Carnegie Institution of Washington, accompanied by Giles Healy—who had instigated this expedition and was its photographer—and by two artists, Antonio Tejeda for the Carnegie Institution, and Agustín Villagra Caleti for the National Institute of Anthropology and History of Mexico. These artists at that time made copies of all paintings in one room; on a return trip the following spring, they completed copies of all murals in the temple. Although painted more than a thousand years ago, the frescoes have been preserved by a thin coating of lime that has formed over all walls; the paintings are further obscured by lichen, which thrives in dampness. Washes of kerosene were applied to surfaces during the period of copying in order to reveal the full brilliance of color.

In 1949 an expedition was sent to Bonampak by the National Institute of Fine Arts of Mexico (Bellas Artes) under the guidance of Carlos Freye—the original discoverer of the hidden city of Bonampak—with whom Giles Healy had first visited the ruins. When the archeologist of the Bellas Artes group, Carlos Margain, the artist, Raul Anguiano, and the photographer, Manuel Alvarez Bravo, had only started to work, Freye and a young artist were drowned while crossing the river. Although this tragedy prematurely terminated the expedition, some valuable material was secured. There have since been various visitors in Bonampak, and much material has been published—including copies, photographs, and descriptions of these most powerfully graphic and best-preserved paintings that have survived from the Mesoamerican cultures.

The Temple of the Frescoes. The largest of nine stone buildings that have remained intact beneath huge trees and dense tropical undergrowth on a small terraced hill near the Lacanhá River, a tributary of the Usumacinta, is the Temple of the Frescoes. This temple is a long building in which a second cornice divides the façade above three low doorways; the upper half had originally been covered with reliefs and paintings. The

three rooms in a row do not communicate; the thick walls of the series terminate in the high, triangular, corbeled false arch of the Mayas. Only the partition walls are vertical throughout; vault faces of all outside walls begin at the height of the doorways and rise twice as high again to the capstones of the vault. A small space is reserved at door level within each room, the remainder being covered by a raised platform. All walls are solidly painted in brilliant colors, and there are indications that masterly outlines, like black lacework, have defined the figures in all paintings.

Room I: You enter the first room (left) as if joining a festive procession directed toward the rear wall, where three priests are featured. From the floor to the peak of the vault, four horizontal friezes extend around the room. Vertical throughout to the height of the doorway, the lowest frieze of processional figures has a background of brilliant turquoise blue, as has also the highest band in the peak; the two intervening friezes on the sloping vault face are painted upon red-orange ochre. The Rain God (Chac to the Mayas) is represented on both sides of the blue apex in an elaborate stylization of a front-view mask of the God flanked by profiles of the same mask; these are painted in red, orange, dark blue, olive green, and yellow, all outlined in black. Symbols, a mask, and a weird animal head with a jaguar claw extending from its nostrils, fill the small triangular vault ends.

Below the turquoise sky of Chac, upon two adjoining walls, stand a row of notables, painted front-view with heads in profile in a high, brilliant red-orange frieze. These figures wear elaborate headdresses and girdles, and long white cloaks which are clasped by shells and hang from the shoulders; one woman is included on the long rear wall. At the right end of this wall, an attendant standing upon a platform holds a child toward these notables, and he looks back to the adjacent vertical wall, where a chief and two women, all dressed in white, sit cross-legged upon a high dais; the chief is giving him instructions. In this same wide frieze, on the vault face above the doorway, the three priests are being dressed by attendants. Only one is in full regalia: placed above him a huge crest of green feathers frames his white, plantlike headdress; he wears a jaguar skin as a skirt, a collar of jewels, earplugs, and bracelets; his body is painted orange. Two priests, similarly attired, stand in profile, whereas the first is presented in front view except for his head. Immediately under the priests busy craftsmen sit or kneel in a narrow frieze that is partly destroyed; black hieroglyphs fill this narrow red band extending around the room. These friezes represent preparations for the actual ceremony, which occurs below upon the wide blue frieze.

Processions of figures, which have just entered the doorway, approach the wall opposite, where the ceremony climaxes. On the left side successive groups of musicians carry rattles in progressively varied positions, play on turtle shells with wooden forks, or blow long horns; one beats a high cylindrical drum. They are accompanied by a group of dancers or actors in aquatic masks—a crab, a crocodile, a fish. Half-hidden by musicians, two figures carry tall feather parasols, shown in front and side view. Similar parasols are carried on the opposite wall in a file of figures so strongly characterized that these must have been portraits. Leaders of both groups turn corners onto the main wall, where the three priests noted above—now fully attired—fill this principal wall of the room; they sway as if in dance. Unfortunately, in this portrayal of the climax of the ceremony these figures are almost destroyed. The stance of a figure seems to indicate its category. It is not possible to see whether the heads of the dancing priests, like their bodies, were painted full-view; otherwise, this honor of full face belongs only to the central masks of Chac painted high in the vault.

Room 2: Upon the walls of the second, or central, room are described with extraordinary realism scenes of a battle or of a surprise raid. An attack rages over the large wall opposite the doorway and extends onto the adjoining end walls, on which prisoners are being captured by their hair. The composition ascends from lower to upper levels through related figures, the entire wall being woven together visually by diagonals of violent body action, by spears pointing centers of interest, and by trumpets blaring above the din. Nothing resembling this freedom and realism of the human body or the variety and unity of composition has appeared elsewhere in early American art. Many warriors wear masks with plumes of brilliant feathers as headdresses, and costumes include girdles, capes, bodices, necklaces—but the vanquished are unadorned, and, instead of the variety of red and yellow ochres used for flesh of the victors, their skin is of deepest brown. An occasional figure among the victors is painted black (the Mayan God of War is painted black). Dark green, patterned as if with foliage, forms a background of forest, and a blue sky shows above. High in the vertical right end wall food is carried aloft in a covered basket; against the blue of the similar left end wall men stand above the battle holding prisoners and wing-shaped shields or banners.

The painting on the entrance wall succeeds the battle.

Unlike the doors of the two end rooms, the door of this middle room is centrally placed. Painted pink halfway up and striped with red to represent steps, this wall becomes a pyramidal platform. To either side, warriors holding spears face the doorway; near-naked Prisoners (Plate 25) with bleeding hands sit upon steps above door level; a severed head lies on a step. Directly above the doorway reclines a Captive, the nude figure drawn with mastery (Plate 26, color, opposite). Upon the highest level stand richly dressed victors—including two women; they face toward the chief, before whom a terrified captive pleads. A spear held by this chief marks the center of the wall.

Nude figures and large insects framed in ovals decorate the yellow peak of the vault.

Room 3: The third room represents a ritual dance. Processions of triumphant figures with trumpets and rattles and staffs have entered from the doorway and are directed toward a pink pyramid with red steps, which covers the lower half of the large wall opposite the door. Profile steps ascend on both end walls to the flat summit of this pyramid. Here the final ceremony takes place.

Opposite, in a band just over the doorway, an audience of warriors sit cross-legged; in a higher frieze notables in white capes stand at ease, with arms crossed or subtly gesturing.

In the continuing frieze of the vertical end wall to left, white-robed women sit upon a green table decorated with red disks; one woman holding a child sits on the floor; another stands between the table and the wall; an attendant kneels before them. At this same high level, on the inclined end wall to right, a double row of figures carry a litter holding a single adorned figure, who reaches high up into the yellow band that fills the peak of the room; otherwise, this highest space is decorated with masks of Chac, similar to those in Room I.

Before the pyramid seven figures stand at floor level. Each is fitted with wedge-shaped wings extending horizontally from waists, and above all heads rise huge headdresses of dark green feathers, long plumes extending. Three principal priests stand against the sky upon the summit of the pyramid; they wear towering headdresses and outstretched wings similar to those of the figures below, and each of the three holds a feather fan. In the center of the pyramid steps a captive is held outstretched for sacrifice, and, above him, a priest holds a knife. It is a moment of anticipation.

The paintings of Bonampak depict the pomp and refinement of Maya culture near the end of the Classic

26. Prisoners (detail). Room 2, Temple of the Frescoes, Bonampak, Chiapas.

25. Captive Figure. Room 2, Temple of the Frescoes, Bonampak, Chiapas.

Horizon, and they record a victory that occurred at a given moment; also, they conserve the esthetic message of the Mayas and establish that wall painting was a highly developed art during the great period of Mayan culture.

Dr. Caso noted in a lecture (1960) the realistic character of the paintings of Bonampak, where men are dealing with affairs of this earth and not with mythical regions, and the distinctiveness of this painting, which has reached full maturity and represents the high quality of a great artist. He observed also that the steps in development of this advanced art are missing, so that we cannot trace its origin.

These paintings indicate a golden age of Mayan painting, when artists knew the laws that rule mural decoration and employed precision in determining the strong points of the composition, to create quality commensurate with the architecture and the astronomical knowledge of the ancient Mayas.

Many details of these paintings are reproduced in photographic color and on a large scale in, *Mexico: Pre-Hispanic Paintings,* published in UNESCO World Art Series, 1958. The Mexican government is taking every possible precaution in order to preserve these murals in the original site.

Classic and Post-Classic Horizons

Peninsula of Yucatán

Certain ceremonial centers of the Northern, or New Mayan, Empire, although for centuries contemporary with centers of the great Southern Empire, outlived the fall of the theocratic societies. In A.D. 1194 Toltec warriors overcame the northern part of the Peninsula of Yucatán. With the resulting fusion of Mayan and Toltec cultures, the Post-Classic Horizon was brought to Yucatán; this horizon is registered in the representation of new gods in new art forms found here.

John Stephens and Frederick Catherwood crossed Yucatán after they had explored Palenque in the Usumacinta Valley. The following year, 1841–1842, they returned to the Peninsula, where they visited in all forty-four sites of ruins, only a few of which had been reported previously. Stephens noted fragments of fresco painting in existence at that time in various buildings. In Xul, Yucatán, Stephens found processional figures painted in profile in horizontal bands (1843):

. . . some having their heads adorned with plumes, others with a sort of steeple cap, and carrying on their heads something like a basket; and two were standing on their hands with their heels in the air. These figures were about a foot high and painted red. The drawing was good, the attitudes spirited and lifelike, and altogether even in their mutilated state, they were the most interesting paintings we have seen in the country.

In Zibilnocac, Yucatán, Stephens found some figures painted in procession. Stephens mentioned seeing in Uxmal, Sayil, and Tambuche fragments of brilliantly colored frescoes and indications that buildings had been elaborately decorated throughout, but he seldom gave the subject of a painting. Of various frescoes that he noted, only those in Chichén Itzá and Tulum survived to be more amply recorded.

Chichén Itzá, "Mouth of the Wells of the Itza," Yucatán (Archeological Zone; Site 27)

Chichén Itzá, one of the oldest cities in Yucatán, flourished first during the fifth and sixth centuries of our era. The name derives from a ruling tribe of the Mayas, the Itzás, who made their home in this city built around *cenotes*—huge natural wells furnishing the all-important water supply. When the Toltecs arrived in Yucatán at the end of the twelfth century, Chichén Itzá became the center of Mayan-Toltec culture. Paintings from before and after the Toltec Conquest have been found here.

Elaborate frecoes doubtlessly have existed upon both exterior and interior walls of the numerous temples of Chichén Itzá. Existing copies and descriptions record paintings that were found in three sites of New Chichén, but, unfortunately, these indications of a rich mural art have not been preserved on the walls. An exception may be fragments of murals still remaining in the Temple of the Tigers. Otherwise, all of this art that still exists is guarded in museums.

Las Monjas, "The Nuns' Palace." Wall paintings found in this largest and most elaborate building of Chichén Itzá, which dates from the Classic Horizon of the city, were first reported by John Stephens in 1843:

The two extreme doorways open into chambers, in each of which are three long recesses in the back of the wall, extending from the floor to the ceiling, all of which, from the remains still visible, were once ornamented with paintings. . . .
(Above) . . . an apartment 47 feet long and nine feet deep, having nine long niches in the back wall; all the walls from the floor to the peak of the arch had been covered with painted designs, now wantonly defaced, but the remains of which present colors in some places still bright and vivid; and among these remains detached portions of human figures continually recur, well-drawn, with heads adorned with plumes of feathers, and in the hands bearing shields and spears.

About 1900 Teobert Maler made numerous tracings of frescoes in this and other buildings in Chichén Itzá, and a few years later Theodore Willard took photographs of the murals or made copies for the Peabody Museum.

At the end of the century A. P. Maudslay reported on the paintings (1895–1902):

. . . battle scenes and other designs; a very few small patches of these paintings still adhere to the walls, and it is just possible to make out figures of warriors ten to twelve inches high, with shields and lances in their hands. Blue, red, orange, and green were the colours used.

Adela C. Breton, in 1906, described the murals more amply:

In two of the upper rooms of the building, called the Nuns' Palace, the wall and the vaulted ceiling were entirely covered with scenes which had backgrounds with thatched houses and trees, also temples with high-pitched roofs enclosed within battlemented walls. There were groups of warriors armed with spears, atlatls (throwing sticks), and round shields, and others seated on the ground with ornamental tails hanging from their girdles. The drawing was firm and spirited, and the coloring vivid and harmonious.

Theodore Willard (1926) reproduced a copy of a warrior standing on a pyramidal structure, in his right hand a shield and battle-ax, and in his left, an atlatl, from which he has just thrown two lances tipped with firebrands into an enclosure. Willard describes horns and hornblowers as being conspicuous upon the walls.

In 1928 Jean Charlot carefully copied remaining fragments on the vaults of Las Monjas, which included several figures. (These copies in oil color are in his possession.)

Today no painted plaster remains in this building.

Temple of the Warriors Group. During seasons between 1925 and 1929, the Carnegie Institution of Washington excavated a complex of buildings: the

Chac Mool Temple, the Warriors Temple, and the Northwest Colonnade, and in 1931 there was published *The Temple of the Warriors*, containing the written reports and the copies of all frescoes found in the ruins made by the staff artists, Ann Axell Morris and Jean Charlot. Today no mural paintings exist in this group of buildings with the exception of fragments of a huge serpent on a wall of the Chac Mool Temple. This temple, one-half of which had been filled with rubble and incorporated into the base of the superimposed Warriors' Temple, is related to the Classic Horizon of Chichén Itzá.

Chac Mool Temple: Fragments found on the walls of the Chac Mool Temple indicate that the adjoining chambers had been decorated with four similar, highly conventionalized snakes. The sinuous serpent body is enclosed by broad blue lines and painted with successive areas of flat colors: blue, red, yellow and white. Triangles, judged to be radiating light, decorate all margins. The mouth of the serpent shows teeth and "a long reptilian tongue in the shape of a decorative double scroll" (Charlot: 1927). Headdress and tail and successive curves of the snake's body are decorated with clusters of flowerlike forms (Plate 27).

In the Temple of Chac Mool two side benches were reconstructed from frescoed stones discovered in the rubble filling the temple. The decorated fronts of the benches, including a slightly jutting seven-inch cornice, were forty inches high and twenty-five feet long. Ann Axell Morris, in 1928, described the paintings as representing files of seated priests and warriors framed by broad blue bands. On one bench priests were seated upon benches covered with jaguar skins; on the other, warriors were seated upon jaguar stools with jaguars shown front view and the human figures in profile.

Warriors' Temple: This partially restored temple, built over the Chac Mool Temple, stands upon a pyramidal base of four receding terraces. A wide flight of steep steps leads to the triple temple entrance, which is divided by two columns in the form of huge feathered serpents, with heads on the ground and tail rattles raised to support a lintel, a construction introduced by Toltec builders. This large temple's restored high walls are now bare. However, when the fallen stones were taken from the rubble, painted plaster still adhered to many surfaces. By putting together the pieces the Carnegie staff made remarkable reconstructions of several large frescoed panels and determined what the entire decoration had been. Copies of these panels are reproduced in color in *The Temple of the Warriors*.

One panel, twelve and one-half feet by seven feet,

27. Serpent Detail. Temple of Chac Mool, Chichén Itzá, Yucatán.

shows a village by the sea with thatched houses, trees, and men and women going about their daily tasks. In each of three canoes, paddled by Maya workers in breechcloths, ride two darker Toltec warriors dressed in tunics and armed with atlatls and shields and darts. Also of darker skin is a priest seated within a temple, where from an inner sanctuary rises a feathered serpent. Another reproduction shows an attack on a seacoast village and also a temple on an island; the victors lead stripped captives to be sacrificed.

In the course of reconstructing the fragments of plaster it was determined that the temple interior had been entirely covered with paintings. The lower walls were covered to a height of five and one-half feet with bands of different colors, above which rose the scenic strips like those described. The vaults were decorated with great serpents, trees, humans, and scrolls, "lined in with rough sweeping strokes." Ann Axell Morris, who made the copies, noted that the figures increased in scale on the highest levels so that no change in size was noticed by the eye looking upward.

The Northwest Colonnade: Leading from the steps of the Warriors' Temple and along the right-hand side of its base is a colonnade formed by a great number of squared columns. Each column is decorated on all four sides with life-sized figures of warriors in painted bas-relief. Similar columns, with warriors and priests sculptured in low relief and painted in brilliant colors, were found in the Chac Mool and Warriors' Temples, where they served to support the roofs. This same type of pillar is found in the ruins of Tollan, the Toltec city in

Central Mexico. The Colonnade of the Warriors Group is still resplendent with these painted reliefs of warriors dressed in tunics, headdresses, and armaments endlessly varied in design, but the only fresco found here on an exterior wall has not been preserved. Ann Morris left this description: "The back wall of the Northwest Colonnade, immediately to the south of the Stairway leading to the Temple of the Warriors [shows] a double file of warriors in gorgeous and variegated costumes. The technique is different in having the entire background in deep rich red, and the whole design painted thereupon in opaque colors, giving to the whole an unusual and rather startling brilliancy."

Large, bold, polychrome figures were uncovered on some sections of the Temple's base between coatings of lime wash, but these show now more as drawings in black.

Some fragments of frescoed plaster from the Temple of the Warriors Group are preserved in the Museum of Yucatán in Mérida.

Temple of the Tigers. The beautiful little Temple of the Tigers overlooks the Ball Court and belongs to this complex of buildings. The name derives from a bas-relief frieze of a procession of jaguars walking in pairs, which decorates an elaborate cornice around the Temple. The entrance to the Temple is between two pillars formed as feathered serpents which support the façade of the building upon upraised tails. Both of these motifs, jaguars in pairs and feathered serpents, were contributed by the Toltecs, but the construction of the Temple is the usual corbeled vault of the Mayas. There were indications that the exterior of the temple had been brilliantly colored, and it is assumed that the panels into which the wall surfaces are divided were originally decorated with paintings. The interior of the Temple's two rooms had been covered with painted designs, but complete murals were extant in only the inner room.

The paintings of the Temple of the Tigers were first reported in 1843 by John Stephens:

We entered an inner chamber, the walls and ceiling of which are covered, from the floor to the peak of the arch, with designs in painting, representing in bright and vivid colors, human figures, battles, houses, trees, and conspicuous on one of the walls is a large canoe; but the first feeling of gratified surprise was followed by heavy disappointment, for the whole was mutilated and disfigured . . . . In some places the plaster was broken off; in every part deep and malignant scratches appeared on the walls; and while individual figures were entire, the connection of the subjects could not be made out.

Catherwood's drawings of separate figures were published by Stephens.

Augustus LePlongeon made numerous imaginative copies of successive groups of figures that he found on the walls of the Temple of the Tigers in 1875, and later he published two books with his interpretations of these murals.

Various copies, tracings, and descriptions have been made of the frescoes in the Temple of the Tigers. Today almost nothing remains on the walls, but this little shows the scale of the figures that in balanced compositions covered all lower walls to a height of about nine feet; also, it indicates the fine quality of this work. These were the first paintings to give a clear mural message from the Early Mayas, and they have inspired much serious consideration by artists. The paintings in the Temple of the Tigers proved that a strong mural tradition had existed in Yucatán.

These panels most probably record the Toltec Conquest.

The Battle: On the vertical wall to the right of the doorway as you enter, the panel, though incomplete and badly marred, is better preserved than those on other walls. A tracing made fifty years ago by Teobert Maler (retraced and published by Theodore Willard) shows about 150 figures eight or nine inches high distributed over a square panel, as if upon a map of the scene represented. This depicts a battle. Across the upper section of the panel is shown a village with women standing among thatched-roof houses; some of them urge on the warriors engaged in combat across the center of the wall (Plate 28). It is a strange battle— no horror, no death; it is more like a battle ballet. Against a dark green field, figures converge toward the center of the panel, but in irregular movements of short files of armed warriors, whose oblique spears, or atlatls —poised for throwing—often are placed at right angles to bundles of darts carried with their shields, so that the movement is visually arrested (Plate 29). Lines of warriors, weaving back and forth and up and down, easily carry the eye into each section of the panel, balance and counterpoise directing the movements. Long, straight, flying spears, repeated diagonally, also unify the pyramidal composition. Two leaders on the right side of the panel are armed like the rest, but above their heads rise snakes with darting tongues; a chief on the opposite side also has his protecting serpent. In the center of the lowest section a timekeeper kneels before a calendar wheel, and important personages sit in consultation in shelters along the lower border of the panel. In the upper lefthand corner above the houses, a fantastic file

28. Battle Detail. Temple of the Tigers, Chichén Itzá, Yucatán.

29. Battle Detail. Temple of the Tigers, Chichén Itzá, Yucatán.

30. Three Musicians. Temple of the Tigers, Chichén Itzá, Yucatán.

of armed figures enters the picture horizontally, like a dancing chorus. Warriors on this battlefield wear short tunics and helmets surmounted by turniplike forms with single long plumes; notables wear ornamented cloaks, probably of feathers.

End panel: The adjoining end wall was described by Adela C. Breton in 1906 as "a scene of attack, with high scaffold towers and a ladder of a notched tree trunk, on which some of the assailants are perched. Here the men are taller and more athletic than in previous scenes." Tall yellow buildings still show faintly in this panel.

Long wall: The long wall that faces the doorway was elaborately decorated in this right-end section. Miss Breton records "some more important houses, forming a town, with a forest on both sides in which are animals, snakes and birds." A copy, reproduced in color by Maudslay, shows delightful details of this forest and includes two figures. Though all of the recorded paintings

were gone in 1934, it was from this section of the wall that the fragment containing three musicians was photographed (Plate 30).

From the center of this long wall, opposite the doorway, two standing life-sized figures have entirely disappeared.

On the left end of the long wall were undulating red hills over which "warriors of the blue feather" advanced. Theodore Willard, in *The City of the Sacred Well*, reproduces a beautiful copy of this painting, in which defenders are indicated in the foreground. It is now entirely erased. Also gone are "personages against a background of blue sky" that were painted upon the adjacent end wall.

To the left of the entrance, the companion panel to The Battle still contains the curved brown form designated by Stephens as a canoe. It looks like a large canoe, but Miss Breton considered it to be a defensive barrier, similar to one in Las Monjas, built about a group of houses which had been captured by blue warriors in feather cloaks. The figures are almost gone.

Copies of these wall paintings made by Miss Breton belong to the University of Pennsylvania. Of the composition she has written (1911): "The positions of the shields . . . are not haphazard, and it might be worthwhile for a mathematician or an astronomer to study them." A. P. Maudslay, who visited Chichén Itzá at the end of the century, has left a description of a picture of human sacrifice painted over the doorway. He reproduced in color a copy in which the victim's body, shown stretched backwards over a stone and held in place, awaits the knife of the serpent-priest standing above. Other victims wait in line. Unfortunately all heads had been destroyed.

Shields sometimes cover faces in the paintings; where an eye was exposed it has often been destroyed—suggesting that for the modern Mayas of Chichén Itzá, as for those in distant Bonampak, the glance of a painted figure is baneful.

Frescoes from both before and after the Toltec Conquest have been reported in other cities of Central Yucatán, notably Chacalal and Santa Rosa Xtampac. Paintings discovered in 1890 by Edward H. Thompson in Chacmultún and Tzulá are known through his descriptions and copies.

Chacmultún, Yucatán (Site 28)

In Chacmultún traces of figures painted in red and blue can still be seen in three horizontal bands that divide the walls in one room of a building that originally was completely decorated. Thompson's copy of one long

31. Mayan Gods. Temple of the Frescoes, Tulum, Quintana Roo.

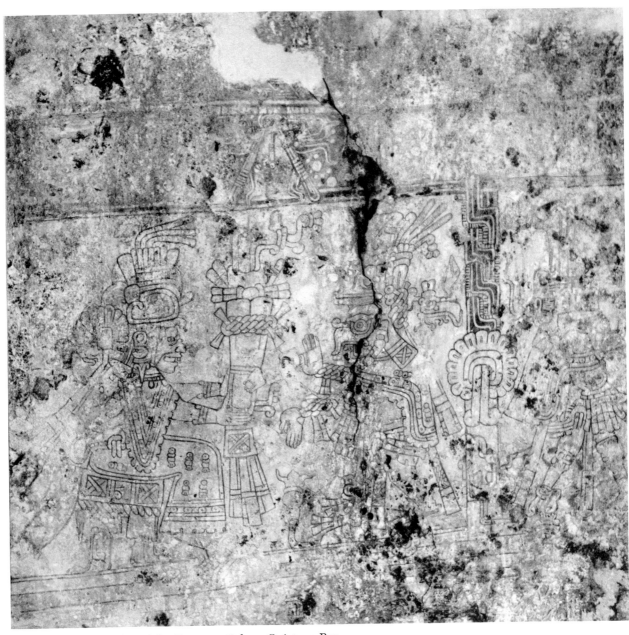

32. Itzamma. Temple of the Frescoes, Tulum, Quintana Roo.

panel shows groups of slender warriors with small heads approaching central steps, upon which several figures are mounting; they carry a variety of banners and spears, that tower above them. In this copy there is great variety of action among the figures. Costumes consist of elaborate headdresses and of breechcloths with ornamental tails attached. Apparently, here there had been no Toltec influence.

Tzulá, Yucatán (Site 29)

In nearby Tzulá all wall paintings have disappeared.

Thompson found traces of frescoes in several rooms, and in one room he was able to make copies. These show scenes similar to the friezes in Chacmultún. One panel represents a chief receiving a file of figures bearing gifts or tribute in baskets. In other Mayan sites all figures are drawn with heads in profile, but in Tzulá one full face was copied. The forms were nine to eighteen inches in height, filled in with various colors and outlined in red. The paintings in Tzulá have been classified as Classic Maya, a style anterior to the Toltec invasion.

Tulum, "Walled City," Quintana Roo (Site 30)

Tulum, a city standing upon a high cliff on the east coast of the Peninsula of Yucatán, has a stele with the date equivalent to A.D. 564. A period of prosperity, enjoyed by Tulum during the Maya-Toltec period, some five hundred years later, accounts for paintings in three temples which show varying degrees of fusion between the conventionalized and symbolic art of Central Mexico and the refined realism of Mayan painting.

The frescoes of Tulum were discovered in 1842 by John Stephens and his party. Stephens was not particularly impressed by what he saw in Tulum until, just as they were to leave, the Temple of the Frescoes was found accidentally by a member of the party.

Temple of the Frescoes. Stephens wrote of it graphically (1843):

The exterior had been richly decorated, and above the cornice were fragments of rich ornaments in stucco. The lower story has four columns, making five doorways opening into a narrow corridor, which runs round and encloses on three sides a chamber in the center. The walls of the corridor on both sides were covered with paintings, but green and mildewed from the rankness of the vegetation in which the building is smothered . . . A small doorway in front opens into the chamber which measures eleven feet by seven; of this, too, the walls were covered with paintings, decayed and effaced, and against the back wall was an altar for burning copal.

Salvador Toscano has interpreted paintings (Plates 31, 32, 33) which still remain in the Temple of the Frescoes (1944):

On the best-preserved wall the mythological scene is arranged in friezes: to the east in the upper band we find, successively disposed, a symbol of the god of Corn, what may be the image of the god of Wind, and a goddess who grinds corn on a metate (perhaps Cinteotl, the goddess of Corn of the Aztecs, or else Xochiquetzl "Our Lady of the Flowers"). In the second file, separated from the adjoining figures by the undulating body of a serpent adorned with lovely flowers, we find the god of Vegetation and Rain . . . Chac; and the god of the Night Sky, Itzamma; in the band appears a goddess who carries in her hands the infant God, Chac; and in front of her appears a jar and a god seated on the back of an animal; and last, in the lower band, a goddess with the aged face of Itzamma . . . On the west wall is a diving god, the sun that falls to the dark earth—to the sky of the dead . . . It appears to be a temple dedicated to Night and Hell, but the presence in the paintings of the benevolent gods mixed with vegetation, corn, and flowers, seems to indicate that the building was dedicated to germination and to rain, and that the fresco represents the agricultural Olympus of the Mayas.

33. Itzamma (detail). Temple of the Frescoes, Tulum, Quintana Roo.

The figures are outlined in black on backgrounds of white and dull black, the only color that shows being turquoise blue. The richness of detail, delicacy of drawing, and restraint in the use of color in this decoration are characteristic of Mayan rather than of Toltec art.

Temple of the Diving God. Toscano has identified paintings in this temple as those portraying the God of the Firmament and the Night, Itzamma; the God of Rain, Chac; and the God of Corn. Figures painted on an inner wall of the Temple are a little larger than those of the Temple of the Frescoes and more geometric in design. They are painted with a great wealth of detail in outline onto a background of strong turquoise blue, parts of figures being done in red. Broad bands of white-flower designs on black enclose the panels.

El Castillo, "The Castle". The remaining paintings in El Castillo show only "the god of rain, Chac, and a crocodile from which gushes a spring of blue water."

The figures are about twice as large as those in the Temple of the Diving God, and of bolder outline; both orange and turquoise are used. These paintings are more Toltec than Mayan in character.

Other frescoes found in Tulum by Miguel Angel Fernández include a god in a turquoise mask, the copy of which was reproduced by Toscano and identified as the Mexican God of War, Huitzilopochtli.

The paintings of Tulum have little in common with other Mayan and Mexican murals but show relationship to the three known Mayan codices in subject matter and in technique; many figures on Tulum walls have been identified through these codices. Most of the ruins found on the east coast of Yucatán are judged to have been painted both inside and out in either solid color or with designs.

South of Tulum, in Santa Rita, British Honduras, a frescoed frieze was uncovered on all four sides of a mound. Copies were made, and one section of this most elaborate painting from Maya-Toltec culture was removed and saved. It recorded the end of a cycle of time, symbolized by processional figures.

It is interesting to note that paintings were recorded by Bernal Díaz del Castillo as having been seen by him on his first visit to the mainland of Mesoamerica in 1517 under Francisco Hernández de Córdova. Bernal Díaz described a stop at Campeche on the west coast of Yucatán when the natives led them to "large temples well built of stone. Upon the walls were painted many serpents and figures of evil-looking idols, with more paintings around something like an altar covered with blood. In another place were symbols like signs of crosses, and all painted at which we marveled as something never seen nor heard of" (1568).

There are various legends of hidden paintings on the Peninsula of Yucatán. More than a hundred years ago John Stephens spent some time trying to trace the source of a rumor of a wonderful painted temple buried in the jungle. Stephens was to spend his last years under the spell of this tropical land of the Mayas and to die a victim of its lure. A couple of generations later Teobert Maler, equally enchanted by the Mayan tradition, claimed to have discovered mural paintings of great beauty, but the secret of the location of his hidden temple was buried with him in 1923. The wonderful frescoed temple discovered in Bonampak, in the Usumacinta River Basin, revives hope that a similar treasure awaits discovery in Yucatán.

PART TWO: COLONIAL MEXICO

Background

Wall painting was practiced lavishly in Mexico during the first century of Spanish rule. Sixteenth-century murals have been discovered in many of the monasteries built by mendicant friars in the wake of the Conquerors, and at times in advance of them. More than two hundred of these fortresslike monastic foundations exist throughout Mexico, and many are still in good condition. Washes of lime over the walls during intervening centuries have preserved many of the paintings. From the prevalence of this art it can be assumed that all monasteries originally had painted decoration and that much of the remarkable mural work now being uncovered was done by Indian artists working under the direction of friars. Mural painting, a traditional form of expression for natives of Mesoamerica, was a highly developed art in Europe at the time of the Conquest of Mexico.

Our record of mural sites begins in the Valley of Tlaxcala.

Hernando Cortés and his small army, after having burned their ships at Veracruz, had traveled up into the highland of Central Mexico with Indian guides. In order to avoid territory held by the Aztecs, the Spanish invaders climbed through rugged, uninhabited country and between great volcanic mountains to reach the fortified Valley of Tlaxcala. Here they met with fierce resistance. Cortés was aided by an intelligent Indian woman, Malinche, or Doña Marina, who spoke the Nahuatl language of the highland and also Maya, which a shipwrecked Spaniard, rescued by Cortés, had learned while enslaved in Yucatán. Through this chain of communication Cortés was enabled to make allies of the Tlaxcaltecas, enemies of the Aztec or Mexica nation, who had arrived late from the northwest and recently had gained control of the Valley of Mexico. From this vantage point they held the principal trade routes of the country, exacted tribute, and captured sacrifices to their gods from the neighboring tribes.

Starting from Tlaxcala, Cortés struck for the heart of the Aztec Empire. The route to the Aztec stronghold lay through the elaborate ceremonial center of Cholula, where the invading Spanish, as a preventive measure, massacred priests and princes, caught off guard, and thus made sure that a disoriented populace lay behind them as they passed between the snow-capped volcanoes, Iztaccihuatl and Popocatepetl, into the Valley of Mexico. A legend of the promised return of Quetzalcoatl, Culture God of the Toltec (could this bearded white man be he?), and omens of doom fatally slowed the Aztec Emperor's defense against the invaders. Two years after Cortés had burned his ships Tenochtitlan—island city of the Aztecs in the Valley of Mexico—had been destroyed; all populous areas of the country were soon to be conquered. Mural sites are dotted along the paths of this conquest.

Chroniclers of the Conquest of Mexico noted with wonder the great pyramidal temples and huge courts which they found in this land. "Magnificence" is a word that recurs in first reports. Everything was built on a large scale, and something of this scale was to enter into colonial buildings and city plans. Mexico City, capitol of New Spain, was to rise upon the ruins of Tenochtitlan as the first great city of the New World.

Mural painting was used by the Spanish for the psychological conquest of the Indian—fear, wonder, and awe being evoked through this medium for the Conqueror and his invisible support: Torquemada related that after the fall of Tenochtitlan, on the walls of its Tecpan, or Governor's Palace, the victors painted the massacre which Alvarado had perpetrated there. Robert Barlow, in his study of Tlatelolco, has recorded that on the walls of the Church of Tlatelolco was painted in fresco the miraculous appearance during the Battle of Tlatelolco of the Virgin and of Santiago (Saint James), whose reputed presence on the battlefield at the crucial moment was believed to have turned the tide of fortune in favor of the Spanish; Santiago was represented as rescuing Cortés from a ditch in Tlatelolco. Mendieta mentions in the Foreword to his *Historia Eclesiástica Indiana* that he had painted in the portico of the Convent of Xochimilco a large picture representing administration of first sacraments to a great multitude of natives. As a painting the dark Virgin of Guadalupe entered into the cult of the Indian to displace Tonantzín, Goddess of the Earth, and to occupy a shrine built on the hill of the temple of this goddess.

In Spain young Charles V, influenced by reformist thought of his time, conceived of the conquest of the New World as a crusade to convert the heathen; the mendicant orders were enlisted for this purpose. These international orders of preaching friars, many of whom were influenced by the philosophies of Erasmus and Sir Thomas More, came with the hope of establishing Utopia in New Spain. The Indians were made "vassals of the Crown," and the friars, as their protectors, gathered the people into communities in order to govern them, and to teach them, and to have them build the monasteries and churches. The friars jealously exercised their powers and privileges, and mendicant missions soon became centers for control of the native population.

Franciscans, first of the mendicants to arrive, in 1524 began to build missions in Tlaxcala, Huejotzingo, México, and Texcoco. The founders included two Franciscans who had accompanied Cortés, three Flemish friars sent by Charles V, including Fray Pedro de Gante, and the twelve "Apostolic" friars who had arrived from Spain in 1524, disembarking on May 13. Included among Los Doce ("The Twelve") was Fray Toribio de Benavente, named by the Indians Motolinía, "the poor one," their friend and historian. Another group of Franciscans came in 1525 to found a monastery in Cuernavaca. Dominican friars arrived the following year, and Augustinians, in 1533; the whole country was then apportioned among the three orders. The Franciscans shared the populous central region with the other orders, headquarters of all mendicants being in Mexico City. These religious orders proved of such powerful aid in controling the people that by 1550 fifty Franciscan missions alone had been established in Central Mexico and westward through Toluca into the high lake country of the Tarascans, Michoacan. Dominicans accompanied Pedro de Alvarado on his conquests to the south and became the first missionaries to the Mixtecs and Zapotecs of Southern Mexico and to the Mayas of Chiapas, Yucatán, and Guatemala. Augustinian monasteries extended from Central Mexico south through the Valley of Morelos to Guerrero and north into the mountainous country of the Huastecs and the Otomis; also, Augustinian friars followed the Franciscans to Western Mexico. The monasteries of the three orders formed chains along Colonial roads throughout the country; they served to consolidate the Conquest.

For a native of Mesoamerica, life before the Conquest had been a succession of elaborate ceremonies under priestly keepers of the calendar; his every art was in service of his religion. After the Conquest all connection of the Indian with his former life and art was deliberately destroyed. Whole libraries of codices were burned, these records of history, science, religion, and art of Mesoamerican cultures being obliterated. With the growth of native culture cut off, onto its roots was grafted the Mediterranean culture, then in full flower. As early as 1525, in San José, the first convent built in Mexico City, Fray Pedro de Gante opened a school of painting where native artists were taught European form. Indian masons likewise were trained in new building techniques in Mexico City. Perhaps it was through enchantment by strange new forms of music, architecture, painting, and sculpture that these civilized, skilled people were first conquered. Some chance similarities in the practices of Indian religions and the Catholic faith made the transition from old ceremonies to new easier for the natives.

A great surge of building took place. The first missions were small and provisional; they were also colorful. Indian temples soon became quarries of cut stone for construction of permanent, fortified Christian temples raised on their sites. The earliest churches were built like basilicas, simple oblong buildings with gabled roofs and clerestory, or were roofed with beams, trabeated, Indian style; but native masons had learned to build arches by 1550, vaults and domes by 1570. High, single-nave, Spanish-Gothic structures soon became the general type. Churches usually face west with cloisters to south. Open chapels—an invention of the time for the accommodation of multitudes accustomed to rituals held under the open sky—were built either as separate units, or annexed to churches, or were incorporated into façades of monasteries. The large courts of Indian temples became churchyards enclosed by high walls with arched gateways, and these retained much of the ceremonial importance of the temple courts.

Mural painting was used in churches and shrines for the instruction and delight of the natives, but often it was of especial richness in the privacy of cells and cloisters made for the friars. The earliest paintings uncovered—simple outline drawings in black or warm gray on white plaster—have been assumed to be copies of woodcuts in prayer books of the period. However, art historians (with a few exceptions) have not found the originals. An immense enthusiasm for the new art took hold of native painters and every image available was copied repeatedly. "Bishop Zummaraga in a letter of 1531 described the Indian as 'mui igenioso, especialmente en el Arte de Pintura'" (Torquemada, III, 456). It is probable that pigments and techniques employed on walls are mainly of Indian origin. Many of the murals may be in true fresco: water color applied to a surface of lime and sand plaster while still wet. Native artists were proficient in this medium and knew the colors appropriate to it; moreover, fresco painting had been used throughout Europe for centuries. Tempera, color mixed with an agglutinant, was also used; oil color was at times employed and most probably combinations of media.

There was rapid expansion by all orders. In the middle of the sixteenth century Renaissance canons of proportional composition in architecture and decoration reached New Spain, to be reflected especially in the great monasteries built by the Augustinian and Dominican orders, which were more ambitious and costly than those built by Franciscans. Spanish Renaissance, or Plateresque, architecture attained fine quality in Mexico; also, many mural paintings record arrival of the High Renaissance in the New World. Undated and unsigned, and also undocumented (with the exception of Tecamachalco, 1562), it is a matter of conjecture as to who painted these walls. Some excellent European artists arrived in the country—enough to form an Artist's Guild in 1556 in order to control Indian competition. The laws of the Artists' Guild, by excluding Indian painters, assured to Spanish artists a monopoly of all negotiable religious statues and paintings. But these laws did not apply to wall paintings. In 1686 an ordinance which granted Indians the right to be examined for the office of painter went into effect.

Upon a few walls Old World art traditions are registered; for the most part, however, paintings of this period are by artists who developed their craft in the New World. Retables—altar pieces formed by an arrangement of various oil paintings within ornate over-all frames—were being installed in all churches at that time. George Kubler, in his intensive study of the period, notes: "the presence of rich architectural forms in the painted frames of many Mexican murals suggests an influence upon the muralists from retable-makers." The elaborate mural art found on monastic walls may, therefore, derive from this phase of church ornamentation as well as from literary sources. Certainly, upon these walls true mural character is achieved in a variety of styles. Native masons in one generation had mastered essentials of European building techniques; during the

second the great monasteries were being built; the third generation must have seen flowering on these walls an art to which native artists made their contribution.

Conflict arose among mendicant orders and secular clergy and Spanish colonials for control of the Indian and his labor. Toward the end of the sixteenth century, with the people gathered into communities and the country relatively at peace, control of the native population passed from the friars to the parish priests. Educational programs for the Indian were discontinued permanently. Segregated in pueblos, the Indians were to a degree protected; they were also severely limited; inevitably, deculturation took place.

The Barefoot Carmelites, the fourth mendicant order, did not arrive in New Spain until 1585. The Jesuit Fathers, who were to become the educators of Mexico, first came in 1572. The building of monasteries ended with the sixteenth century; many were ceded to the secular clergy. The college Santa Cruz de Tlatelolco, "First College of America," conducted by Franciscans under Fray Bernardino de Sahagún for the higher education and indoctrination of native nobles and for the study of Indian cultures, was soon afterwards abandoned. Missionaries, especially Franciscan and Jesuit, aided in conquering new frontiers among rude tribes to the north. Parish churches then supplied religious ceremonial life for the settled populace. During the first century of the Colony of New Spain great depopulation occurred among the natives, due not only to tragedies of the Conquest and to excessive forced labor but especially to repeated devastating epidemics of imported diseases, against which the Indian had developed no immunity. Close proximity in pueblos increased the contagion. The Church filled a great need of the people; it was their only salvation from despair.

Colonials had become very rich in New Spain, and they spent their wealth lavishly in building and decorating churches. The restraint and precision of Renaissance design, reflected in Colonial Mexico during the last half of the sixteenth century, by 1630 had yielded to the drama and emotion of Baroque decoration as developed in Mexico. Spanish Baroque, strongly influenced by Moorish design, acquired lively and distinctive characteristics when executed by Indian craftsmen. Also, choice objects of Chinese and Japanese art, brought in Spanish ships from Manila, crossed Mexico from Acapulco to Veracruz on the way to Spain; this art, in passing, contributed an influence from the Orient to the evolving art of the Colony of New Spain. In Mexican Baroque mural tiling often extends over entire façades, domes, and towers; carved and painted wood

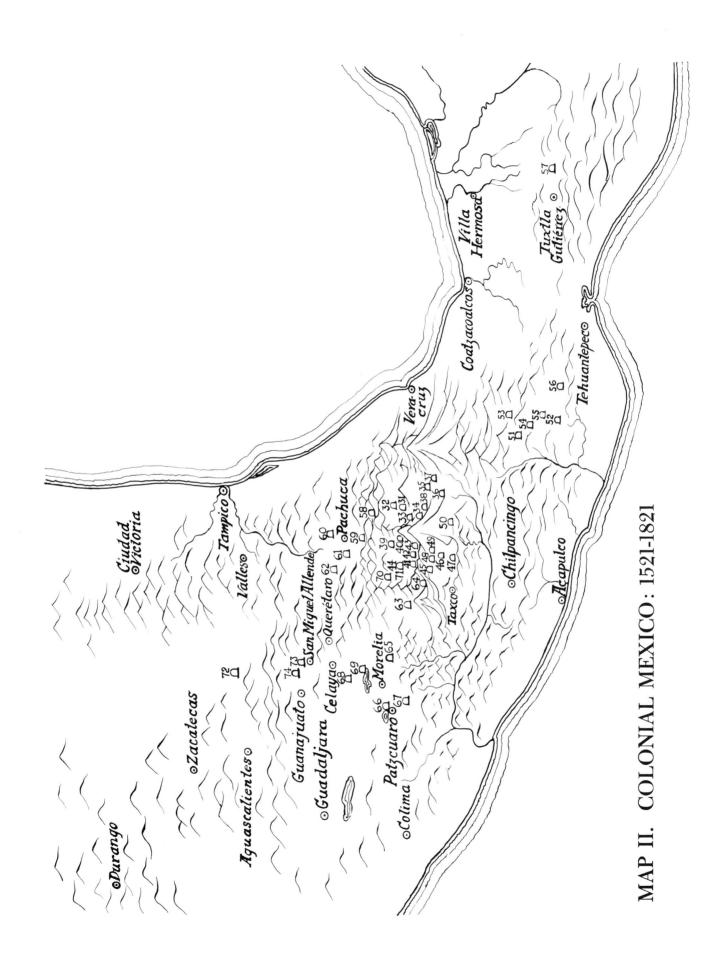

MAP II. COLONIAL MEXICO: 1521-1821

MURAL SITES (in order of appearance in text)

16th and 17th Centuries

Central Mexico

31. Tlaxcala
32. Tizatlan
33. Huejotzingo
34. Cholula
35. Tepeaca
36. Cuauhtinchan
37. Tecamachalco
38. Puebla
39. Acolman
40. Tepetlaoztoc
41. Culhuacan
42. Tlalmanalco
43. Ozumba
44. México

Southern Mexico

45. Cuernavaca
46. Oaxtepec
47. Tlaquiltenango
48. Tlayacapan
49. Atlatlahuacan
50. Matamoros
51. Yanhuitlan
52. Cuilapan
53. Teiticpac
54. Etla
55. Oaxaca
56. Tlacochahuaya

Southeastern Mexico

57. San Cristóbal Las Casas

Northern Central Highland

58. Tepeapulco
59. Epazoyucan
60. Atotonilco
61. Actopan
62. Ixmiquilpan

Western Central Highland

63. Zinacantepec
64. Malinalco

Western Mexico

65. Charo
66. Tzintzuntzan
67. Tupátaro
68. Yuririapúndaro
69. Cuitzéo

18th and 19th Centuries

Central Mexico

70. Tepozotlan
71. México

Mid-Western Mexico

72. San Luis Potosí
73. Atotonilco
74. Dolores Hidalgo

MURAL SITES (in alphabetical order)

Actopan (61)
Acolman (39)
Atlatlahuacan (49)
Atotonilco (60, 73)
Charo (65)
Cholula (34)
Cuauhtinchan (36)
Cuernavaca (45)
Cuilapan (52)
Cuitzéo (69)
Culhuacan (41)
Dolores Hidalgo (74)
Epazoyucan (59)
Etla (54)
Huejotzingo (33)
Ixmiquilpan (62)
Malinalco (64)
Matamoros (50)
México (44, 71)
Oaxaca (55)
Oaxtepec (46)
Ozumba (43)
Puebla (38)
San Cristóbal Las Casas (57)
San Luis Potosí (72)
Tecamachalco (37)
Teiticpac (53)
Tepeaca (35)
Tepeapulco (58)
Tepetlaoztoc (40)
Tepozotlan (70)
Tizatlan (32)
Tlacochahuaya (56)
Tlalmanalco (42)
Tlaquiltenango (47)
Tlaxcala (31)
Tlayacapan (48)
Tupátaro (67)
Tzintzuntzan (66)
Yanhuitlan (51)
Yuririapúndaro (68)
Zinacantepec (63)

and also stucco decorations cover interiors of churches and, with gold leaf generously applied, give Christian temples of the period great splendor. As three-dimensional ornamentation took precedence over painted walls, mural painting fell into disuse. The preferred style of oil paintings on canvas or wooden panels enhances expression of the gay Baroque period in retables, wall altars, and chapels. The greatest flowering of Mexican Baroque occurred in and near the colonial city, Puebla de los Angeles, established in the valley of the huge ceremonial city of Cholula, where numerous Christian churches replace former Indian temples. In this art, a synthesis of the cultures of the Old World and the New World took place and became the expression of New Spain. An independent taste had developed in the Colony.

During the seventeenth and eighteenth centuries an immense number of parish churches were constructed throughout the country. Built cruciform with a tiled dome placed over the intersection and towers to the sides of a decorated façade, these churches still dominate towns and countryside, and their bells continue to call the people together. With official church decoration no longer under direction of the mendicant orders but in the hands of more or less independent craft guilds, wall painting became the art of the populace. Interiors of parish churches have been repainted so often that it is difficult to classify work as belonging surely to any one period; in very few sites has the original decoration survived.

Mexican Baroque, growing more colorful and "exuberant" in character, persisted through the eighteenth century, but about 1730 in the larger cities this style developed into ultra-Baroque, or Churrigueresque— an extravagant sculptured ornamentation that covers façades and interiors of churches, where, very heavily gilded, it reflects the taste of a too-rich ruling class. Churrigueresque expression lacks the "religious ecstasy" of the earlier baroque.

Canvases painted in oil color were the vogue during the eighteenth century. Colonial wealth had continued to bring artists and paintings from Europe, and canvases painted in Mexican cities were in great demand in monasteries and churches throughout the country. In the eighteenth century it became the fashion to white-wash murals where these existed so as to make hanging space for the numerous framed canvases being acquired, and it is due to this practice that many sixteenth-century murals are preserved. Side altars and chapels multiplied during this period, and canvases often fill their walls. As a rule these paintings were conceived and executed independently of the walls they adorn and thus do not conform to the definition of mural painting. However, mural decoration was never completely abandoned, although artists in Mexico, as in Europe, had lost the knowledge and the inspiration of the Renaissance.

In mid-century a short-lived school of painting under Miguel Cabrera added volume rather than quality to the work of the eighteenth century. The school included only students of pure Spanish descent. Contemporary with Cabrera's school of art, the wall canvases of Francisco Antonio Vallejo constituted a revival of mural painting. The Jesuit priests, educators of Mexico, were principal patrons of the arts, but in 1767 they were expelled from Mexico by the Spanish Crown.

Mission churches in the expanding provinces to the north were always gaily painted, inside and out; these decorations have rarely survived. Franciscan missions stemmed from Apostolic colleges, the headquarters of all being San Fernando in Mexico City. Built in 1775, this large church was elaborately decorated with murals, showing that wall painting at this date was still favored by Franciscans, "wedded to poverty and unostentation." Just a century later an earthquake badly damaged the building, and the work of restoration obliterated all murals.

Among popular shrines the Sanctuary in Atotonilco, Guanajuato, established in 1748, is remarkable for mural paintings that date from Colonial times to the present. Paintings in the various chapels suggest that an artists' guild may have persisted in Western Mexico after guilds were discontinued in Mexico City. Subtle transition is noticeable in these paintings—from an established Baroque tradition to the informality of Popular Art. We cannot doubt that throughout the whole Colonial Period wall painting was a living art among the people of Mexico and that this art, although disregarded, was found wherever people gathered and there was a wall to paint.

With Churrigueresque extravagance flourishing in the architectural decoration of Colonial cities, and with religious paintings being reproduced wholesale, almost as a copyist's trade, while others of a spontaneous popular character were being produced, the Spanish Crown took measures to bring the Colony into line with neoclassic standards as currently practiced in Spain. Accordingly, in 1785 the Royal Academy of San Carlos of New Spain was established in Mexico City as an extension of the Royal Academy of San Fernando in Madrid.

Academic standards were to dominate Mexican art throughout the turbulent nineteenth century and into the twentieth; the walls painted under this influence record the period of transition between the Colonial Period and contemporary mural painting, and form another chapter in Mexican art.

Monasteries were built by all religious orders in the large cities but in practically none of these have original decorations survived the erasing hands of time and of changing fashion. Some churches in remote regions retain sixteenth-century paintings. Church buildings still in use, however, continue to be redecorated.

The Department of Colonial Monuments, established in 1916 under the direction of Jorge Enciso, is responsible for the recovery of many Colonial frescoes, usually from under many coatings of lime. Under the supervision of this Department the work of exploration and preservation of paintings has continued, and monasteries with important murals are maintained as Colonial museums. Manuel Toussaint, late former director of the Department of Colonial Monuments and distinguished historian of Mexico's Colonial art, investigated and published many Colonial wall paintings existing in isolated regions of Mexico and has greatly facilitated the process of record making.

The Sixteenth and Seventeenth Centuries

Central Mexico

VALLEY OF TLAXCALA

The first monasteries built by Franciscans may all have been elaborately decorated with paintings in fresco. Allied with the Conquerors, Tlaxcala was less destroyed both physically and culturally than the conquered regions. Manuel Toussaint, in his authoritative study of Colonial art in Mexico, has noted that Tlaxcalan artists were distinguished as muralists decorating convents and also as painters of post-Conquest codices, their work showing a distinctive style.

Tlaxcala, Tlaxcala (Site 31)

San Francisco. No original decorations have been uncovered in the church of the Monastery of San Francisco in Tlaxcala, where a beautiful timbered roof is still intact, or in the ruined cloisters, but an early description of frescoes painted upon walls of the open chapel of the Mission of Tlaxcala has been left by Motolinía, in recording a Tlaxcalan religious festival held in 1539:

For Easter they had finished the chapel in the patio which turned out to be a very grand place called Bethlehem. The outside was painted right away in fresco in four days, as thus the rains never fade it: in one space they painted the works of the creation of the world in the first three days, and in another space the works of the other three days; in two other spaces, in one the Tree of Jesse with the lineage of the Mother of God, which placed high is very beautiful; in the other is our Father Saint Francis; in another part is the Church: His Holiness the Pope, cardinals, bishops, etc.; and in the other group, the Emperor, kings and nobles. The Spaniards who have seen the chapel say that it is like the most charming works of this sort that are in Spain.

(Toussaint: 1948, pp. 32–33)

Tizatlan, Tlaxcala (Site 32)

San Esteban (Open Chapel Enclosed by Church of the Ascension). Near the city of Tlaxcala a painting from the early Colonial Period has been preserved in an open chapel built high on the Pyramid of Tizatlan (where the altars with battling Toltec gods are also found). As this is the reputed site of the palace of the old blind chief, Xicotencatl, Cortés' strongest ally and one of the four tribal chiefs baptized in the Franciscan church in Tlaxcala in 1520, this chapel on the pyramid is called El Palacio de Xicotencatl. According to the legend in the Church of San Francisco in Tlaxcala, Xicotencatl was baptized Esteban; the decorated open chapel is named for his patron saint. This chapel is enclosed behind the present parish church of La Asunción, three of the five arches that define the chancel of the chapel are now walled in, and the other two open into the sacristy of the church. This open chapel, built of archeological material, is roofed with dark beams—trabeated (or placed horizontally), Indian fashion—that rest upon an ornamental entablature divided by a Franciscan cord, and are bracketed by carved and painted cherubs. On both sides of the chancel a choir loft is sim-

34. Proscenium of Open Chapel. San Esteban, Tizatlan, Tlaxcala.

ilarly beamed at a lower level in the opposing direction. All walls of the chapel were originally covered with paintings, but now only rows of small figures on the walls of the apse remain, imperfectly preserved.

The principal decoration of the chapel is over the wide arch that spans the apse: God is painted in Heaven surrounded by clouds and accompanied by a choir of angels who play various instruments, sing, and burn incense. On one side is painted a face of the sun; on the other, the moon—symbols that recur often in early Colonial decoration. This panel is framed above (under the entablature) and below (over the turn of the arch) by decorative borders of winged cherubs. At some time during the centuries the original fresco painting has been retouched with tempera, but the primitive character of the forms has not been destroyed. Brilliant indigo, yellow, and *almagre* (orange-ochre) are prevailing colors (Plates 34, 35, 36 [color, p. 72]).

VALLEY OF PUEBLA

Huejotzingo, Puebla (Site 33)

San Miguel Arcángel (Colonial Museum). "The old people of the town remember when the church, before it was whitewashed and afterwards covered with the paintings in tempera which Fray José Martínez accomplished with such great determination and sacrifice, exhibited in its pristine richness the decorations left by the first Franciscans" (García Granados: 1934).

Church: Partially uncovered on the high, smooth walls of this church are two similar horizontal friezes from the original decoration that pass around the building, one just above a six-foot dado of polished red plaster, the other at the level of the choir loft. Upon a background of light blue between two Franciscan cords, an elaborate design of angels, shields, and foliage fills these bands. These friezes are in the Renais-

35. Proscenium of Open Chapel (detail). San Esteban, Tizatlan, Tlaxcala.

37. Franciscan Friars. Behind Altar in Church, Huejotzingo, Puebla.

sance Arabesque common in Europe early in the six-teenth century. Accidentally preserved behind a side altar, a section of decoration shows three rows of small figures of friars in procession: just above the lower orna-mental frieze, Franciscans chastise themselves with whips; the next row up shows them carrying symbols of the Crucifixion; the third row of larger figures is still partly painted over (Plate 37). Above the entrance to the choir a Crucifixion has been uncovered.

Monastery: In the convent, the decoration of cloisters, cells, corridors, and stairway is profuse around openings, above dustguards, and as friezes, a vase of flowers being a principal motif. A painting of the Virgin stands upon a crescent moon above a doorway of the lower cloister, and distributed over the surface of the panel, as in a codex, are the symbols of her Litany. Saints painted in narrow panels to either side form a triptych. This doorway leads through a passage to the meeting hall of the friars, de Profundis, and a fresco of the three archangels is painted large over its entrance, Michael in armor in the center. Above this entrance within the hall is painted a cross, at the sides of which kneel Los Doce, the Twelve Franciscan Apostles, with names inscribed and a legend telling of their arrival. An arched panel high on the left wall represents Christ washing the feet of his Apostles (Plate 38). A frieze of griffins that change into foliage goes around upper walls; on the right side it frames a series of frescoed arches within which stand Franciscan saints: Saint Francis, against a background portraying various inci-dents of his life, fills one panel (Plate 39); standing in pairs are Saint Beneventura and Saint Anthony of Padua, Saint Clara and Saint Helen, Saint Catherine and another saint.

Court: Four small open shrines, or *posas*, placed in the corners of the churchyard retain in their domes frag-mentary figures of angels painted in brilliant indigo and vermilion.

Cholula, Puebla (Site 34)

Monasterio de San Francisco (Franciscan Monastery). Wall paintings with the date 1530 inscribed were found in the cloister of the Franciscan Monastery in Cholula. However, this may be a commemorative date, the paint-ings actually having been made at a later time.

Represented are scenes from the Life of Saint Francis, and also the Mass of Saint Gregory, in which articles for use in the service and symbols of the Crucifixion are disposed over the surface above the altar exactly as in a codex. Here the Indian usage agrees with a medi-eval European theme.

Tepeaca, Puebla (Site 35)

San Francisco (Parish Church). The fortress-monas-tery of Tepeaca, established originally by Cortés in 1530 as a rude fort, was built after 1550. The church of the monastery, which serves the parish, still retains some decorations from different periods.

Evangelists depicted within circles in pendentives of the dome of the church may date from the end of the sixteenth century. A small section of decoration found behind a wall altar on the south wall shows scenes from the Life of Saint Francis. Toussaint reports that it is painted in oils, on a ground of clay mixed with straw about one-half centimeter thick, and notes that both Francisco Morales and Simón Pereyns were in Tepeaca between 1566 and 1568. In this panel small figures are

36. Proscenium of Open Chapel (detail of angel). San Esteban, Tizatlan, Tlaxcala.

38. Christ and His Apostles. Sala de Profundis, Monastery, Huejotzingo, Puebla.

carefully composed within squares arranged in all-over pattern. Blue and red of brilliant hue suggest the jewel-like quality that these crumbling paintings once possessed.

The façade of the church is entirely covered with a painted floral pattern of red on a pink ground. According to the inscription, this decoration dates from the beginning of the eighteenth century.

In the ruined convent can be seen fragmentary friezes of flying cherubs with garlands of roses, also of a later date.

Cuauhtinchan, Puebla (Site 36)

San Juan Bautista (Parish Church). A rocky road leads down from Tepeaca to Cuauhtinchan. The great temple of this Franciscan monastery remains intact and dominates the region, but the cloisters are in ruins. Decorations have not been uncovered in the church as this record is made.

39. Saint Francis (detail). Sala de Profundis, Monastery, Huejotzingo, Puebla.

40. The Annunciation (with Jaguar and Eagle). Cloister, San Juan Bautista, Cuauhtinchan, Puebla.

41. Vault of Choir Loft. Franciscan Church, Tecamachalco, Puebla.

Mendieta wrote at the end of the sixteenth century: ". . . and in particular in the entrance to the Convent of Cuauhtinchán there is painted the memory of the story that they had."

Cloister: In the lower cloister above an arched doorway an area of fresco shows a jaguar, an eagle, and a square picture of the Annunciation (Plate 40). It seems that the Annunciation was painted into an earlier decoration; the Indian animals appear to hold this painting between them with mouth and beak. The jaguar and the eagle (which represent the two orders of Knights of the Aztec Empire) are similar to figures that occur in the important codex from this pueblo, *Anales de Cuauhtinchan* or *Historia Tolteca-Chichimeca*, of 1544. In the small panel, figures of the Virgin and Gabriel are expressed in true Renaissance style with rich costumes and lively grace.

The portico of this ruined monastery retains fragmentary murals showing large figures of sainted friars.

Tecamachalco, Puebla (Site 37)

Asunción de Nuestro Señora (Parish Church). A tall, austere Franciscan church stands on the side of a hill near the pueblo of Tecamachalco, its adjoining convent in ruins. This church contains mural paintings dated 1562. The decoration, painted on the vault that sustains the choir over the church entrance, consists of a number of large, oval medallions placed within spaces formed by convolutions of the ornate ribbing of the vault (Plate 41); these radiate from a centrally placed Franciscan shield. Mrs. Elizabeth Wilder Weismann, in a special report to the authors of this book, says of the sources of these murals:

The subjects of the sotecoro vault are from the Apocalypse and the Old Testament, and they are the only examples of such subjects in sixteenth-century mural painting in Mexico. Sixteen medallions between the ribs at the corners of the vault are from the Apocalypse; the eight panels nearest the center show scenes from Genesis and Ezekiel; symbols of the Four Evangelists occupy the middle panels of the four sides. These paintings are also unique in that they are nearly all derived fairly literally from European woodcuts. Except for the Witnesses in the Temple (which may have an Italian source) they come from woodcuts of a group of North European engravers such as Holbein and Hans Burgkmair, and go back to such sources as the Wittenburg Bible of 1552, the Lübeck Bible of 1494, and Quentell's Bible (Cologna, 1499). Thus this decoration stands apart from other surviving murals in being clearly dated and associated with the name of the artist, Juan Gersón, who chose subjects unusual for Mexico. Even the Sun with the Columns of Jasper is literally out of the Apocalypse and the engravings

of these literal North European interpreters of it. It is not by chance that the painting on the vault below the choir at Tecamachalco has always held the cardinal position in whatever argument one made about the European painter and sixteenth-century murals. It is an important, unique, and indeed a beautiful work. Formerly we took it to be the proof that a European might occasionally do such painting: Juan Gersón, obviously a Fleming, working from well-known Flemish and German woodcuts, using a full palette instead of the monotone of most mural decoration, mentioned by name under the date 1561 in the local chronicle, the *Anales de Tecamachalco*.

Now, after only a little more thorough reading of the documents, the picture reverses itself. Juan Gersón is obviously an Indian, from an Indian family which is mentioned more than once. A relative, Tomás Gersón, was made governor of nearby Tepeji de la Seda by the Spaniards. Both Tomás and Juan were recognized in 1592 by the viceroy Luís de Velasco the Younger. They were given permission to go on horseback with saddle and bridle, wearing Spanish clothes, including sword and dagger. The name does indeed come from Europe, where it belonged to a French theologian whose principal work had been published in Mexico by Bishop Zumarraga in 1544. The subject-matter is Christian, of course; though it is unique in treating subjects from the Old Testament and Apocalypse. The models for the pictures also come from Europe—from Flemish and German woodcuts in illustrated Bibles—presumably provided, like the painter's name, by the Franciscan friars. The tracery-enclosed spaces of the vault came from Spanish Gothic architecture, the paintings are not in fresco, but in an oil medium on canvas. But the hand that painted them, using the bright colors of the pre-Conquest codices, and dating them 1562 in a Nahuatl inscription, is without any doubt an Indian's.

Considered as the work of a Flemish painter, these recapitulations of the old iconography were disappointing; as the work of an Indian they are fascinating and winning. His manipulations of the alien models, the ingenuous rendering of human and animal forms, the way he bridges the gaps of what is not clear or intelligible—all of this brings the Indian in his plumed hat very near.

Tecamachalco is in the region of Mixtec-Puebla culture, from which most codices, including the Borgia Group, derive. Xavier Moyssén, in a carefully documented study of the paintings of Tecamachalco, notes that the colors used here are similar to those found in codices from this region.

The vault of paintings has suffered some refurbishing, and the paintings nearest to the entrance are concealed by a vestibule, installed at a relatively recent time. Strong white ribs, ornamented with red and blue, support a background of deep ochre, like gold; the medallions are framed in terracotta; turquoise-blue of sky and water predominates in the paintings, with different reds,

42. Apse of Church, Acolman, México.

yellow ochre, white, and black used also in these compositions, but no green. The entire vault is covered between ribs with fine cloth to receive the color. As a whole this decoration is astonishingly beautiful and each separate painting is fascinating.

Puebla, Puebla (Site 38)

Casa del Dean de la Plaza. A most interesting fresco has been uncovered in the residence of Dean don Tomás de la Plaza in Puebla, the date on the impressive entrance to the fine old building being 1580. The sumptuous decoration shows a chariot mounted by a bearded and winged figure with flying robes and drawn by a horned beast, as if rising in flight. Castles decorate the background, and sleeping angels inhabit the foreground. Elaborate Renaissance friezes are painted above and below the panel, in which speech spirals appear before mouths of Indians dressed in jaguar

skins, a continuation of indigenous art in a civilian Colonial building.

During the seventeenth century, in these privileged regions of Tlaxcala and Puebla, there grew from the roots of sixteenth-century mural painting a very different art of fantastic beauty, in which different traditions combined with great freedom of invention and imagination to produce Mexican Baroque. However, this three-dimensional decoration dominates all surfaces and one looks in vain for a painted wall amidst the golden splendor. This Baroque art spread to all Colonial centers, and wall painting was continued as an art only in remote regions.

Valley of Mexico

Acolman, México (Site 39)

San Agustín (Colonial Museum). San Agustín Acolman, a great, decorated Augustinian monastery in the

43. Apse of Church (detail). Acolman, México.

Valley of Mexico, lies on the road to Teotihuacan. It was first built on a modest scale by Franciscans in 1539 and rebuilt by Augustinians in 1558, when a handsome plateresque, or Spanish-Renaissance, façade was added to the church and a larger cloister was also built. Until 1920 both convent and church were filled with about six feet of sediment from the Dam of Acolman.

Church of Acolman: The principal decoration of the Church of Acolman is upon the five walls that form the apse: above the reredos, an altar piece formed of a series of canvases, is painted an elaborate shield; the short and long walls at either side of the altar are divided into four wide, horizontal bands, within which colossal figures rest upon monumental square thrones (Plates 42, 43). In the two lower bands, black-robed figures of popes, cardinals, and bishops sit as if in meditation; within the upper bands, prophets and sibyls hold shields with Latin inscriptions, and nude figures

unfurl large scrolls. The rows of figures are separated by narrow friezes of a floral pattern. Great size and architectural order distinguish the figures, the decoration being boldly drawn in black upon the white plaster. Slight color survives in the gold ochre of thrones; earth red in the shadows of thrones, faces, and hands; faint flesh pink in the high nude figures; and rose and indigo in the floral friezes. The entire church interior frames this decoration. It has been partially restored.

The high ogival vault of the church is covered with a corrugated pattern incised in the plaster, and, in contrast to this gray surface of the vault, two medallions are painted in brilliant colors: one is of the hieroglyph of Acolman—a bare arm with the symbol of water over the shoulder—and the other is a design of flowers.

Early cloister: Excavation of the small early cloister revealed frescoes that may date from before the middle of the sixteenth century: Large figures, finely drawn onto white plaster, represent incidents from the Life of the Virgin and, also, several saints, among whom are Saint Luke and Saint Ambrose, who holds a book in reverse. Indian symbols—the head of an Eagle Knight painted beside Saint Luke, and a figure of a jaguar in a decorative border—seem frankly included as if they were signatures. On the side walls of the church be-

44. The Damned. Upper Cloister, San Agustín, Acolman, México.

45. The Crucifixion. Upper Cloister, San Agustín, Acolman, México.

hind reinforcing pillars, fragments of similar figures indicate that these walls had been decorated at the same time.

Upper cloister: The larger cloister retains elaborate frescoes in the upper story. A wide frieze, firmly placed like an entablature around the upper walls, unites panels in angles of the cloister, five of which have been preserved (Plate 44). Done almost exclusively in black on white, these paintings show the precise use of compass and rule as employed by Renaissance artists. A square panel of the Crucifixion (the best-preserved) shows Mary and John standing beside the Cross and

Magdalen kneeling at Christ's feet (Plates 45, 46). A background of trees, mountains, and churches rises in superimposed units, and symbols of the sun and moon are placed in the upper corners. The companion wall in this corner represents the Last Judgment with many tortures of Hell. All panels rest upon a heavy black band that goes around the walls of the cloister and makes an occasional loop (Plate 47). Where interrupted by openings, the two ends differ: one seems to be a very stylized head; and the other, a tail, converting the black band into a succession of Indian snakes boldly supporting the Christian decoration. As the loops are carefully

46. The Crucifixion (detail). Upper Cloister, San Agustín, Acolman, México.

47. Detail of Border, Upper Cloister, San Agustín, Acolman, México.

48. Augustinian Martyrs. San Matias, Culhuacan, D.F.

related to the compositions, surely they were designed as a unit.

Tepetlaoztoc, México (Site 40)

Santa María Magdalena (Parish Church). Northeast of Texcoco on the road to Otumba, the Dominican convent of Tepetlaoztoc, established in 1529 and rebuilt after 1549, retains in its cloisters frescoes painted within large circles to represent scenes from the passion of Christ. Mrs. Elizabeth Weismann says further: "Here we have also one of the few surviving examples of mural portraits of early missionaries: Fray Domingo de Betanzos, painted on amate paper where the Indians could see him."

Culhuacan, D.F. (Site 41)

San Matías (Colonial Museum). In Culhuacan a Seminary of Languages was established by the Augustinians near El Cerro de la Estrella (the "Hill of the Star"), where the New Fire of the Aztecs was kindled every fifty-two years. The monastery had been ceded to the Augustinians by the Franciscans in 1554.

The large three-nave church, begun in 1562 with construction well underway around 1576, is destroyed, but the cloisters have been restored. Distinctive borders in the cloisters show the stepped spiral so dear to the worshippers of Quetzalcoatl; and "this suggests that we can consider the paintings here, more surely than in most places, as the work of Indian hands. Murals in the west rooms show curious attempts to translate European perspective, which suggests a bold native artist not completely in control of the devices of three dimensionality, but excited by them" (E. W. Weismann).

Here, as in other Augustinian foundations, mural decoration is found in abundance. In wide arabesque friezes, griffins hold medallions with symbols of the Crucifixion, and small, gay angels hold symbols of Death. Figures of friars are painted in arches, one large panel (Plate 48) being filled with elongated figures of Augustinian martyrs, whose successive tonsured heads suggest a multitude—a solution found also in the woodcut that decorates the first scientific book printed in Mexico (1557). The three front figures in this panel hold books and pens.

Continuing exploration has uncovered panels and friezes in the entrance to the convent and throughout the cloisters. One large painting of the Adoration of the Christ Child by the Three Kings, is judged to be from the hand of an European master, but much joyous decoration by Indian artists is also found here (cf. Gorbea Trueda: 1961).

49. Los Doce (detail showing Cortés). Portico, San Francisco, Ozumba, México.

Tlalmanalco, México (Site 42)

San Luís Obispo (Colonial Museum). South of Culhuacan on the road to the Valley of Morelos, Tlalmanalco is one of the earliest sites occupied by Franciscans
in the Valley of Mexico. However (according to Manuel
Toussaint), this convent was not finished until 1585.

Los Doce are painted in arches of the portico. The
decoration of the cloisters is most graceful: wide Renaissance friezes filled with foliage, birds, animals, and
an occasional figure of a child pass around upper walls,
frame panels, and decorate piers. Fray Martín de Va-
lencia, the leader of Los Doce, who was buried here in
1534, and Saint Clara, founder of the Franciscan Order
of Poor Clares, are represented in two panels arising
from flowering forms encircled by foliage. In the upper
cloister, among other decorations, is a painting of the
Devil as a goat, alluding perhaps to the meeting of
Saint Anthony with a monster half-man and half-goat.

Cloisters and the high delicate arches of a large open
chapel are roofless. A native date, interpreted as 1560,
records when the sculptured decoration was made.

Ozumba, México (Site 44)

San Francisco (Parish Church). South of Tlalmanalco
near the southern rim of the Valley of Mexico, the
Franciscan Convent of Ozumba preserves in its large
portico paintings that record incidents following the
Conquest.

The paintings cover the upper half of all walls of the
portico and, with exception of a panel over the entrance,
these figures are life-sized. To the left of the inner doorway, Los Doce (Plate 49) stand in procession faced

50. Indian Martyrs. Portico, San Francisco, Ozumba, México.

away from the entrance; half of the twelve turn onto the side wall, where the leader receives Cortés, kneeling and accompanied by attendants. A bishop's mitre lies at the feet of each friar. These figures are finely though thinly painted; a legend indicates that they were retouched in 1848.

A large panel to the right of the doorway pictures the martyrdom of three Christian Indian boys from Tlaxcala, imposed by Indians of Cuauhtinchan, whose idols they have broken, an incident of 1531 related by Motolinía in 1541 (Plate 50). Filled with action and representing natives strongly characterized, this painting contributes new elements of realism and of mural composition. The movement swings around a vertical axis formed by an upraised hammer, from which radiate oblique lines, centers of interest being indicated by

lines of opposing directions; the whole panel is unified by inclined divisions of the landscape. Apparently, sometime during the centuries some simple religious soul, outraged with the executioners, has stoned them, so that the surface about the Indians' heads is damaged.

In the smaller panel over the entrance to the monastery, Saint Francis, accompanied by sainted monks and angels, upholds the Virgin on three spheres, and over the background are distributed the symbols of the Litany of the Virgin—wall, tower, rose, lily, etc.

Elizabeth Weismann attributes the murals in Ozumba to the seventeenth century—"the whole manner of painting suggests the free invention of artists already accustomed to European modes of representation—I should assume these at Ozumba to be more historical in mood, carrying on that early tradition in what is beginning to be a folk art." The Litany is certainly later; probably late seventeenth or eighteenth century.

Most of the apparitions of the Virgin of Guadalupe, painted at an even later period, are destroyed.

The paintings in Ozumba, in filling the portal of this Franciscan monastery with earliest traditions of the missionaries, preserve a link in thought between Tlaxcala and Mexico City, where Los Doce labored.

México, D.F. (Site 44)

Palacio Real. The great buildings that rose in the City of Mexico during the sixteenth century may all have been decorated with murals. Manuel Toussaint has noted that wall paintings once decorated the National Palace. Viceroy don Gastón de Peralta, as soon as he arrived in New Spain in 1566, ordered that the Palace walls were to be covered with frescoed battle scenes, which gave rise to the canard that he had an army of 30,000 men ready to revolt against the King. Toussaint judged that the painter involved was Simón Pereyns, as the Viceroy had brought this Flemish artist with him from the court of Spain. Because of numerous conflicts Gastón de Peralta soon departed and of his painted army nothing remains. Pereyns stayed on to have a varied career in Mexico and to influence the painting of his time.

This report of mural art in the Palace, added to the frescoed wall discovered in the residence of the Dean in Puebla, indicates that extensive use of wall painting was customary in nonreligious buildings during the sixteenth century. In the metropolitan area almost nothing has survived.

Hospital de Jesús Nazareno (Hospital). The Hospital de Jesús, established by Hernándo Cortés in Mexico City in 1524 under the name Hospital de la Purísima Concepción y Jesús Nazareno, was built in part before 1550; it has never ceased to function as a hospital. This is the only building in Mexico City that is known to retain sixteenth-century painted decoration.

An upper corridor of the second patio shows a large section of a Renaissance frieze with cherubs, griffins, and shields interwoven with foliage; it includes also a recurring figure of an Indian bearing a hamper on his back.

Many small panels between the beams in this corridor are painted with heads—apparently portraits—which are of unusual interest for the freedom and assurance with which they are done.

San Felipe y Santiago, Atzcapotzalco (Parish Church). A Dominican monastery, built upon ruins of

51. Frieze (detail). Santo Domingo, Atzcapotzalco, México, D.F.

the great temple of Atzcapotzalco, was completed in 1565. The lower cloister has original decorations of small friezes around upper walls, arabesques with angels above and beside openings (Plate 51), and strange bird forms painted in spandrels of arches that enclose angles of the cloister.

Indian symbols included in the design of friezes give the whole decoration a native flavor, though derived literally from Renaissance grotesque design.

The early church, which still serves the parish, has seen many transformations in its decoration, and no original murals have been discovered.

Santiago Tlatelolco (Parish Church). The church of Santiago was first built in the sixteenth century upon ruins of the great Pyramid of Tlatelolco, "Place of Built Land." This church adjoined the former College of Santa Cruz, established by Franciscans for Indian youth. In 1609 Santiago Tlatelolco was rebuilt cruciform and with a dome.

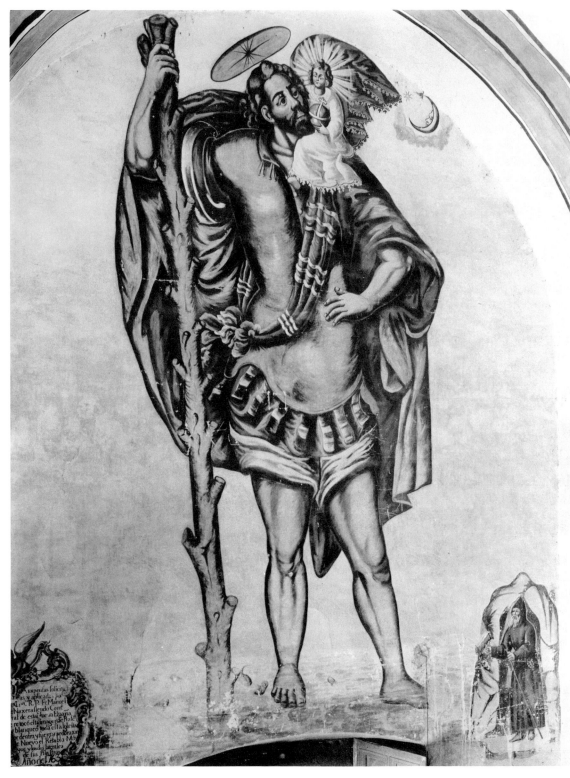

52. Saint Christopher. Santiago Tlatelolco, México, D.F.

Its principal decoration, a huge mural of Saint Christopher painted over the side entrance, may reproduce an image from the earlier church (Plate 52). Saint Christopher became the symbol of the Conquest, as of Christopher Columbus—the man who crossed over the water to bring the church, symbolized by the Christ Child, to the New World. This figure, painted as a colossus in various churches of Colonial Mexico, derives from the Middle Ages: "A pious tradition assured that no one would die a sudden death if during that day he had contemplated this Saint. . . . In harmony with this belief the size of the image and the place chosen were such that anyone leaving mass would receive the desired benefits without seeking them" (Charlot: 1945).

The figure of Saint Christopher, about twenty-five feet in height, is painted upon an arched panel that rises high above the side entrance of the church. In his right hand the saint holds a huge staff, upon his left shoulder he carries the Christ Child, and a halo is shown above his head as he turns to the shining Child. He walks in water with trousers rolled and a mantle thrown over his shoulders. A crescent moon shines nearby; a hermit stands in a cave below. As the proportions of this figure diminish upwards, exaggerating perspective, the figure of Saint Christopher appears even taller than it is.

An inscription on the wall records that the church was redecorated and the painting retouched in 1763. At that time a "new skin" was given to Saint Christopher, and the Holy Child was repainted to accord with eighteenth-century taste.

Colorful floral designs uncovered on walls of the church are typical mural decoration of the eighteenth century. Large patterns in black decorating arches of the dome accord with sculptured evangelists in pendentives, also of a later period.

Santa María, Churubusco (Colonial Museum). Built in 1678 by Dieguitos (Barefoot Franciscans from the Province of San Diego in Spain), this small monastery is delightfully decorated with friezes painted in imitation of the ornamental tiling used extensively in Puebla, a simplified expression of Mexican Baroque.

Southern Mexico

VALLEY OF MORELOS

Immediately south of the high Valley of Mexico mountains descend steeply to the semitropical Valley of Morelos. Here the Spanish, like their predecessors, were to find refuge from the altitude of Central Mexico. This Valley became the special domain of Cortés, at whose request the fifth establishment of the Franciscan

Courtesy EXCELSIOR

53. Capture of Missionary Boats. Catedral de Cuernavaca, Cuernavaca, Morelos.

missionaries was made in Cuernavaca. The warm Valley of Morelos was divided between the mendicant orders: to Franciscans was assigned the west; to Dominicans, the central part; and to Augustinians, the east. Throughout this region large monasteries were soon being built by the three orders. In a few of these foundations original wall paintings have been found, each of the orders being represented in characteristic style.

Cuernavaca, Morelos (Site 45)

Nuestra Señora de la Asunción (Cathedral). The Franciscans reached Cuernavaca in 1526, and the first mission was built on a modest scale. By order of Cortés, the present Cathedral, Our Lady of the Assumption, was begun in 1529; a side door is dated 1552.

Open Chapel: Fragments of design show that the open chapel has been painted throughout. Above the

54. Transport of Missionaries (detail); Crucifixion of Missionaries (detail). Catedral de Cuernavaca, Cuernavaca, Morelos.

doorway that leads from here to the cloister a fresco in black outline shows a figure of Saint Francis framed with a Renaissance border design called *de Romano.*

Cloister: A fresco in the lower cloister of the monastery undoubtedly is among the earliest Colonial murals. Arranged like two pages of an illumined manuscript, successive rows of small half figures of sainted monks and nuns hold shields bearing their names. Between these panels a series of three smaller panels, one below the other, depict scenes from the life of Saint Francis. Angels bear scrolls in the outer borders, and the whole is limited by a Franciscan cord. Toussaint has compared this composition to an Indian manuscript genealogy.

A design of pomegranates upon a red ground forms high friezes and frames doorways in this cloister. In a passage from here to the sacristy a Crucifixion is painted with figures above life size: Mary stands beside the cross with a hand raised to her head, and John in doublet and hose is on the other side, but the figure of Christ has disappeared from the cross. Small churches are distributed over the landscape. This panel, like those in the cloister, is drawn rather than painted.

Cathedral: While the early Franciscan church was being reconditioned in 1957, with great respect for its original beauty of construction, removal of coatings of lime and paint down to the original plaster uncovered mural paintings of a character different from those discovered from the sixteenth century. A great continuing mural covers the long, high side walls of the Cathedral, from choir to triumphal arch, with scenes of the martyrdom of San Felipe de Jesús and his twenty-five companions in Nagasaki on February 5, 1597.

Spread over the walls of the side entrance are boatloads of Japanese soldiers taking missionaries, with hands bound, to their martyrdom—a storm having driven them from their course to the Philippines onto these Islands (Plate 53). A great crowd awaits their arrival in Nagasaki, where they are to be judged. The prisoners are then transported on foot and in oxcarts through streets full of people to the hill, where a long row of crosses receives them (Plate 54).

Luís Islas García notes that all figures are of oriental type and costume—even the prisoners—and oriental form is very well known to the painter, that the walls are conceived as successive units, and that the color is of distinctive quality; all of these characteristics are different from anything we know of painting in New

Spain but coincide with work done by Japanese artists of the persecuted Christian church, "against whom a fierce bamboo curtain was raised in 1639."

Islas García remarks that La Asunción de Cuernavaca was the last Franciscan stop on the way to the Orient; from here travelers to the Philippines, China, or Japan bid the friars goodby on their way to Acapulco: "This same convent was the first cultural stop for all who returned from those far lands, not only to the capital of New Spain, but to the Court of Spain or beyond—to St. Peter's in Rome to see the Pope." Therefore, he considers it natural that here we find first evidence of oriental influence and that a Japanese painter, a Christian leaving the land of persecution, has painted here "this most important happening between New Spain and the Orient—the martyrdom of San Felipe de Jesús and his companions."

The decorated side walls are about twenty-five feet high and seventy feet long. The boats, bristling with spears and banners and Japanese soldiers, increase in size as they ascend the wall. Informally grouped figures, rising in tiers to cover great wall spaces, include, in successive scenes, armed guards, women, and children, with rows of buildings in the background, and culminate in the row of crucified figures. The soft blue of the water contrasts with a variety of warm colors on land, among which red-orange is conspicuous. Fish of various kinds appear in the wàter, the arch under the side door being included in the ocean. (Plate 55).

Oaxtepec, Morelos (Site 46)

Santo Domingo (Colonial Museum). This Dominican monastery, established in 1528 in Oaxtepec near the Garden of Montezuma, administered the Hospital of Santa Cruz for Indians, now in ruins. The church was begun after 1561; its well-preserved monastery retains many original frescoes, probably painted soon after 1562. All vaults of the large portico, the passage to the cloister, and oratories of the friars are elaborately decorated in Moorish design—*artesonado*, painted in imitation of coffers, with more lavish use of *almagre* (red ochre) and turquoise blue than is usually found. In each end panel of the lower cloister a fresco in full color represents a scene from the Passion of Christ: the Arrest, the Flogging, Carrying the Cross (Plate 56), the Crucifixion. Though poorly preserved, these paintings are of unusual beauty. Large figures of saints finely painted in black decorate piers of the cloister (Plate 57). Side walls of an oratory for initiates are painted with a frieze of arches that enclose angels as if running; the Trinity fills the arched wall of this chapel. The vault of the

Courtesy EXCELSIOR

55. Fish (detail). Arch of door, Catedral de Cuernavaca, Cuernavaca, Morelos.

56. The Way of the Cross. Cloister, Santo Domingo, Oaxtepec, Morelos.

57. Saint Dominic. Cloister, Santo Domingo, Oaxtepec, Morelos.

refectory is richly decorated with three-dimensional coffers; large paintings of the miracles of the Loaves and Fishes and the Wedding Feast fill the arched end wall. These decorations confirm the extensive use of wall painting in sixteenth-century monasteries.

The seventeenth-century church of this monastery retains in the vault of a transept a circle of flying cherubs; an angel musician is seated upon a cloud in each corner of the vault (Plate 58).

Tlaquiltenango, Morelos (Site 47)

San Francisco (Parish Church). South of Yautepec near Jojutla is the monastery of Tlaquiltenango. Eliza-

beth Weismann says of it: "This establishment, originally Franciscan, was taken over by the Dominicans between 1570 and 1586, and from that period dates a fresco over the cloister entrance representing Dominican friars and nuns. All the vaults and walls were painted somewhat crudely with geometric designs."

Other sites

Dominican monasteries of Tepoztlan and Yautepec near Cuernavaca retain fragments of paintings which show that these also have been richly decorated.

Augustinian monasteries were established throughout the eastern part of the Valley of Morelos soon after the arrival of this order in 1533, and a number of imposing foundations exist short distances apart; in a few of these wall paintings have been found.

Tlayacapan, Morelos (Site 48)

San Juan Bautista (Parish Church). North of Oaxtepec, near mountains in the northern part of the Valley of Morelos, the high, massive church of Tlayacapan, heavily buttressed and with its adjoining monastery, looks almost like a pyramid. Many hermitages dot the surrounding country. Although here the Conquerors had met with fierce resistance, Tlayacapan evidently became an important center of the Augustinians.

Monastery: Elaborate paintings uncovered in chapels of the monastery are being most carefully restored. Unfortunately, the painted surface had been picked in order to make a coating of plaster adhere, but the strong black-and-white design was not destroyed. The sala of the friars, De Profundis, is richly decorated in fresco: figures of saints, above life-size, stand in painted niches beside a doorway, above which is painted a Crucifixion; two flying angels meet above on the high arched wall. Groups of figures showing the Passion of Christ extend on the walls from a waist-high dado to a wide frieze of Renaissance floral design that goes around the upper walls. Large painted imitation coffers decorate the vault; similar decorations appear in upper corridors. The grace and opulence of the Renaissance are reflected here.

Atlatlahuacan, Morelos (Site 49)

San Matéo (Parish Church). The handsome monastery of Atlatlahuacan, also in the northern part of the valley, is easily reached by the highway from the Valley of Mexico to Cuautla.

Decorations in this large monastery have a strong Moorish flavor: friezes of flower arabesque upon cloister walls, exquisite designs of foliage in angles of clois-

58. Vault of Chapel, Santo Domingo, Oaxtepec, Morelos.

ters, deep coffers painted terra cotta and turquoise over the vault of the refectory. The vault of the open chapel to the north of the church is covered with a wonderful painted star design. Within the church, high upon the proscenium of the apse, a large painting of the Last Supper shows strong reds and greens. The rich decoration of this monastery is from the period when Renaissance design merges into Baroque.

Dominican friars traveled south through Matamoros and the Alta Mixteca, or Mixtec Highland, to Oaxaca with the Conquerors. Inaccessibility of this far region assured to the Dominican Order a practical monopoly of this civilized area, and, with skilled Mixtec labor available, a chain of monasteries were built like inns along the way.

Matamoros, Puebla (Site 50)

Santo Domingo de Izucar (Convent). In Izucar de Matamoros—gateway to Oaxaca—roads from the Valleys of Puebla and Morelos converge below the volcano, Popocatepetl, and continue south. The partially ruined Dominican Convent of Izucar, first established in 1528, is now occupied by Franciscan nuns, who in restoring it have uncovered frescoes in the cloisters. High upon walls of the lower cloister a number of por-

traits of sainted monks and nuns, framed within varied shapes, have been underpainted in black—with later application of earth red, yellow ochre, and indigo blue. Cross vaults in this cloister show stars on a light-blue ground. In the upper cloisters colossal female figures decorate the heavy piers. Unfortunately, some of these have been retouched, but two remain drawn with authority.

Yanhuitlan, Oaxaca (Site 51)

Santo Domingo (Parish Church). The highway to Oaxaca, as it winds through the highlands, passes the beautiful monastery of Yanhuitlán, one of four great Dominican centers built in this region between 1550 and 1575. The large, massive church and its cloisters, with difficulty, have survived earthquakes and civil wars. A frescoed figure about fifteen feet in height painted on the great stairway represents Saint Christopher, symbol of the Conquest, carrying upon his right shoulder the Christ Child toward whom his face is turned. He holds a tree trunk for a staff as if mounting the stairs. The bearded Saint is dressed in doublet, puffed breeches, and hose; he wears a cloak that hangs in many folds from his shoulders and another cloak envelops the Child. Primitive and strong in treatment, this Saint Christopher, in spite of his beard and outfit,

59. The Crucifixion. Open Chapel (ruin), Santo Domingo, Cuilapan, Oaxaca.

60. Baptism. Open Chapel (ruin), Santo Domingo, Cuilapan, Oaxaca.

looks very Indian and varies greatly from other known representations of the saint.

Cuilapan, Oaxaca (Site 52)

Santo Domingo (Church, Ruin; Convent, School). Southwest of the city of Oaxaca near Zaachila (once the regal seat of the Zapotecs) the Monastery of Cuilapan was established in 1555. This large foundation had a complex architectural history in the sixteenth century, and decorative paintings of various types can still be seen on walls.

Convent: "Paintings include typical arabesque decorations and a family-tree type of an allegorical representation of the Dominican Order in the convent."

Open Chapel: The large ruined chapel attached to the north side of the church was probably at first an open chapel. Mrs. Weismann says of the murals:

The fragment of a narrative mural (apparently on a Biblical theme) may be from the earliest period; if the Crucifix [Plate 59] is contemporary, it is one of the oldest examples of the Indian mood in Mexican painting. Burgoa (*Geográfica Descripción*, 1, 401–402) says that the "pinturas de tinta al temple" at Cuilapan were the work of an Indian. The Baptism [Plate 60] is, in contrast, an affecting example of folk-art from some later period.

Church: The building of the great basilica seems to have been abandoned in the 1570's by command of the Audiencia. In the sacristy there remains a Crucifixion (Plate 61) framed in Renaissance decoration from this period.

Teiticpac, Oaxaca (Site 53)

San Juan (Parish Church). Near Tlacolula the small church of Teiticpac preserves some fine sixteenth-century murals; one of these represents the Descent from the Cross. (Islas García: 1946)

Etla, Oaxaca (Site 54)

Santo Domingo (Parish Church). North of the City of Oaxaca the Monastery of Etla retains from the seventeenth century small paintings of exquisite quality. In angles of the lower cloister large arabesques decorate vaults, and the arched panels are painted with small

61. The Crucifixion. Sacristy, Santo Domingo, Cuilapan, Oaxaca.

62. A Saint. Cloister, Santo Domingo, Etla, Oaxaca.

figures of saints (Plate 62) placed within decorative frames of plaster.

Oaxaca, Oaxaca (Site 55)

La Collada. A former charity hospital, La Collada, in Oaxaca, preserves a large mural painting of the Virgin, La Purísima (what we now call the Immaculate Conception). In style it is related to panel paintings rather than murals and most probably dates from the seventeenth century. Slight retouching of the original fresco painting through the centuries has not destroyed its ecstatic beauty (Plate 63)

Santo Domingo (Parish Church). The huge Dominican monastery in Oaxaca, first established in 1529, has undergone much rebuilding, and its beautiful church belongs to the seventeenth century. The entire interior covered over with ornamental relief (Plate 64) is an example of a church *not* frescoed but decorated in the new three-dimensional style.

Cloisters: Bits of decorative friezes show in cloisters. Painted upon the heavy piers of the lower cloister, a succession of single almost life-sized figures of saints of the Dominican Order date from the seventeenth century; these suggest transition to panel painting.

Tlacochahuaya, Oaxaca (Site 56)

San Jerónimo (Parish Church). Although this is a sixteenth-century establishment of the Dominicans, they were restrained from building the convent they had begun in 1580. The present buildings are from the seventeenth century.

The church of the Monastery of San Jerónimo, built cruciform with towers and dome in typical Colonial style, is perfectly preserved, and the church interior, entirely covered with painted decoration conceived and executed as a unit, is integrally a part of the building. This decoration expresses the unity and gaiety of Baroque design through painting alone, stuccoed design

63. The Virgin. La Collada, Oaxaca, Oaxaca.

64. Adam and Eve. Santo Domingo, Oaxaca, Oaxaca.

being absent and gold showing only in the frames of panel paintings of altars.

Upon walls and vaults of the church, units of small cherubs alternate with large flowers in all-over patterns painted in brilliant reds and blues and dull green upon a surface of graded white. Around upper walls a frieze of large ornamental vases of flowers is painted in the same gay colors (Plate 65); floral border designs frame arches, altars, and medallions of painted figures—no section of the church but is included, evangelists in pendentives of the high dome being part of the large design. Brilliantly colored archangels poise with spread wings in pendentives of the choir loft's dome (Plates 66, 67). The whole decoration is delightful for the ease and pleasure with which it seems to have been done. It is like spring in a garden.

In comparison with the gilded Baroque churches of Oaxaca and of Tlacolula, this painted decoration is subdued; as painted design it is very rich and expresses strong native character.

Tlacochahuaya was a first stop for the Dominicans on the road from Oaxaca through Tehuantepec to Southeastern Mexico.

65. Saint Luke. San Jerónimo, Tlacochahuaya, Oaxaca.

66. Vault. San Jerónimo, Tlacochahuaya, Oaxaca.

67. Archangel. Choir Vault, San Jerónimo, Tlacochahuaya, Oaxaca.

68. Mass of Saint Gregory. Santiago, Tepeapulco, Hidalgo.

Southeastern Mexico

From Oaxaca a line of Dominican monasteries extended south through Tehuantepec into Chiapas and continued along the ancient highway of the Indians, later of the padres, to Antigua, Guatemala. Thomas Gage followed the old route in the seventeenth century. Future investigation may disclose wall paintings in monasteries and Colonial churches in this land of the Mayas.

San Cristóbal las Casas, Chiapas (Site 57)

La Merced (Ruin). The heavy mission church of La Merced, before which the Indians of the region hold their market, retains a few decorations that are an integral part of the structure. Three-dimensional and painted designs mingle here on a low double arch; flowering arabesques, painted in vivid red, blue, and green, cover the arch and are enriched by a modeled and painted sun and moon near the central, heavy, sup-

porting pillar, which is carved and painted with a spiral design.

This fragment of design suggests the rich, native Baroque character of the decoration that has existed in the region.

Northern Central Highland

North of the Valley of Mexico and beyond the limits of the region that had been controlled by the Aztecs, early missions extended into populous valleys of this mountainous country, La Huasteca of the Huastecas and the Otomis in Hidalgo. Between diverging lines of Franciscan missions, the Augustinians built successive large, fortified monasteries in this rich mining area; in some of these sites important murals have been uncovered.

69. Christ Crowned with Thorns. Cloister, San Andrés, Epazoyucan, Hidalgo.

70. Christ Carrying His Cross (detail of Tormentors). Cloister, San Andrés, Epazoyucan, Hidalgo.

LA HUASTECA

Tepeapulco, Hidalgo (Site 58)

Santiago (Parish Church). The enchanting town of Tepeapulco, lying on the main line to Veracruz, is an important site for sixteenth-century murals. Mrs. Weismann reports that two periods of decoration are visible in the cloister: Figural panels have been uncovered, square narrative panels such as a Nativity, and an instructive Mass of St. Gregory with arabesque borders (Plate 68). "All but the frieze was whitewashed and a Franciscan cord pattern painted over it; the cord also seems to be sixteenth-century. The panels have the innocent linear quality that seems so concerned with presenting the story. No one has really worked out the

dates and the sequence but it is all there." This Franciscan monastery was founded in 1528 and finished in 1586.

Epazoyucan, Hidalgo (Site 59)

San Andrés (Parish Church). Near the mining center of Pachuca and north of the road to Tulancingo, the Monastery of Epazoyucan was established in 1528 by Franciscans, who in 1540 ceded it to Augustinians. The church was built in 1541, in about eight months. The convent was built in 1556 and the mural paintings in the cloister date from approximately this period. Uncovered in 1922, the frescoes of Epazoyucan are among the finest Colonial murals that have been found.

71. The Crucifixion. Cloister, San Andrés, Epazoyucan, Hidalgo.

Cloister: The Death of the Virgin, with many saints in attendance and small angels below, is painted in a wide arch above an opening. In four arched panels in angles of the cloister are represented incidents from the Passion of Jesus: Christ Crowned with Thorns is accompanied by a strange, impersonal bearded figure (Plate 69); Christ Carrying His Cross falls, pushed and pulled by His tormentors (Plate 70); the Crucifixion appears to be an unfinished panel with blank spaces left below for two figures, or these may have peeled off (Plate 71); the Descent from the Cross, or Pieta, shows, below the cross and ladder, Christ's body in the arms of His blue-robed Mother and surrounded by friends (Plates 72, 73). There is rich color in these paintings: indigo, pink, ochre, and sienna; they are distinguished by geometric precision of composition, strong characterization, and able handling of forms and costumes. These panels have the authority of original paintings and may be by a European artist. Manuel Toussaint surmised that Juan Gersón, the painter of the *sotecoro* (choir loft) of Tecamachalco (described above), may have done these paintings. However, the panels may not all be by one painter, and Juan Gersón is proved to have been an Indian.

72. Descent from the Cross. Cloister, San Andrés, Epazoyucan, Hidalgo.

73. Descent from the Cross (detail). Cloister, San Andrés, Epazoyucan, Hidalgo.

Courtesy Instituto Nacional de Antropología e Historia

74. Descent from the Cross. Cloister, San Agustín, Atotonilco el Grande, Hidalgo.

Atotonilco el Grande, Hidalgo (Site 60)

San Agustín (Colonial Museum). North of Pachuca in the Monastery of *Atotonilco el Grande,* important sixteenth-century murals have been uncovered in cloisters. Square panels with elaborate painted frames depict the Passion of Christ in very different technique from the murals of Epazoyucan. In the Descent from the Cross it is interesting to note similar elements meticulously drawn rather than painted (Plate 74).

Paintings that decorate a doorway show an interest in Humanist philosophy: above the doorway is painted a figure of Saint Augustine; in tiers of three at either side of the doorway are represented half-figures of pagan philosophers with their names painted: Socrates, Plato, Aristotle, Pythagoras, Seneca, and Cicero. The Renaissance was present in New Spain.

Actopan, Hidalgo (Site 61)

San Agustín (Colonial Museum). The great fortress-monastery of Actopan, begun in 1550, lies on the eastern highway to Mexico City. This is the most elaborately decorated of all sixteenth-century structures so far explored. The frescoes uncovered in the Mon-

75. The Holy Life. San Agustín, Actopan, Hidalgo.

76. The Holy Life (detail). San Agustín, Actopan, Hidalgo.

77. The Holy Life (detail). San Agustín, Actopan, Hidalgo.

78. Saints of the Church. Stairway, Convent, San Agustín, Actopan, Hidalgo.

79. Don Pedro Ixcuincuitlapilco (detail). Stairway, Convent, San Agustín, Actopan, Hidalgo.

astery of Actopan have been painted at different times and by various artists. High upon the walls of the portico or open chapel, ships and groups of people represent arrival of the Spanish; the vault is covered with arabesques of flowering design that frame medallions of saints.

The earliest painting may be that which covers the arched end wall of the entrance *sala:* a panorama or allegory of eremitic life (Plates 75, 76, 77). Through a landscape of streams and trees, a road leads to a church placed on a hill; black-robed friars gather in groups, wander on roads, or sit in numerous hermit caves; animals, birds, and snakes fill odd spaces. There is great intimacy between Heaven and the saintly life: God overhead within a circle of clouds wears the mitre of a pope; He sends an angel with a spoken message. Speech scrolls show also before mouths of authoritative figures below. Turquoise blue distinguishes water, gray-green is in trees, but the modeled underpainting is firmly done

in black. On the ascending road in the center the Devil appears in the guise of a *cargador* bowed down by a heavy load, perhaps the first native touch to appear on a Mexican wall. Drawing of figures and details of the landscape are reminiscent of the famous Map of Uppsala, representing the Valley of Mexico, believed by Dr. Sigvald Linné (1948) to have been painted about 1550 by an Indian of Tlatelolco. This large panel could have been done by the same hand.

Decorations of the monumental stairway of the Monastery reflect the Italian Renaissance (Plate 78). The walls of the stairwell, about fifty feet high and twenty feet square, are completely covered by five horizontal bands of large figures painted in black with additions of yellow ochre, red ochre, and green earth. In each of the four highest arched panels of the dome, a saint stands in a landscape; in three successive bands of painted arches, saints sit at desks, three to a wall. Wide Renaissance friezes separate these rows of saints, who appear as if within balconies surrounding the stairwell. On the lowest level a tonsured monk in black, Fray Martín de Acevedo, and two Indian *caciques* in white, Don Juan Irica Atocpa and Don Pedro Ixcuincuitlapilco (Plate 79), kneel before a crucifix.

Elaborate and varied decorations are painted upon the walls and vaulted ceilings of cloisters, corridors, and cells. In upper corridors, friezes are formed of shields with different symbols of the Augustinian Order painted in red and black; in cells, wide friezes filled with fantastic animals, birds, and flowers, and a nude figure mounted on a griffin that dissolves into foliage are painted in black on turquoise blue. In arched panels over openings, frescoes represent scenes from the Passion of Christ: Gethsemane, the Flogging, the Crucifixion, and also the Last Judgment with Christ and the Blessed standing above, and tombs opening below. Partially uncovered upon a wall of one corridor, large figures of angels with green wings hold ribbons to garlands of flowers. A fresco of Christ at the monastery entrance to the choir is painted in color. Cloister vaults are decorated with geometric Moorish designs. In the refectory of the Convent, deep coffers painted in turquoise and terra cotta cover the great vault.

An elaborate floral pattern decorates the vault of the sacristy. A tempera painting of the Baptism of Christ found here does not date from the earliest period. As yet no frescoes have been uncovered in the great church, but the vault of an adjoining open chapel is covered with an elaborate geometric design, like complicated wood paneling of Moorish origin.

83. Tiger Warrior (unit of frieze). Church, San Miguel Arcángel, Ixmiquilpan, Hidalgo.

80. Tiger Warrior (unit of frieze). Church, San Miguel Arcángel, Ixmiquilpan, Hidalgo.

Ixmiquilpan, Hidalgo (Site 62)

San Miguel Arcángel (Parish Church). North of Acto-pan, on the highway from Mexico City, the Augustinian monastery of Ixmiquilpan, founded at the same time as San Agustín at Actopan, was built on a similar plan by Fray Andrés de Mata.

Sacristy: The sacristy contains many frescoes, painted in black onto the white plaster, which represent the last days of Christ; among them are Entrance into Jeru-salem, and Gethsemane, with numerous large figures of a distinctive human type strongly composed in panels on lower walls. In a finely painted, wide panel over the entrance of the sacristy, small figures walk upon a rough sea filled with fish; above another doorway Jerusalem is represented by buildings, small animals fill the fore-ground, and the Three Crosses of Calvary stand on a hill in the distance.

Some of these panel paintings of the sacristy are partly destroyed; others have been retouched at some former time and have a popular character, but enough of the original painting exists to be of importance as sixteenth-century mural art.

Large decorative units painted in full color cover the

81. Dragon (unit of frieze). Church, San Miguel Arcángel, Ixmiquilpan, Hidalgo.

ribbed vault of the sacristy, some motifs suggesting Indian symbols. High upon the walls a foliated frieze on a turquoise background repeats a snakelike form with a human head, whose red hair is being pulled by a cherub.

Church: Murals found in the great temple of Ixmiquilpan are of very different character from any that have been discovered elsewhere in Mexico. Before 1960 the paintings on the sacristy walls and sections of a frieze in an upper corridor of the Monastery were about all that could be seen of what obviously had been rich Renaissance decoration. It was, therefore, a great surprise when mural designs uncovered on walls of the great plateresque church proved to have strong native

characteristics. These high walls had been redecorated at different times during the centuries; during repairs discovery was made of the original decoration, in which Indian warriors battle with monsters and with humans. No reference is made in these paintings to the new religion or to heavenly spirits, but here are represented the eagle and the jaguar—Indian emblems of the Aztec orders: Caballeros Aguilas and Caballeros Tigres—and also medieval grotesques.

Visible from the entrance of the church, high in each lunette of the choir vault, is painted a great spread eagle, flanked by spotted jaguars with speech scrolls. The right wall includes the arch of the baptistry; here the composition varies as the eagle turns slightly aside

82. Centaur (unit of frieze). Church, San Miguel Arcángel, Ixmiquilpan, Hidalgo.

and the jaguar, instead of leaping, sits upon this arch.

Above a high dado, a wide frieze extends on both sides from the front walls down the length of the church. It is formed by undulations of a large design of acanthus leaves and blossoms (prickly herb of the Corinthian capitol) painted green-blue, or turquoise, on a background of red-orange. Within this sinuous net of verdure, the curves of the acanthus frame and separate scenes in which Tiger Warriors, with insignia of leaders and armed with native weapons, battle with dragons, centaurs, and other Indians (Plate 80).

The serpentine pattern, a familiar form of Renaissance design, is obviously traced in repeated units; the battle scenes likewise are repeated—sometimes in reverse. Tiger Knights carry shields with bows and arrows and quivers of jaguar skin, or they wield *macanas,* the two-edged obsidian sword of the Aztecs. Prisoners are being captured by the hair.

A yellow dragon has a headdress of feathers, a scaled body, an open mouth with sharp teeth and a spiral tongue; its long lower jaw undulates like a snake. An Indian, half over-thrown by this fabulous animal, carries a *macana* and holds a stone; an armed person appears behind the dragon—almost the only figure superimposed (Plate 81).

The centaur—with serpentine neck, head adorned with quetzal feathers, hoofs in sandals, a human head worn on his belt—carries a shield in one hand; three monsters as Evil and the victims of the warriors as Sin. It is probable that a medieval bestiary inspired this native interpretation. The Otomís were famed as warriors and this is an Otomí region.

No one knows when this work was done; Renaissance design was used into the seventeenth century in Mexico.

An upper frieze, passing along the high walls at choir-loft level, is also of acanthus pattern; it is much narrower than the lower frieze and more intense in color. Angels, centaurs, horses with fish bodies—Italian grotesques, all are harmonized here against deep orange. In a band that frames this frieze, colors are reversed: on a blue background, tendrils of orange end in fabulous heads, birds, cupids. These friezes are all painted in tempera—color mixed with an agglutinant.

The Gothic barrel vault of the church is painted in imitation of elaborate carpenter work—*artesonado* such as exists in the vault of the open chapel of Actopan —with hexagonals, crosses, etc. Acanthas leaves are included in the design over the angular apse.

Western Central Highland

Western Mexico is approached through the Valley of Toluca. At the time of the Conquest this region of Toluca had been recently conquered by the Aztecs. The Tarascan people of the high lake region to northwest, however, had successfully repulsed Aztec aggression. Franciscans, invited to the beautiful lake country of Michoacan by the Tarascan king, had as their first occupation the destruction of great numbers of temples and idols. Spanish Conquerors under Nuño de Guzmán soon treacherously devastated the land and outraged the people. Later the friars and the appointed governor of Michoacan, Bishop Vasco de Quiroga, worked to restore an orderly life to the people, the Governor using *Utopia*, by Sir Thomas More, as his guide.

This account begins with earliest penetrations to the west.

VALLEY OF TOLUCA

Zinacantepec, México (Site 63)

San Miguel (Parish Church). West of the Valley of Mexico and beyond Toluca, the Franciscan Convent of Zinacantepec has been interestingly decorated. In the portico is a poorly preserved mural, a rare example of a once important type—an instructive genealogy, the Tree of Jesse, showing the lineage of the Virgin. On the other side of the portico, the figure of Saint Francis is painted reclining; a tree is shown rising from his heart, sainted monks and nuns disposed along the branches. These paintings of the Tree of Jesse and of Saint Francis

Courtesy Instituto Nacional de Antropología e Historia

84. Angelic Saint. Cloister, La Purificación, Malinalco, México.

arrows in the other hand are held like the Augustinian insignia (Plate 82). Grotesque heads sprout from acanthus stems; speech scrolls and hair turn into leaves.

The figures (Plate 83, color, p. 104), drawn in profile —Egyptian fashion—are painted flatly; shading occurs only in whirls of the leaves. Flesh is painted light brown; costumes are worn by Tiger and Eagle warriors, but the victims are often nude. These figures began as tracings but were not developed equally; some have the same two hands, and certain units are painted with more authority than are others. This painting was surely done by Indian hands.

Carrillo y Gariel, in his study of the Ixmiquilpan murals, remarks that some details "seem taken from illustrations of the codex of Sahagún." He interprets the relate to the earliest description of paintings by Indians, as recorded by Motolinía in the open chapel of Tlaxcala, with which this record begins.

Malinalco, México (Site 64)

La Purificación (Colonial Museum). South of Toluca in a mountainous region famous even now as a center of pilgrimage for Indians, the Augustinian Monastery of Malinalco retains in its cloister fragmentary frescoes of strongly realistic character, such as one of a bishop (Saint Augustine) surrounded by a crowd of people. Figures of angelic saints appear in decorations of the vault of the church (Plate 84). One figure with flying drapes carries a sleeping child as if to Heaven. Unfortunately these strong paintings are greatly deteriorated.

Western Mexico

Charo, Michoacan (Site 65)

San Miguel (Colonial Monument). Interesting and well-preserved frescoes exist in the sixteenth-century monastery in Charo, which lies between Morelia and Acambaro in the state of Michoacan northwest of Toluca. It was populated by Matlatzinca Indians captured by Tarascans from the Valley of Toluca a short time before the Spanish Conquest. First established by Franciscans, the mission was ceded to the Augustinian Order by Bishop Vasco de Quiroga, governor of Michoacan, in the middle of the century.

The Augustinian monastery is built on a rise overlooking a wooded area and is reached by a short flight of steps. A passage leads from the portico of the convent

Courtesy Instituto Nacional de Antropología e Historia

85. Martyr. Cloister, San Miguel, Charo, Michoacan.

to the arcaded cloister, which is one-storied and light. All walls of the passage and cloister are covered with murals drawn onto the white plaster in black, that served also for the robes of the friars. The rose color of flesh is complemented here and there with blue.

Incidents from the Passion of Christ fill the panels of the passage: Gethsemane; Jesus Seized; Jesus Scourged; Christ the King, Mocked. On the continuing wall of the cloister are scenes of Augustinian Martyrs being stoned or pierced with arrows, and groups of agonized spectators, and all walls are framed with

Courtesy Instituto Nacional de Antropología e Historia

86. Santa Mónica and Tree; Saint Augustine and Tree. Cloister, San Miguel, Charo, Michoacan.

87. The Virgin. Open Chapel, San Francisco, Tzintzuntzan, Michoacan.

friezes *de Romano* (Plate 85). Past the door that leads to the church is painted "Ecce Homo"—Christ crowned with thorns and wearing a long monk's cape, with two prophetic figures emerging from clouds above. The adjoining wall is covered with a painting of a mountain retreat, a subject dear to the Augustinians. This is quite destroyed.

The inner side of the cloister is divided by a central doorway into two large panels which glorify the Augustinian Order. On one side (Plate 86) a tree rises from the bosom of Saint Augustine; white flowers, placed symmetrically on horizontal branches, open to show half figures of Saints of the Order praying. On the other side (Plate 86), a tree grows from the heart of Santa Mónica, mother of Augustine, her figure reclining, her head resting on one hand while the other holds a book. From a braided trunk, branches of this tree extend in curves, upon which flowers, fewer and larger than in the other panel, hold small kneeling figures of nuns. Pomegranates, leaves, and a large black bird vary the composition in this charming panel. These trees representing spiritual genealogy are among the earliest form of decoration introduced by the friars, but elsewhere these designs are even less well preserved.

LAKE REGION

Tzintzuntzan, Michoacan (Site 66)

San Francisco (Parish Church). In 1533 a mission was established by Franciscans in Tzintzuntzan, seat of government and sacred city of the Tarascan people beside Lake Patzcuaro. The convent faces a large court filled with a grove of ancient olives. The walls of a small church adjoining the convent were distinguished by colossal painted figures of Saint Christopher, Saint Peter, and Saint Paul until these were destroyed when the church burned in 1944. The fresco of Saint Christopher—bearded, the Christ Child on his shoulder, a staff held diagonally in his hands, and a mantle caught over his arms—was painted with singular vigor.

In both upper and lower cloisters of the convent, illustrations from the Life of Saint Francis painted in imitation of canvases are spaced upon the walls. These poorly preserved tempera paintings in black and red from a late period show popular character. Fragmentary decorations from an earlier period exist in the stair well.

Near the present parish church an open chapel, established with the mission and later enclosed with adobe as a shrine of the Virgin (Plate 87), has now been restored to its original form. As a chapel it had on each side of the rear wall a saint as if in Heaven, semipopular in character.

These slight remains of paintings in Tzintzuntzan indicate the continuing use of mural art in this region.

Tupátaro, Michoacan (Site 67)

Santiago (Parish Church). Beautiful decorations exist in the small church of Tupátaro, a pueblo a few miles southwest of Patzcuaro. This adobe church has a hipped roof covered with tiles; it is ceiled to form large panels —horizontal down the center and following roof-sheds to sides. Each panel (Plate 88) encloses a tall, militant

88. Archangels. Ceiling Panels, Santiago, Tupátaro, Michoacan.

angel supported by clouds and framed by ornamental borders that extend over the whole ceiling, the entire decoration being painted in brilliant primary colors. These angels form a very orderly vision of heaven. Saints and an occasional Spanish soldier appear in small panels over the choir loft, cherubs being included in the foliated design that encloses these (Plate 89).

The wooden panels are masked with cloth covered over by a thick coat of lime or gesso and are painted with watercolor mixed with lime or another agglutinant; because of the clarity of color it was believed to be done in lacquer, such as is used in craft work of Michoacan. As this small church has but three diminutive windows and the door is shaded by the choir loft, it is always almost dark.

Yuririapúndaro, Guanajuato (Site 68)

San Pablo (Parish Church). One of the most distinguished monasteries in Mexico is the large Augustinian

89. Choir Loft Ceiling (detail). Santiago, Tupátaro, Michoacan.

foundation near Lake Yuriria, which was built after 1550. The sculptured façade is boldly decorated with floral designs and includes two figures of Indians with drawn bows—all of strong native character. However, paintings in small arched panels of the cloisters show groups of figures painted with sophistication. In two dark, golden-hued paintings of fine workmanship are represented the Virgin of Candelaria and Christ in the arms of God the Father. These may be oil paintings. In the lower cloister, more freely done—almost popular in character, a small, poorly preserved panel represents the Massacre of the Innocents by Herod.

Cuitzéo, Michoacan (Site 69)

Santa María Magdalena (Parish Church). Shortly after Yuriria was established, the Augustinians founded another great monastery beside nearby Lake Cuitzéo, north of the city of Vallodolid (now Morelia). The plateresque façade, more restrained in treatment than those at Yuriria, was also executed by native craftsmen; the small paintings in lunettes at angles of the cloister are similar to those in the companion monastery. Most probably these date from the seventeenth century. Geometric patterns of red and black form dados in cloister and stair well; a large Archiepiscopal Cross is painted above the stairway.

A Renaissance frieze decorates an upper corridor; the motif, a figure with a human head and a snake body that dissolves into foliage, has been copied in recent redecoration of the church.

The Eighteenth and Nineteenth Centuries

Central Mexico

Tepoztlan, México (Site 70)

San Francisco Xavier (Colonial Museum). In the Valley of Mexico a short distance north of Mexico City, the former Jesuit Seminary of San Martín de Tepoztlan contains a great complex of cloisters and chapels built during the seventeenth and eighteenth centuries. In these is illustrated the triumph of Baroque decoration during this period; the subservient, almost nonexistent role of mural painting is also indicated here.

The large church of the Seminary, San Francisco Xavier, includes the Chapel of Loreto with its famous Camarín de Loreto, in which is registered the magnificence of Mexican Baroque during the latter half of the seventeenth century. The vault of this small high chamber, behind the altar of the Chapel of Loreto, is entirely covered with rich, three-dimensional decoration showing architecture, sculpture, and painting inextricably mingled in a brilliant representation of Heaven. A gilded vault of double crossed arches (of Moorish derivation), with stuccoed background of cherubs, stars, sun, and moon, is upheld by four similar, large sculptured angels poised around the central lantern in the attitude of flight.

The main church, San Francisco Xavier, dating from the eighteenth century, contains great reredos that exemplify the golden splendor of flamboyant Churrigueresque decoration; it retains painted borders of flowers and cherubs over arches and cornices and around windows. Arched vaults above the three elaborately carved and gilded reredos of this church are painted to suggest the nearness of Heaven: over the main altar is a vision of Paradise (partly destroyed), and above the two side altars, the Apparition of the Virgin of Guadalupe and sainted monks being visited by the Virgin and by Jesus. Like the sculptured figures and painted canvases of the altars they crown, these mural paintings are realistic in detail and restless in design. Around the large central dome of the church a painted pattern of deep red encircles the lantern, from which issue dark rays.

Few wall paintings exist in the huge monastery. A partly destroyed tempera painting of the Annunciation in the portico probably dates from the eighteenth century. The cloisters show fragmentary decorative friezes, painted to enrich the large framed canvases that still fill many walls.

The Chapel of the Novices is covered over with decorations painted on canvas, as is also a small chamber near the portico.

México (Atzcapotzalco), D. F. (Site 71)

Santo Domingo. The decoration of the Chapel of the Rosary of the old Dominican church of Atzcapotzalco dates from the eighteenth century. Above a great sculptured Churrigueresque altar heavily covered with gold leaf, the wide vault is painted with a Vision of Heaven: In the center, the Virgin being crowned by the Trinity

90. Francisco Antonio Vallejo. Descent of the Paraclete (detail of Mary). Library, Escuela Nacional Preparatoria, México, D.F.

is framed by a circle of cherubs; in window vaults intersecting either side joyous angels carry musical instruments. At some more recent time these angels have been repainted in gay colors, giving a popular character to the whole decoration. Evangelists in pendentives of the dome also have been repainted, and these make transition from the eighteenth to the nineteenth century.

Colegio de San Ildefonso (School Library). The sacristy of the former chapel of the handsome eighteenth-century Jesuit College of San Ildefonso, now converted into the library of the National Preparatory School, retains upon two walls mural canvases painted by Francisco Antonio Vallejo in 1760. Expressed in terms of the time, Vallejo's work was a mural revival for his generation.

The paintings fill adjacent walls with intrinsic arches in the small, high, former sacristy. On one wall is painted a very youthful Holy Family with the Seven Archangels holding symbols in an architectural setting. A Vision of Heaven fills the high arch, where God the Father is surrounded by cherubs and winged musicians; the Holy Dove is suspended between Heaven and Earth. The other wall is painted with the Descent of the Paraclete, in which Tongues of Fire fall from the Holy Dove suspended above Mary, and women are grouped about her (Plate 90), with the apostles seated to sides or rising above the Baroque doorway, which interrupts the wall low on the left side.

Templo de la Enseñanza (Parish Church). The large Churrigueresque Church of La Enseñanza, "the Teaching," in Mexico City, also retains mural canvases painted by Vallejo. Three large consecutive wall canvases decorate this elaborate church, built in 1754, which is all that remains of the old conventual college of that name.

91. Gethsemane. Vault, Santuario de Jesús Nazareno, Atotonilco, Guanajuato.

Mid-Western Mexico

San Luis Potosí, San Luis Potosí (Site 72)

Convento del Carmen (Convent). A series of paintings by Francisco Antonio Vallejo in the Convent of Carmen in the Mid-Western city of San Luis Potosí has been judged by Manuel Toussaint to be Vallejo's best work. These large mural canvases represent incidents from the Life of Saint Elias. Vallejo, a painter from Mexico City, reflects the Romantic period of art in his work.

Atotonilco, Guanajuato (Site 73)

Santuario de Jesús Nazareno (Sanctuary). A Baroque tradition of mural painting appears with vigor upon the walls of church and chapels of the pilgrimage shrine of Atotonilco, situated about ten miles north of San Miguel Allende. The Sanctuary of Jesus of Nazareth —established in 1748 by the priest, Luis Felipe Neri de Alfaro, to commemorate the Life and Death of Christ— still serves as a center of penitence. Here all walls, vaults, window arches, and *camarines* of the various units included in the Sanctuary are covered with murals, painted at different times during the past two centuries, in which a Mexican tradition of mural art has been preserved and perpetuated.

All walls being closely decorated, this complex of paintings confuses the visitor and cannot be appreciated when seen quickly. The murals range from sophisticated examples of Mexican Baroque tradition to provincial solutions—all having Mexican character. Colonial and Popular mural art exist here side by side and sometimes merge; also, in the cupola of the last chapel to be built appear figures derived from Academic painting. Together, these painted walls form a graphic history of Mexican art as it has existed in this remote mining region from the middle of the eighteenth century into the twentieth—a transition independent of the Academicians.

Church: Large painted figures of angels show faintly on the plain façade of the entrance to the Sanctuary. Within, the portico is adorned with painted devils and is darkened by a vestibule covered with small Popular

92. View of Church Exterior. Vault, Capilla del Rosario, Santuario de Jesús Nazareno, Atotonilco, Guanajuato.

93. Battle of Ships. Vault, Capilla del Rosario, Santuario de Jesús Nazareno, Atotonilco, Guanajuato.

paintings of different kinds of self-inflicted suffering. A series of murals, grown dark from torch processions and candle smoke, cover walls and vaults of the church and are seen with difficulty. Most easily visible are the paintings on vaults above and below the choir, which represent the Passion of Christ (Plate 91). Life-sized figures in decorative compositions of rich pattern suggest the sophistication of eighteenth-century painting. Earliest murals have been attributed to the artist Miguel Antonio Martínez de Pocasangre, a contemporary of the founder, Felipe Neri, who inspired the work. But the various Baroque decorations and paintings have undoubtedly been made by different hands.

Capilla de Betlem: Opening from the church on the right, the Chapel of Bethlehem is decorated in "exuberant Baroque." Roses and scenes woven with arabesques cover the walls. Three large gilded sunbursts of stucco decorate the vault; tall angels are painted in folds of the golden radiations, the Virgin and Child being enshrined in one center. The remaining spaces of vault and cupola of this chapel are filled with angels and cherubs, saints and shepherds, and scrolls with legends.

Capilla del Rosario: Also opening on the right side

of the church, nearer the main altar, the smaller Chapel of the Rosary contains most interesting murals. In the oblong, intersected vault of the Chapel the narrow triangular sections, to front and rear of the lantern, are filled by exterior (Plate 92) and interior views of a church with figures in procession. The wide triangular spaces to the sides contain ships that battle in rough seas (Plate 93). This is The Battle of Lepanto of 1571. In these panels, forms accommodate to spaces with great sureness of design.

The small room behind the altar of this chapel, El Camarín del Rosario, contains three large windows that flood with light the polychrome sculptured angels and painted saints filling every space of this small chamber.

Capilla de Loreto: The small Chapel of the Virgin of Loreto, at the left side of the church, must have suffered the neoclassic reformation of the nineteenth century, as it is very bare, but behind the altar a tiny octagonal oratory is completely covered with a succession of groups of small figures which rise in tiers into the cupola. This Baroque decoration is reported to have been painted early in the nineteenth century by José María Barajas. On the lowest level, painted within medallions, a suc-

94. (above) Miracle of the Marriage Feast; (below) Miracle of the Loaves and Fishes. Vault, Templo del Calvario, Santuario de Jesús Nazareno, Atotonilco, Guanajuato.

cession of scenes is accompanied by verses illustrating the miracle of the transported house.

Capilla del Intierro Sagrado: To the left of the church entrance, the door to the Chapel of Holy Burial is carved with separate members of the Body of Christ. This small chapel, which forms a vestibule to the later principal chapel of the Sanctuary, is delightfully decorated with arbors of roses painted upon its walls and also with stuccoed arabesques spread over the vault. Above the doorway are paintings with small figures, where three illustrations of the Crucifixion probably have been repainted.

Templo del Calvario: Beyond the small Chapel of Holy Burial is the long, narrow Temple of Calvary, built cruciform, with a dome over the intersection and cross-shaped windows opening high on the side walls. Three huge altars, more like stages, face toward the intersection; these support colossal figures of the Way of the Cross. Paintings cover all available wall space in the church and behind the altars. The window vaults intersect the barrel vault of the Chapel on both sides and divide it into four wide segments, in which four miracles of Christ are interestingly composed in relation to the architecture (Plate 94). However, each window vault contains also another painting, which cuts into the central murals, the effect being over-rich, as of paintings on top of paintings. Around the drum of the cupola are painted standing figures of saints of the Church; flying angels fill the dome, which opens to Heaven as in Academic mural art. Gold leaf is not used here; many verses from the Bible are inscribed upon the walls; devils recur in the decorations as the paintings of this pilgrimage center become more popular in character. Atotonilco shows the transition from the Baroque of the eighteenth century to the Popular of the nineteenth with a dash of Academic art in between.

Dolores Hidalgo, Guanajuato (Site 74)

Capilla del Señor del Llanto (Parish Church). The Chapel of the Lord of Sorrows near Dolores Hidalgo (where Mexico's revolt from Spain began) is reported to be decorated with paintings by Pocasangre, poems by Felipe Neri being interlaced with the designs. These paintings from the mid-eighteenth century were restored with oil color in 1812.

Felipe Neri, the founder of the Sanctuary of Atotonilco, died in 1776. He is revered in Mexico as a saint.

PART THREE: ACADEMIC ART

PART THREE: *Academic Art, 1785-1915*

Background

In the struggle for freedom from Spain, Mexican nationalism has been closely related both to the assertion of Indianism and to the development of art, relationships clearly registered throughout the turbulent nineteenth century. The people of Colonial Mexico had realized a degree of cultural independence from Spain long before the armed uprising early in the nineteenth century, but, strangely, cultural colonialism in art was to outlive by another century the winning of political independence.

The long period of colonialism had witnessed the gradual amalgamation of races and cultures in New Spain. Mexican Baroque—in its barbaric splendor so different from Rococo expression found elsewhere— shows that the cultural tree had grown distinctive New World characteristics. A new European graft was felt to be needed; so in 1785 the Royal Academy of San Carlos of New Spain was established in Mexico City by the Spanish Crown. Modeled after the Royal Academy of Madrid and made dependent on it, the Academy of San Carlos was a measure to control the self-assertion in taste which had developed in the Colony. Directed by artists from Spain, the Academy was designed to insure a disciplined approach to the fine arts in accord with the neoclassic Academic tradition current in Europe.

The school started in 1781 with classes in engraving under a Spaniard, Don Gerónimo Antonio Gil. Departments of Architecture, Sculpture, and Painting were added in 1785; Gil was appointed general director of the Royal Academy of San Carlos for life, and all departments were to be under the direction of Spanish artists. First instructors for the new school were found in a group of painters inherited from the earlier school of Miguel Cabrera in Mexico City.

Gil proved autocratic and difficult for the artists working under him. The first director of Painting, Andrés Ginés de Aguirre, a Spanish muralist, stayed only long enough to decorate the vault of the baptistry of the Sagrario Metropolitano. There were other defections until, in 1790, Manuel Tolsa arrived from Spain as director of Sculpture; in 1793 Rafael Ximeno y Planes, another muralist, replaced Andrés Ginés as director of Painting, and the Academy achieved a new vigor. Upon the death of Gil in 1798, Tolsa became general director of the Royal Academy, a position he held until his death in 1816.

Under Tolsa's leadership the Classic revival in architecture and art soon became the official style in Mexico, with Tolsa working as both architect and sculptor and Ximeno y Planes painting important murals. Reaction against Churrigueresque ornamentation and the desire of the ruling classes to share in European fashion were added to official pressure to make this new art sweep the country; gay, lawless Mexican Baroque architectural decoration was often replaced by its antithesis in severe pediments and columns. In many churches huge carved reredos filled with statues and paintings were replaced by altars like small Greek temples, built to hold a single canvas or figure.

At the San Carlos Academy plaster casts of Greek and Roman sculpture, and drawings of these made to be copied, introduced students to the disciplines of Academic art. As a concession to the revolutionary spirit of the time, the charter of the Academy specified that four pensioned students of pure Indian blood must always be included, all pensions being valid for twelve years. Baron von Humboldt, describing a visit to the San Carlos in 1802, noted its democratic character. Humboldt (1810) brought native American art and architecture into focus with world cultures; he was the first to do so.

The political and social revolt that spread over the Western World at the end of the eighteenth century was touched off in Mexico by the Indian uprising in 1810 in Dolores, Guanajuato, under Padre Miguel Hidalgo, whose cry for freedom, "El Grito de Dolores," reverberates today. The first Banner of Revolt—a painting of the dark Virgin of Guadalupe—was taken from the nearby Sanctuary of Atotonilco, where first soldiers of the Revolt found shelter.

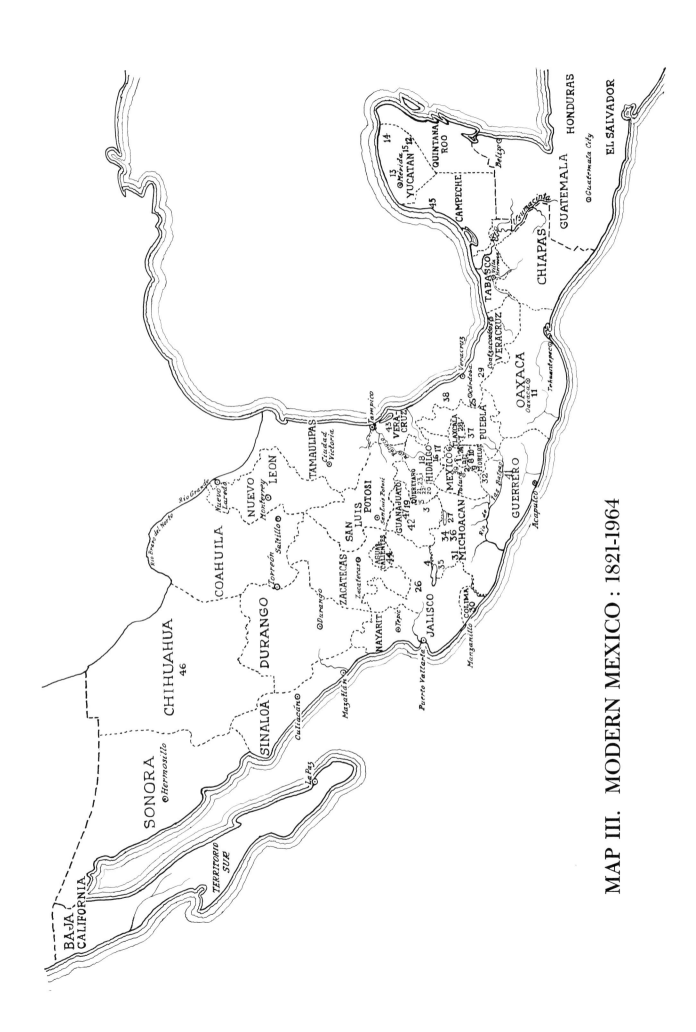

MAP III. MODERN MEXICO : 1821-1964

MURAL SITES (in order of appearance in text)

Part Three

1. México
2. Tenancingo
3. Celaya
4. La Barca
5. Querétaro

Part Four

(1) México
6. San Juan Teotihuacan
7. San Martín Texmelucan
8. Cuernavaca
9. Alpuyeca
10. Tlayacapan
11. Cuilapan
12. Valladolid
13. Motul
14. Tizimín
15. Tzitás
16. Ixmiquilpan
17. Actopan
18. San Antonio Ametusco
19. Atotonilco
20. Caderéyta
21. Tolimán
22. Bernal
23. Madelena

Part Five

(1) México
24. Chapingo
25. Orizaba
26. Guadalajara
(8) Cuernavaca
27. Morelia
28. Ayotla
29. Axochio
30. Manzanillo
31. Uruapan
32. Taxco
33. Coyoacan, D.F.
34. Janitzio
35. Jiquilpan
36. Patzcuaro
37. Puebla
38. Jalapa
39. Atarasquillo
40. Ciudad Universitaria, D.F.
41. Chilpancingo
42. Guanajuato
43. Poza Rica
44. Aguascalientes
45. Campeche
46. Chihuahua
47. Dolores Hidalgo

MURAL SITES for Parts Three, Four, and Five (alphabetically listed)

Actopan (17)
Aguascalientes (44)
Alpuyeca (9)
Atarasquillo (39)
Atotonilco (19)
Ayotla (28)
Axochio (29)
Bernal (22)
Caderéyta (20)
Campeche (45)
Celaya (3)
Chapingo (24)
Chihuahua (46)
Chilpancingo (41)
Ciudad Universitaria, D.F. (40)
Coyoacan, D.F. (33)
Cuernavaca (8)
Cuilapan (11)
Dolores Hidalgo (47)
Guadalajara (26)
Guanajuato (42)
Ixmiquilpan (16)
Jalapa (38)
Janitzio (34)

Jiquilpan (35)
La Barca (4)
Madelena (23)
Manzanillo (30)
México (1)
Morelia (27)
Motul (13)
Orizaba (25)
Patzcuaro (36)
Poza Rica (43)
Puebla (37)
Querétaro (5)
San Antonio Ametusco (18)
San Juan Teotihuacan (6)
San Martín Texmelucan (7)
Taxco (32)
Tenancingo (2)
Tizimín (14)
Tlayacapan (10)
Tolimán (21)
Tzitás (15)
Uruapan (31)
Valladolid (12)

Tolsa, as general director of the Royal Academy, was vigorous in defense of the Spanish Crown and busily constructed cannon, mortars, and cannon balls to put down the insurrection. Upon his death in 1816, Ximeno y Planes became general director.

Yielding to the spirit of revolt, King Ferdinand in 1820 granted constitutional reforms to New Spain— reforms little to the liking of those dominant in the land. The concessions were resisted by conservatives who, thinking to govern the country as an empire, declared independence for Mexico in 1821. Don Agustín de Iturbide, President of the Regency, soon became Emperor Agustín the First, only to be exiled two years later. The reforms proposed by the King of Spain under pressure of revolutionary action were not easily to be denied, and a whole century of revolutions was to result.

During these first years of independence from Spain, the San Carlos, neglected, fell into disuse. A triumvirate of generals, ruling the new republic, rescued the Academy in 1824, and named Pedro Patiño Ixtolinque director of the National Academy of San Carlos. Patiño, an able Indian artist trained in the Academy, had served as a lieutenant to General Vicente Guerrero in the War for Independence. With Mexico no longer a colony, a national art began with the nation itself; after independence American subject matter was honored in lithographs and in paintings.

Spanish Colonial barriers against non-Spanish travelers being down, various foreign artists and writers visited Mexico during the first decades of independence and made records of the land and its people. In 1826 an Italian artist, Claudio Linati, introduced lithography into Mexico, and, through his own work, published in Brussels in 1828, made typical Mexican life known to Europeans. Other artists followed. Through lithographs of Mayan ruins by Frederick Waldeck, a Bohemian, and Frederick Catherwood, an Englishman, and in *Antiquities of Mexico*, published by Lord Kingsburough, hitherto unrecognized values of pre-Spanish Mexican cultures became known.

In Mexico the National Academy of San Carlos, without support and without interference, from 1824 to 1843 was "free to strive toward the elaboration of a national art." In 1840 Philomino Mata, an independent, became director of Painting and taught the able young painters, Primitivo Miranda and Juan Cordero, who were soon afterwards to study in Rome, where each won high honors in painting large historical compositions. While they were abroad General Antonio López de Santa Anna, Provisional President of the Republic, decreed reorganization of the Academy: It would be supported

by a national lottery, good salaries would be paid, and its directors would be selected "from among the best artists to be found in Europe."

Pelegrín Clavé, a Spanish painter influenced by German artists, who was finally selected as general director, became "official dictator of taste in Mexico"—with contempt for all things Mexican. Clavé introduced living models and art exhibits. Miranda returned from Europe in 1848 to find the Academy moved under foreign control with no place for him. Although the disastrous war with the United States had occurred, the Academy continued to grow until, when Cordero returned in 1855 covered with glory, he found that the San Carlos had a whole foreign staff, including two from England and two from Italy, with no official opening for his talents.

Clavé, dedicated to "the moral and the beautiful," undertook to refine Mexican painting. This "intentional throw-back to Colonial status" was opposed by Mata. Cordero, making a bid for the directorship of the Academy, was supported by decree of Santa Anna; Don José Bernardo Couto, conservative president of the Directing Board, defended Clavé. But as at this time Santa Anna found it advisable to flee the country, his decree was disregarded, and Clavé retained his post. The struggle for position between Clavé and Cordero was tied to the political fortunes of the time and is registered in mural paintings.

Left without an office, Juan Cordero, between 1855 and 1860, painted three important murals in Mexico City.

In 1860 Benito Juárez, a Zapotec Indian, renewed Mexico's Revolution and, with victory, inaugurated reforms. Two years later the invasion forces of Napoleon III landed in Veracruz. Jean Charlot, in his scholarly study of the Academy of San Carlos, from which these facts are drawn, reports that at this time Juárez presided at the commencement of the Academy; when Mexico was slurred, he dissolved the Governing Board, cancelled the Lottery, and demoted Clavé. Santiago Rebull, Clavé's most gifted student, who had also studied abroad, became director, selected by Juárez as a Nationalist. Oaths were demanded and dismissals followed.

In 1863 the Liberals were defeated; Juárez fled and Rebull resigned. Clavé and others were reinstated in the Imperial Academy of San Carlos under Maximilian.

Emperor Maximilian, a highly cultured European, was sensitive to the quality of the art of Early Mexico. Rebull, the Liberal, was employed by him to paint his and Carlotta's portraits and to paint mural panels in

Chapultepec Castle. Maximilian respected the art of Mexico.

During the years following Cordero's impressive revival of mural painting, Clavé undertook, with the assistance of students, to decorate the dome of La Profesa, the great church of the Jesuit Order in Mexico City. This decoration was finished in 1867 as civil war raged near the City. The following year, with the Imperialists defeated, Maximilian executed, and Juárez reinstated as President, Clavé departed for Spain. However, he was able to have his disciple, Salomé Pina, recalled from Europe as general director, a position he held until 1880.

After Juárez' death, Porfirio Díaz, as President, looked to France for Mexico's culture, and for almost twenty-five years Don Ramón Lascurain was general director of the National Academy of San Carlos. It was during this period that Leandro Izaguirre matured to become teacher to both José Clemente Orozco and Diego Rivera, great muralists of the twentieth century. Landscape painting had been introduced into Mexico, and José Luis Velasco was painting with great distinction his strangely lovely land.

The century of revolutions and invasions had coincided with an authoritarian and international development in art, but the way was being prepared both at home and abroad for other developments. From the Academicians, mural painting in Mexico during the nineteenth century had acquired skill and realism and the drama of great figures in movement; through the unrestricted use of perspective, mural art was weakened, however, in its relation to architecture. Even in work of Academic intention, personal solutions by Mexican muralists insidiously replaced authority, so that religious murals of the century show native taste. The popular art of lithography, escaping dictatorship by the Academicians, went directly to the people. Derisive caricatures on single sheets, giving scope to unregulated talents, poked fun at the pretensions of officialdom and, observed by young artists, prepared the way for change. Most especially, José Guadalupe Posada's engravings were of revolutionary character and influenced the work of future muralists.

Academic painting continued throughout the nineteenth century and into the twentieth as the expression of authority and sophistication, but side by side with this imported style flourished a mural art that is closer to the Mexican people—essentially folk painting distinguished by keen observation and meticulous execution, which derived from the Mexican Baroque tradition of free invention. At the turn of the century, however, young Mexican painters brought back from their study abroad wide understandings of art that sensitized them to the popular painting of Mexico. In their work the two developments were to come together.

Central Mexico

1785–1850

México, D.F. (Site 1)

Sagrario Metropolitano (Parish Church). The first director of painting of the Royal Academy of San Carlos, Don Andrés Gines de Aguirre, a Spanish muralist, decorated the vault of El Sagrario during his stay in Mexico. This probably was the first Academic mural painted in Mexico. El Sagrario, a beautiful example of Churrigueresque architecture, is built beside the Cathedral of Mexico in the form of a Greek cross. In the four sections of the intersected vault, Gines Andrés painted four Baptisms, including the Baptism of Christ.

Toward the end of the nineteenth century these paintings, having deteriorated, were covered over after having influenced other paintings of the century.

Catedral de México (Cathedral). The finishing touches were put upon the great Cathedral of Mexico from 1793 to 1813 by Manuel Tolsa, working as both architect and sculptor. Begun in the sixteenth century, this largest New World cathedral, over the years, acquired whatever was offered by each period, and, in form and decoration, registers the successive Colonial styles. The vaults, built cruciform, rest on huge columns, and the dome arches high above their intersection. The great cupola, rising from an octagonal drum, is well lighted by windows placed here and in the shaft of the lantern. This dome was remodeled by Tolsa, and in 1810 it was decorated by Ximeno y Planes.

The painting of the Assumption of the Virgin represents Mary, accompanied by numerous angels and

95. Ximeno y Planes. Angels (detail). Cupola, Catedral de México, México, D.F.

cherubs (Plate 95), riding upon a circle of clouds against a light-blue sky; lower, upon the upright sides of the cupola, various classic figures sit or recline upon a second ring of clouds (Plate 96). A ladder makes a connection between the lower and upper groups. Cherubs flying against a darker sky encircle the lantern. The small figures of the decoration (from the distance they seem small) are solidly painted and foreshortened with great realism, but because of the height of the cupola, individual figures are seen with difficulty. Opening visually into unlimited space, the dome does not confine the mural to its vault. The tempera color has not lasted well and has been partially repainted.

Santa Teresa la Antigua (Secularized). Capilla del Señor: The Chapel of Christ, built in the Church of Santa Teresa between 1798 and 1813, was designed by the director of Architecture of the Academy and

decorated by Ximeno y Planes, but the dome and the half dome with Ximeno's paintings were destroyed in 1845 by a violent earthquake. The Chapel was built to enshrine the miraculous crucifix of Ixmiquilpan. In the cupola above the intersection, Ximeno's decoration represented the story of the Renovación, the sixteenth-century miracle of the self-renovation of this figure of Christ. In the half dome over the apse he painted the battle that took place when the villagers, "2000 Indians armed with bows and arrows," recaptured the Crucifix from representatives of the Archbishop who had come to claim it. In the existing decoration of the restored chapel (now secularized) all that remains from Ximeno's work is a painting of Saint Matthew in a pendentive (Charlot: 1946, p. 257).

Colegio de Minería (College of Mines). The famous neoclassic College of Mines, built by Manuel Tolsa

Courtesy Jean Charlot. Archivo de la Dirección de Monumentos Coloniales

96. Ximeno y Planes. Classic Figures. Cupola, Catedral de México, México, D.F.

from 1797 to 1813, retains upon the ceiling of its chapel two large paintings by Ximeno y Planes: the Miracle of the Well with the Virgin of Guadalupe presiding above, and the Assumption of the Virgin in a heaven of angels and clouds. These two square scenes entirely cover the chapel ceiling. As they are painted without reference to the horizontal space they occupy, they are difficult to appreciate.

Monte de Piedad (National Pawn Shop). A Crucifixion painted in an arched panel above the altar of the former Chapel of the National Pawn Shop is by Ximeno y Planes, probably done in his latter years. The Chapel can be seen upon request.

1850–1915

When the earthquake of 1845 destroyed the domes of the Chapel of Christ in the Church of Santa Teresa,

decorated by Ximeno y Planes in 1813, the commission to redecorate the Chapel was given to the painter Juan Cordero, a student of the Academy of San Carlos in its more nationalistic period, who was then studying in Rome. In 1855 this able mestizo returned to Mexico to revive mural painting and to enter into long conflict with the Spaniard, Pelegrín Clavé, the new director of the National Academy of San Carlos.

México, D.F. (Site 1)

Jesús María, 3a Calle de Jesús María (Secularized). Juan Cordero's first mural fills a large lunette in the arch behind the main altar of the former Church of Jesús María. This painting, Jesus among the Doctors, "is a transition work of a technique still close to easel painting." A painted architectural setting divides the semicircular panel symmetrically, figures being grouped to

97. Juan Cordero. God and the Virtues. Dome, Capilla del Señor, Santa Teresa, México, D.F.

the sides of an empty center. The doctors, elaborately wrapped in mantels, are arranged in varied groups of three; Mary and Joseph enter at one side; the whole is dominated by the seated figure of the Child Jesus.

. . . isolated areas of local color, deep green, loud violet, metallic blue, minium red, saffron, all condensed chroma intensities that contrast with the diluted tints reserved for the Holy Child. The geometrical construction is defined by the horizontals and verticals of a severe architecture that is but a pretext for the mathematical partitioning of the plane. The effect is of color stencils superimposed upon a geometrical diagram. The subject dated at least from Italian days.

(Charlot: 1946, p. 255)

Santa Teresa la Antigua, Lic. Verdad (Secularized).
Santa Teresa marks Cordero's development into a real

muralist in both technique and conception. Jesús María was a single arched wall, but Santa Teresa offered the special problems of a central dome, the curved surfaces of pendentives, a half dome over the apse, vaulted arches, and vertical walls. The artist solved these spatial relationships by enlarging the figures and intensifying the color in the higher sections, in order to make all areas more equally visible under different lighting, and by relating the various figures to the central theme.

Capilla del Señor: Cordero's decoration is painted directly on the wall in what seems to be a glue tempera. Originally it covered every part of the Chapel of Christ. Some of the panels have been whitewashed, but the domes, three pendentives (the fourth by Ximeno), and four panels beside the windows remain intact.

98. Juan Cordero. The Immaculate Conception (detail). Dome, San Fernando, México, D.F.

In the narrow vault that leads to the apse, an angel with stars above head and hands spreads his arms, dark wings, and drapes to fill the star-shaped space created by cutting in of side window vaults. These vaults, in turn, are filled with cherubs and framed to reinforce the architectural form. High in the half dome of the apse, accompanied by cherubs, two silhouetted angels with trumpet and scroll announce the miracle of the Renovación, or self-renewal of the figure of Christ, pictured taking place below in the arms of angels.

Within the dome of the Chapel "God the Father appears, swaddled in Mars violet drapes, silhouetted against a dazzling egg-yellow dawn . . . ," and seated upon clouds around the base of the cupola, great figures of the Virtues (Plate 97), holding appropriate symbols,

are painted in strong, contrasted colors and with uncompromising solidity. Even the milder figures of the Evangelists are filled with unusual vigor of form, color, and movement. More like easel paintings are the sculpturesque symbolic figures of Astronomy, History, Poetry, and Music painted in panels beside the central windows.

These murals painted by Cordero in the Chapel of Christ were too daring in color and in execution to be well received by fellow artists or by the public. He did not receive the full contract price.

Galería de San Carlos (Art Gallery). In 1857 Ramón Sagredo, a pupil of Clavé, painted medallions with heads of famous artists on gold backgrounds upon walls of a remodeled gallery in the Academy of San Carlos.

These medallions were copied from details of a decoration by Paul Delaroche in the hemicycle of the École des Beaux-Arts in Paris. A mural planned for the library of San Carlos was not painted.

These paintings, although of no importance as murals, are mentioned in the *Diálogo*, written in 1860 by Don José Couto Bernardo, Clavé's sponsor, but Cordero's murals are not.

San Fernando (Parish Church). An earthquake in 1858 cracked the eighteenth-century Apostolic Church of San Fernando from dome to floor. During the process of repairs the elaborate mural decoration of the church was destroyed. Juan Cordero undertook, at his own expense, the redecoration of the cupola. After the cool reception given his decoration of Santa Teresa, he seemed eager to try again, and he probably volunteered to do this mural; perhaps it was to redeem himself or merely to have a wall to paint. The painting in the dome of San Fernando won for Cordero the applause denied him with his previous work.

The Immaculate Conception [Plate 98], oyster gray in a dark blue mantle, ascends a heaven of changing hues, ranging from gold ochre to flesh shade, to a kind of bluing blue. A dance of small cherubs in green, red, and purple scarves rings the shaft of the lantern, a motif already essayed in the dome of the Cathedral by Ximeno y Planes. Adolescent angelical musicians fill the dome, plucking harps, blowing trumpets, and playing cellos, while other spirits raise banners and display mottoes on streamers.

(Charlot: 1946, p. 259)

Jean Charlot records of the reception of San Fernando's decoration: "It became the fashion to go to see Cordero's mural as an alternative to a picnic, a concert, or a dance" (1946, p. 258).

The cupola with the radiant Virgin and the pendentives filled with evangelists who float on clouds in the company of angels, all paintings by Cordero, are still intact, but matching wall decorations by Santiago Villanueva have been whitewashed.

La Profesa (Parish Church). The great success of Juan Cordero's mural irritated his rival, Pelegrín Clavé. In 1861 Clavé, with five adept pupils, started to paint the cupola of the fashionable Church of La Profesa. The painting of the dome was interrupted by the rise of Juárez; it was resumed during the short reign of Maximilian. "The dome was uncovered in 1867 to a distracted public and it became the privilege of critics friendly to Cordero to belittle the work." Eight radiating divisions of the dome were painted in oil with the Seven Sacraments and an Adoration of the Cross, and

in its octagonal center was painted God the Father, black-bearded. Each panel was treated as an independent unit, and achitectural features, conceived independently of the dome's structure, were included. The whole conception differed radically from the accepted formula of the dome as representative of the vault of Heaven. The decoration was destroyed by fire in 1914 and today there is nothing left of the paintings of Clavé and his pupils in the cupola of La Profesa.

When Clavé, who had been a partisan of Maximilian, returned to Spain in 1868 he was able to leave a pupil, Salomé Pina, and not Cordero, in charge of what had been for a short time the Imperial Academy of San Carlos.

Castillo de Chapultepec (National Museum of History). Santiago Rebull, considered the best student of the San Carlos Academy under Clavé, was selected by Maximilian to decorate Chapultepec Castle. In the open loggia of the upper floor Rebull painted, in 1865, four panels of Bacchantes (Plate 99). In 1894, after the Empire was only a memory, Rebull painted two more panels, also in Chapultepec Castle.

Pastel tones on black backgrounds characterized these symbolic figures painted in graceful movement. They were accompanied by garlands and vases, where a dominant note was Pompeian red.

All panels were whitewashed in 1930. Later these murals were cleaned and removed to a museum, so now there are no paintings in the loggia.

Escuela Nacional Preparatoria (National Preparatory School). In 1874 Juan Cordero made his final contribution to mural painting in Mexico. Upon the panel on the top landing of the great stairway of the former Jesuit College of San Ildefonso, now the Preparatoria or National Preparatory School, he painted the first mural in Mexico to celebrate the Age of Science. He called it the Triumph of Science and Labor over Ignorance and Sloth. The painting was destroyed in 1900 and replaced by an ornamental window.

A copy of this mural has been preserved and, also, an interpretive description by Cordero's friend, López López. The painting as reproduced by Charlot (1946) shows Minerva, Goddess of Wisdom, seated majestically on a large throne topped by a neoclassic pediment to symbolize Architecture. Two cherubs at rest on the slopes of the pediment offer wreaths of laurel and oak, "emblems of genius and strength." Figures symbolizing Electricity and Steam sit at a lower level. To Minerva's right, sailors unload a ship in the background. On the other side, Cleo, Muse of History, writes

99. Santiago Rebull. Bacchantes. Loggia, Castillo de Chapultepec, México, D.F.

her annals, while ferocious Envy is put to flight; a locomotive draws its cars below distant hills. A golden light spreads from the horizon. A winged cherub in the foreground enjoins silence.

This painting dedicated to Science and Industry was made as a favor for Cordero's Comtist friend, Dr. Gabino Barreda, director of the Preparatoria. Cordero was rewarded for his labor by a eulogistic public ceremony during which he was crowned with a laurel wreath of solid gold. Jean Charlot has noted that upon this occasion Cordero's great admirer, Felipe López López, made a recommendation: "To the good taste and culture of the administration the convenient beautification of public buildings . . . The schools of medicine, law, mining, agriculture, and commerce . . . , the palaces of the Government, of justice, city halls and others that house the administrative sovereignty, all need distinctive marks and wait for the brush and chisel of Mexican artists, dedicated to the study of the fine arts, to the end that such places be spared the trite appearance of private buildings" (1946, p. 265).

Charlot adds: "It was not the lot of Cordero's generation to see the realization of a clearly defined national style, but his merit lies in that he foresaw its coming, and eased the transition with his works" (1946, p. 265).

Basilica de Guadalupe, Villa Madero (Sanctuary). In 1883 the Collegiate Church of Guadalupe was newly decorated by Salomé Pina and Félix Parra, artists trained in the Academy of San Carlos and in Europe, with two large mural paintings in oil. These have more recently been enclosed by gilded frames to make them look like canvases rather than murals. The golden octagonal cupola of the high church is decorated with a figure of the Virgin of Guadalupe, radiant above a representation of the Basilica. Haloed angels, with and without wings, fly with torches against the golden sky and above a Mexican landscape that encircles the base of the cupola. Evangelists with streaming drapery rest upon clouds in the pendentives. The purity of the original painting of the Virgin of Guadalupe, which is in the Basilica, is in great contrast to the realism represented in the dome as her environment. Since G. Carrasco was painting in the Basilica de Guadalupe in 1878, this dome may be his work.

Tenancingo, México (Site 2)

Iglesia del Calvario (Parish Church). In the Church of Calvary in Tenancingo the pendentives are painted with the Four Strong Women of the Old Testament—Judith, Deborah, Esther, and Jael. The medium used is tempera touched with oil. Jean Charlot says that these figures may be by Pedro Monroy, Clavé's pupil, and the decorations of medallions and scrolls, by Santiago Villanueva.

Western Mexico

1785–1850

After the Royal Academy of San Carlos had been established in Mexico City neoclassic architectural design and decoration was enforced officially wherever new construction or reconstruction of importance was undertaken, so that this style spread into the provinces. Throughout the rich mining regions of Guanajuato and Querétaro the Churrigueresque ornamentation of the eighteenth century had reached fantastic expression and there may have been reaction against it.

Celaya, Guanajuato (Site 3)

El Carmen (Carmelite Monastery). In Celaya the reconstruction of the church of the Carmelite monastery, which had burned at the turn of the century, was entrusted to Francisco Eduardo Tresguerras, a versatile genius of that city. Celaya's brilliant, self-taught architect, artist, poet, and musician has become a legend in Western Mexico. Both as architect and as muralist he has been credited with very diverse works. However, the only murals known surely to have been painted by him are in the church of *El Carmen* in Celaya.

As rebuilt by him the church of *El Carmen* represents the Academic reaction. This is a cruciform temple with a triple neoclassic façade; the white and gold interior, lighted from the high cupola, is bright, austere, bare—everything that the other great churches of the region are not. It seems probable that Tresguerras derived the pure and graceful style of El Carmen from a book of architectural drawings published in Paris in 1768 by Jean Charles Delafosse, which is preserved in the library of the National Academy of San Carlos in Mexico City.

Iglesia: On side walls of the apse, at the sides of the main altar, two mural landscapes by Tresguerras are shown within frames, painted so as to resemble canvases (Plate 100). In one painting Saint John of the Cross and Saint Teresa travel on foot through a forest; in the other, Saint Elias, from a soaring chariot of fire, drops a white mantle upon Saint Eliseo. What is to be remarked about these murals is the realism represented in the landscapes and figures. These paintings seem small and isolated on the large walls. The color is rich—possibly done in oil or in tempera touched with oil.

Capilla de Juicio, or Chapel of Judgment: A side chapel opening from the church is decorated with three large mural panels that celebrate Death; designs of skulls and bones fill lunettes and dados. These principal decorations of the church of El Carmen are by Tresguerras.

On one side of the altar a painting of the Raising of Lazarus shows the shrouded figure and the sepulcher, surrounded by dramatic figures against a rocky landscape with distant buildings. On the other side a representation of Tobias Burying the Dead shows the bearded patriarch standing wrapped in a mantle amidst the dead and their graves, with a background of monumental forms built of stone.

The chapel takes its name from the largest and most interesting of the three murals, the Last Judgment (Plate 101), which covers the wall to the left as one enters. High in the center of the wide panel a cross is shown amidst clouds that support the Heavenly Host; at the sides angels trumpet for the souls below. Nude and bewildered, these emerge from the tombs to be judged; they are welcomed by angels on one side or assisted by demons with pitchforks on the other. Low in the center a large tombstone is being raised and a skeleton figure looks out questioningly; this figure is believed to represent Tresguerras himself as the stone

100. Francisco Eduardo Tresguerras. Saints Travel in Landscape. Church, El Carmen, Celaya, Guanajuato.

101. Francisco Eduardo Tresguerras. The Last Judgment (detail). Capilla de Juicio, El Carmen, Celaya, Guanajuato.

bears his initials. The panel is painted in pigment mixed with lime, or "fresco-seco," and is somewhat pale in color. It is reputed to have been left unfinished at the time of his death in 1833.

In the painting of the Last Judgment oblique lines of cross, trumpets, tombstones, spears, arms, and legs weave the wall into a visual whole. The figures are painted with sophistication but a most engaging freshness imbues the entire panel.

Convento: Upstairs in the adjoining convent of the Carmelite Order, a small Chapel of the Virgin of Carmen is entirely covered with mural paintings, reputed to be also by Tresguerras. Interestingly fitted into the divisions of three intersected vaults of the narrow chapel, near life-size figures of angels and cherubs carry legends and symbols of the Litany of the Virgin. They fly in clouds against pale blue, which in the center of each vault changes to color of gold. Arched intrinsic walls of the Chapel follow these small vaults. On one side, in lunettes above a door and two windows, small figures present various subjects: the Nativity, with adoring shepherds; the Child Jesus in the Temple; the Death of Saint Joseph, with Mary, Jesus, and angels in attendance. On the opposite side of the Chapel, in a large panel beside the altar, distorted figures of the two thieves (Plate 102) are painted hanging upon crosses; a light behind clouds suggests the Resurrection of Christ from the bare third cross. A side altar fills the next panel; the third is interrupted by a low door, above and to the sides of which small figures of Carmelite monks follow paths beset by temptations, which lead to the Virgin seated in the arch of the panel as she blesses a monk safely arrived (Plate 103). On one side of the door a youthful figure throws off his habit (Plate (104) as he follows a different path. The adjoining end wall, opposite the altar, includes a niche: above, within the lunette, Christ, seated at a bare table, is attended by Angels. A rocky landscape extends over the wall below; on one side of the niche a monk kneels in prayer; on the other a nun abstains from tempting food (Plate 104).

The new realism of the nineteenth century is suggested in the paintings of this chapel; also, a special respect for its structure is shown in the originality with which the different compositions are accommodated to the walls. The whole decoration is interesting for the unhackneyed style in which it is painted, suggesting that it could have been some of the early work done by the brilliant Tresguerras. The principal colors used are yellow ochre, orange ochre or *almagre,* earth green, and pale indigo; the medium used is tempera.

102. Francisco Eduardo Tresguerras [?]. One of the Two Thieves. Chapel of the Virgin, Convent of El Carmen, Celaya, Guanajuato.

Mons in quo beneplacitum est Deo habitare in eo.

Ybi loquitur Christus.

Ybi coronat Christus.

Liberatus sum

Fratris sicut ihi.

Pericula inferni invenerunt me

Castitat

Mundo et mundo con

erunt animam meam.

103. Francisco Eduardo Tresguerras [?]. Carmelite Monks and the Virgin. Over entrance
in Chapel of the Virgin. Convent of El Carmen, Celaya, Guanajuato.

104. Francisco Eduardo Tresguerras [?]. (left) Carmelite Monks (detail). Beside entrance to Chapel of the Virgin, Convent of El Carmen, Celaya, Guanajuato. (right) Nun Practicing Abstinence. Adjacent Wall of the Chapel.

1850–1915

La Barca, Jalisco (Site 4)

La Casa del Burro de Oro (Hacienda). A hacienda, the House of the Golden Burro, near La Barca, retains murals by a genre painter, Gerardo Suárez. The walls of the open corridors around the patio are covered with large paintings of regional types, shown in city streets, in the countryside, or in gay garden scenes of hacienda life with musicians and dancing (Plates 105, 106, 107). The murals show contrasting costumes of different classes in Mexico, which relate in style to those in the great book of lithographs, *México y sus Alrededores,*

published in Mexico City in 1856 during a nationalist phase of Mexican art.

Well-lighted in the wide corridors and framed by green growth, which is also painted into the pastoral scenes, these walls express the romanticism of the nineteenth century as reflected in Mexico.

Querétaro, Querétaro (Site 5)

Santa Teresa (Parish Church). The church of *Las Teresitas*, a heavy neoclassic edifice built early in the nineteenth century for the Reformed Order of Barefoot Carmelite Nuns, has been attributed to Tresguerras as

105. Gerardo Suárez. Garden Scene. Corridor, Casa del Burro de Oro, La Barca, Jalisco.

106. Gerardo Suárez. Street Scene. Corridor, Casa del Burro de Oro, La Barca, Jalisco.

107. Gerardo Suárez. Countryside Scene. Corridor, Casa del Burro de Oro, La Barca, Jalisco.

architect, although Toussaint doubts that it is his. The church is elaborately painted with murals from a later period; the date 1887 is inscribed outside.

The entire vault of the church is elaborately painted in blue-gray in imitation of carved design. The decoration of the half dome of the apse, also a simulation of wood carving, is filled with cherubs done with hard precision amidst the curves of ornamental details. Below, at the sides of an oval window, two scenes from the Old Testament fill the arched wall. Along both sides of the nave large figures of saints painted in soft tans and pink-gray, sixteen in all, stand guard beside four tall windows. The large intrinsic arch of the choir is filled with three scenes: in the center, St. John of the Cross expels demons; on one side he appears with St. Teresa; on the other, the Virgin confers a scapula on a saint.

These paintings, for all of the Academic ambition shown, have no special quality as art; they may date from late in the century.

Santa Rosa Viterbo (Parish Church). This late eighteenth-century church was partly remodeled in 1849. The pendentives, painted with the Four Strong Women of the Old Testament—Judith, Deborah, Esther, and Jael—reflect similar paintings found in Tenancingo. However, Jean Charlot finds these murals in Santa Rosa to be folk paintings done in lime tempera in 1910.

PART FOUR: PAINTING OF THE PEOPLE

PART FOUR: *Painting of the People*

The Development of a Mexican Art

Dr. Alfonso Caso in writing of Mexican art has observed: "Mexico is not only a region in the world; it is also, and above all, a culture" (1958, p. 123).

During three centuries of growth as a Spanish Colony, Mexico had developed a mixed or mestizo culture, and when Independence brought forth the Mexican nation this distinctive way of life was already flourishing in the land. *Arte popular* is the expression of this new way of life.

The popular arts, constantly being revitalized by fresh hands for daily or ceremonial use, retain the influences that have contributed esthetic experience to the people. Old World traditions, grafted onto native Indian roots, bloom with new vigor and variety in a style of art that is distinctively Mexican and carries the rhythm and color of the land.

In this mestizo culture of Mexico, Christian festivals brought from Europe are celebrated throughout the country with fireworks introduced from the Orient. Elaborate decorations made of tissue paper and papier mâché substitute for pre-Conquest religious or magical decorations of *amate* paper and of corn paste, still to be found in fragmentary form in remote regions of the country. But the festivals and their celebration have taken on a character that makes them quite different from those of the lands from which they came, or of any other land: they are truly Mexican. In every cultural expression of the people some degree of fusion of Old World and New World traditions is present, the result being a new art that has gradually been created by a new people.

Folk art, although constantly changing, is a growth from the soil; it is a spontaneous expression by the people. Essentially, popular art is of the countryside; in Mexico it enters into and revitalizes the art of cities.

Manuel Álvarez writes as a contribution to this chapter:

Popular Art is the art of the People.

A popular painter is an artisan who, as in the Middle Ages, remains anonymous. His work needs no advertisement, as it is done for the people around him. The more pretentious artist craves to become famous, and it is characteristic of his work that it is bought for the name rather than for the work—a name that is built up by propaganda.

Before the Conquest all art was of the people, and popular art has never ceased to exist in Mexico. The art called Popular is quite fugitive in character, of sensitive and personal quality, with less of the impersonal and intellectual characteristics that are the essence of the art of the schools. It is the work of talent nourished by personal experience and by that of the community—rather than being taken from the experiences of other painters in other times and other cultures, which forms the intellectual chain of nonpopular art.

During the Colonial epoch and the nineteenth century painting was largely directed from Europe by European painters, or by Mexicans who had been taught by them, or who themselves had studied in Spain, Italy, Germany, or France; therefore all art not within European tradition was held in contempt. Only in these times of social and political revolution have we come to recognize the artistic and social value of Popular Art in all of its manifestations.

Popular mural paintings are always being created and erased. In the churches of Mexico some expressions of Popular Art from the past century have remained longer than in places of daily use, and interesting work is more likely to be found in communities far from urban centers, which have not lost their characteristic taste, as in Alpuyeca or Tlayacapan in Morelos, or Motul in Yucatán.

The Indian artist, whose traditional style was rigorously suppressed during the Colonial epoch, was compelled to copy, on the walls of churches and convents, the European engravings that were handed to him for that purpose. But, as time went on—or even immediately where circumstances were favorable, as in Ixmiquilpan—his feeling for form and color began to assert itself.

Popular painting is farthest removed from commercial art: it exists for itself. Sometimes it is decorative, as in some pulque saloons, where its only purpose is to give pleasure through color and geometrical design; sometimes it represents satirical scenes, and the name of the establishment is worked into the scheme, or perhaps phrases with double, or Rabelaisian, meaning.

The Reform Laws expropriating all Church property, first decreed by Benito Juárez in 1857, became effective after the fall of the empire of Maximilian ten years later, and the Church buildings passed into the exclusive care of the people who use them. Many Popular paintings register this care. Religious wall paintings of the time show the influence of native taste in technique rather than in subject. Throughout Mexico angels and cherubs, flying in clouds in the cupolas of parish churches, hint of the mysteries of Heaven as revealed in the domes of the Cathedral and of San Fernando in Mexico City; above altars angels may be painted drawing curtains to disclose a cross; upon the walls of churches or sacristies Bible stories may be represented. Decorative elements grow elaborate as Popular painting reasserts Baroque expression.

After the death of Juárez the government of Porfirio Díaz ruled the Republic of Mexico through a clique that excluded all but a favored few, who tended to monopolize land, industry, and commerce. This group looked toward Europe for its values and ignored or despised indigenous art and even the communal culture that nourished it. During this period the taste of city dwellers was in decline.

The many-sided Revolution of the twentieth century, which began with the overthrow of the Díaz regime, destroyed the set patterns of the country and, gradually reaching deep into the life of the people, became to an amazing extent a cultural revolution. Of the many resulting changes, that of most universal importance for the Mexican people is the affirmation of their national culture.

The Mexican poet, Octavio Paz, asserts: "The Mexican Revolution, discovering folk art, gave birth to our contemporary painting; discovering the language of the people, it created our new poetry" (1959, p. 14).

Dr. Caso has written with rare perception of the popular arts of his country. He concludes: "Perhaps one of the fundamental merits of Popular Art is that it presents itself at the same time as an alive and a traditional art. Although it is strongly rooted in indigenous traditions, and shows Spanish and Asiatic influences, unquestionably it has connection with modern Mexican painting and with the most important manifestations of art in contemporary Mexico" (1958, p. 155).

Mexican Baroque expression has persisted in Popular painting. Mexican artists, trained in the Classic tradition of the San Carlos Academy and abroad at the turn of the century, had mastered the disciplined intellectualism of Western painting at a time when this art was being transformed in Europe. They were to return to Mexico to rediscover their country and its native art, and their formal growth, coming together with the emotional richness of Popular expression in Mexico, was to flower upon the walls of Mexico during the period of deep stress, hope, and aspiration of the Mexican Revolution as authentic Mexican art—in great murals that have astonished the world of art.

Popular wall paintings may be found throughout Mexico wherever people congregate: in churches, markets, shops, halls, schools, and homes. This contagious art is likely to appear in regions where Pre-Conquest or Colonial murals have been found. The photographs included here have been taken in different sections of the country between erasures of this impermanent art; they indicate the wide prevalence and general character of Popular mural painting in the various regions. We cannot be certain that any of these paintings still exist, but somewhere new ones come as the people of Mexico continue to paint.

Central Mexico

MÉXICO, D.F. (SITE 1)

The City of Mexico has been notable for Popular paintings on façades and interiors of *pulquerías* or pulque shops, social centers of the workers. During the period when the contemporary mural movement was taking shape in Mexico City, Popular painters shared in the *élan* of the movement. Unfortunately, hygienic regulations in 1930 caused many wall decorations to be painted over, with a resulting discouragement of this fascinating art of the people. Manuel Alvarez Bravo took photographs of some paintings that had escaped destruction, as well as of others in the making.

Pulque Shops

Calzado de los Gallos. On the façades of *pulquerías* along the famous Highway of the Roosters, where cock-

108. Cock Fight. Pulque Shop, Calzada de los Gallos, México, D.F.

109. One Day in the Year. Pulque Shop, Calzada de los Gallos, México, D.F.

110. Request for Soup. Pulque Shop, Calzada de los Gallos, México, D.F.

fighting had long taken place, a series of painted walls have represented various subjects: a railroad station, with a locomotive of a former day minutely painted in every detail; a cockfight (Plate 108), with a circle of spectators; two *aficionados* with cocks under their arms (Plate 109), labeled Un día en el año ("One Day in the Year"); two men demanding soup while a woman reminds them that she is "only now plucking the fowl" (Plate 110). All four of these anonymous paintings appear to have been done by the same hand.

A famous Popular painter, Luis Cienfuegos, decorated many *pulquerías* in Mexico City while the contemporary movement was growing there. Among these paintings by Cienfuegos, in the Barrio of Peralvillo

marked "Lic. Sanitaria No. 3777," the entire façade of one *pulquería* is covered with decorative borders framing curtains, which are raised to disclose jungle landscapes filled with lions (Plate 111) and tigers (Plate 112). On Puente del Rosario, Cienfuegos painted various scenes within wide decorative borders: a landscape with an airplane flying overhead (Plate 113), a sailboat at sea, a *charro* drinking pulque offered by a *china poblana* (Plate 114). Grouped in small panels he has painted with intense realism a drum, cartridges, a fife, a plumed helmet, gloves, a flag (Plate 115). Upon the façade of one *pulquería* Cienfuegos painted a large military horseman, but as the commissioner did not pay for it, he left it as a ghost picture—a horse mounted

111. Luis Cienfuegos. Lions. Pulque Shop, Lic. Sanitaria No. 3777, México D.F.

112. Luis Cienfuegos. Tigers. Pulque Shop, Lic. Sanitaria No. 3777, México, D.F.

only by a military uniform minus face and hands. The Mexican genius for exquisite detail is apparent in all of Cienfuegos' work.

Murals as Symbols for Shop Names. The name of a pulque shop is often indicated by its decoration: Los Brincos de los Changos ("Doings of the Monkeys") is illustrated by a series of panels showing monkeys going through all of the motions of making and selling pulque (Plate 116). La Charrita ("The Little Rider") is decorated with a horse mounted by a lovely *china poblana* and framed by a garden of flowers (Plate 117); Las Fierras ("the Wild Beasts") shows a lion almost catching a rabbit (Plate 118); El As de Bastos ("Ace of Clubs") is pure abstraction with not a club in sight, but it is strangely suggestive of a game of cards (Plate 119).

Store

In Barrio de San Simón, of Mexico City, paintings were made on exterior walls of a store: in one panel, a girl is dressed in the festive costume of a *china pob-*

113. Luis Cienfuegos. Landscape with Airplane. Pulque Shop, Puente del Rosario, México, D.F.

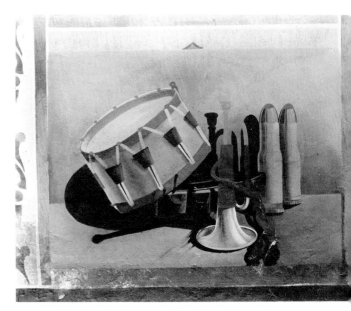

115. Luis Cienfuegos. Still Life. Pulque Shop, Puente del Rosario, México, D.F.

114. Luis Cienfuegos. Stirrup Cup. Pulque Shop, Puente del Rosario, México, D.F.

116. Pulquería Las Brincas de los Changos (Doings of the Monkeys). Pulque Shop, México, D.F.

117. Pulquería La Charrita (China Poblana). Pulque Shop, México, D. F.

118. Pulquería Las Fieras (Wild Beasts). Pulque Shop. México, D.F.

119. Pulquería El As de Bastos (Ace of Clubs). Pulque Shop, México, D.F.

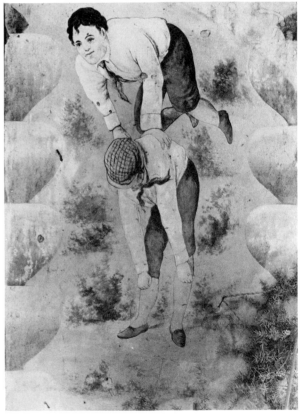

120. China Poblana. Store Wall, Barrio de San Simón. México, D.F.

121. Two Boys at Leap Frog. Store Wall, Barrio de San Simón, México, D.F.

Photo by Pablo Méndez
Courtesy Fondo Editorial de la Plástica Mexicana, Arte Popular.

123. "Farewell, My Love." Restaurant, Villa de Guadalupe (Villa Madero), D. F.

122. Milking Cow with Calf. Dairy Shop, México, D.F.

lana (Plate 120); in another, two boys play leapfrog, head on (Plate 121). This must have been copied from an illustration made elsewhere, but it has taken on the magic of a good painter's hand.

Dairy Shop

A *lechería* (dairy shop) decorated with landscapes related to milk, shows a large cow with a calf tied to its neck being milked by a very small girl (Plate 122); another mural is a landscape of Swiss character with painted minutiae of incredible fineness of execution.

Restaurant

Wall paintings come and go on the façades of shops that serve pilgrims to the shrine of Guadalupe, at the northern extremity of Mexico City. A *fonda* in Villa de Guadalupe, or Villa Madero, is decorated with a Popular painting that must represent a fiesta being prepared in a pueblo: a turkey hen bids farewell to a

124. Satirical Butchering Scene. Butcher Shop, San Juan Teotihuacan, México.

125. White Horse. Bath House, Texmelucan, Puebla.

ease, and women hurrying with *ollas* (kettles) in their hands (Plate 123, color, p. 152).

In Mexico City some young painters entered the mural movement obliquely by painting in *pulquerías*.

SAN JUAN TEOTIHUACAN, MÉXICO (SITE 6)

Butcher Shop

In this town near the archeological zone of Teotihuacan, upon the façade of a *carnicería* (butcher shop) satirical comments on our human ways reverse the roles of swine and men: a man hangs by his belt as he is weighed by a large, competent pig; another is being scalded in a big pot by other swine (Plate 124).

SAN MARTÍN TEXMELUCAN, PUEBLA (SITE 7)

Bathhouse

In a pueblo on the main highway between Mexico and the city of Puebla a great white horse painted on the wall of a *baños* (public bathhouse) facing the highway (Plate 125) makes this a town to be remembered. This painting, in the region where the horse was first used in the New World, is like a ghost of the terror created by the horse among Indians at the time of the Conquest.

huge gobbler who stands beside a *casuela* (large pottery bowl) just waiting for him on a charcoal brazier. These figures are painted against the sky, with small figures in the landscape below—a *campesino* (country fellow) sprawled on the ground, other men seated at

Southern Mexico

CUERNAVACA, MORELOS (SITE 8)

Iglesia de Guadalupe (Parish Church). The Church of Guadalupe, adjoining the Borda Gardens in Cuernavaca, was built as a chapel by Le Borde's son late in the eighteenth century. Of its decorations, two panels painted in tempera are copies of familiar subjects: one The Virgin Enthroned and Saint Roc, with his dog, kneeling before the Virgin, who is seated upon cottony clouds (Plate 126). A third panel placed high above the side entrance is very different. This is a Crucifixion in which the suspended body of Christ is covered with pierced wounds, while from hands and feet and side fall arrows of light (Plate 127). The Cross is set in a Mexican landscape; its base is encircled by a snake, and its top is crowned by cherubs and sun and moon. This painting suggests a form of sacrifice practiced before the Conquest. Dr. Caso (1937, p. 45) has recorded an Aztec ceremony in honor of Xipe in which

126. Virgin Enthroned and Saint Roc. Iglesia de Guadalupe, Cuernavaca, Morelos.

127. The Crucifixion. Iglesia de Guadalupe, Cuernavaca, Morelos.

128. Hell. La Parroquia, Alpuyeca, Morelos.

the prisoner was tied to a frame, raised, and then riddled with arrows until he expired. "In some magical way the rain of blood was thought to induce the fall of another precious liquid, water."

ALPUYECA, MORELOS (SITE 9)

La Parroquia (Parish Church). South of Cuernavaca, in the pueblo of Alpuyeca, the small parish church is entered through the heavy arch of the choir. Wall paintings cover this arch. On the left side, Hell is represented by the seven deadly sins, personified and accompanied by devils in a pool of fire (Plates 128, 129); on the right, conspicuous in the flames of Purgatory, are a king and bishop and lovely ladies (Plate 130), but they look up hopefully as a young girl rises from their midst praying on her way to Heaven (Plate 131). Overhead, in the center of the arch, Jesus and Mary within a frame of clouds welcome the young girl into Heaven (Plate 132). These expressive murals are painted in oil

129. Hell (detail). La Parroquia, Alpuyeca, Morelos.

130. Purgatory. La Parroquia, Alpuyeca, Morelos.

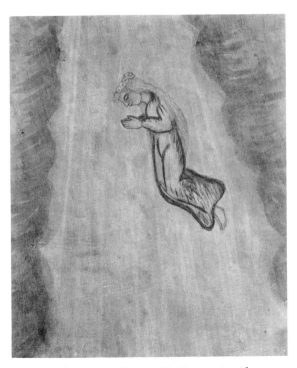

131. On the Way to Heaven. La Parroquia, Alpuyeca, Morelos.

132. Young Girl Received into Heaven. La Parroquia, Alpuyeca, Morelos.

133. Apparition of the Virgin of Guadalupe. San Juan Bautista, Tlayacapan, Morelos.

134. Baptism of Christ in River Jordan. San Juan Bautista, Tlayacapan, Morelos.

157

135. A Baptism. Santo Domingo, Chapel Ruin, Cuilapan, Oaxaca.

paritions of the Virgin of Guadalupe to the Indian, Juan Diego, are painted within large medallions on a lower side wall (Plate 133); high on this same wall is painted a panel of Jesus Praying in Gethsemane while the three Apostles are very much asleep; on the opposite wall above a side altar, a large panel, dated 1905, is painted with the Baptism of Jesus in the River Jordan (Plate 134).

Near the apse, on both sides of the church, painted curtains reach from dado to vault. These are bordered with repeated abstract designs, but on one side alternating spaces are filled with a variety of familiar objects: moon, hat, hand, jar, and so on, painted in red on a yellow ground with no exact repetition. This decoration is reminiscent of the objects found in prayer scrolls in the prehistoric temples of Teotihuacan; however, it was painted before these excavations were made; also, it is far removed in place.

CUILAPAN, OAXACA (SITE 11)

Santo Domingo (Ruin). In the old, ruined chapel of the Dominican monastery of Cuilapan a popular painting of a Baptism must date from very long ago. Costumes and accessories suggest Colonial times, but this painting, in a large arched niche, because of its extreme naïveté belongs to the timeless expression of Popular art. This may well be the oldest Popular mural still existing in Mexico (Plate 135).

color with free use of red-orange or *almagre* in the fires of Hell and Purgatory.

TLAYACAPAN, MORELOS (SITE 10)

San Juan Bautista (Parish Church). The tall, narrow church of the old Augustinian monastery of Tlayacapan contains a variety of popular paintings: the Four Ap-

Southeastern Mexico

In the land of the Mayas, Popular murals painted in homes reflect the taste of their time.

VALLADOLID, YUCATÁN (SITE 12)

Casa Colonial (Dwelling)

A life-sized lion, "which Rousseau might have seen and copied," was painted in the corridor of a Colonial house in Valladolid (Plate 136).

Signed by Roberto Pell (but undated) mural paintings were found in small towns of Yucatán:

MOTUL, YUCATÁN (SITE 13)

Casa Colonial (Dwelling)

In the corridor of a large Colonial house Pell painted

136. Lion. Valladolid, Yucatán.

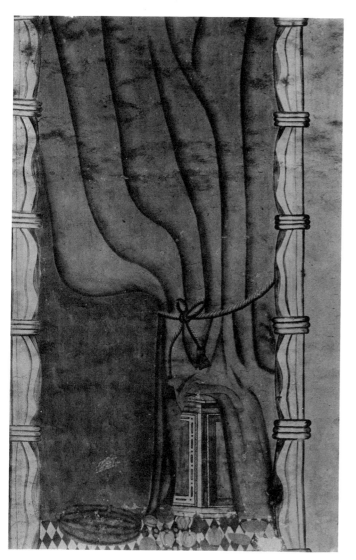

137. Roberto Pell. Draped Curtain. Corridor, Colonial House, Motul, Yucatán.

138. Roberto Pell. Hennequin Worker. Corridor, Colonial House, Motul, Yucatán.

panels twenty feet in height: one is of a draped curtain resting upon a tiled floor (Plate 137); the other, like a window opening onto the landscape, shows a worker cutting hennequin (Plate 138).

TIZIMÍN, YUCATÁN (SITE 14)

Vivienda (Dwelling)

On the walls of a thatched house Roberto Pell painted landscapes with painted frames in imitation of canvases. In the dining room he painted scrolled medallions, one enclosing a cat (Plate 139) and another enclosing a melon and other fruits (Plate 140).

139. Roberto Pell. Cat in Medallion. Dining Room, Tizimín, Yucatán.

140. Roberto Pell. Fruits in Medallion. Dining Room, Tizimín, Yucatán.

141. R. F. Canul. Advertisement. Drug Store, Dzitás, Yucatán.

Tzitás, Yucatán (Site 15)

Drug Store

Advertising becomes wall painting in the hands of the people. A painting on the front of a *droguería* (drug store) in Tzitás, signed by R. F. Canul and dated 1929, advertises a patent medicine by showing two men—one, well, and the other, sick (Plate 141).

Northern Central Highland

In the Otomí regions of Hidalgo, where the great Augustinian monasteries show rich decorations dating from the sixteenth century, various kinds of Popular paintings have been found.

Ixmiquilpan, Hidalgo (Site 16)

San Miguel Arcángel (Parish Church; mural destroyed). Among parish churches decorated after the Colonial Period, the great monastery temple of Ixmiquilpan was unique. By order of the parochial curate the upper walls of the church were painted with murals on a grand scale in the middle of the nineteenth century by a provincial artist, Pedro López. Just one hundred years later, in 1960, the paintings were removed in order to reveal the original decoration of the temple.

These ambitious biblical illustrations, reflecting in semi-Popular style the large historic paintings in vogue with Academicians of the time, were executed with immense vigor. The highest level of the long walls on both sides was divided into four equal panels that extended into the barrel vault; these were filled with large-figure compositions, illustrating incidents from the Life of the Virgin, which included neoclassic architectural forms, all crudely but solidly painted with much realism.

More symbolic were the paintings that covered the choir's walls and vault: on one side priests, on the other, monks, enclosed by huge triangles, received rays from the Holy Ghost above. Upon the arched wall the Virgin Ascending to Heaven was flanked by four bushy-bearded Evangelists accompanied by their very realistic symbols of lion, calf, eagle, seraph.

At first glance these paintings seemed but wearisome and inexpert attempts, but they possessed a popular Mexican savor that had its attraction. These immense murals also gave a hint of the great vitality and boundless courage of Mexican artists, some of whom in the more auspicious twentieth century were to paint the murals of the Revolution.

El Carmen (Parish Church). Decorations in the sacristy of the eighteenth-century church of El Carmen are more Baroque than Popular in character; the original Colonial decoration probably has been retouched. In the arched wall God the Father, robed in red, casts from his bosom rays of light that form a triangular frame to enclose a priest saying mass below. Different scenes fill the side walls, and partly destroyed decorative details enrich all spaces.

Paintings within the church are from a more recent time. In the cupola heavy curtains drawn by angels open the way to Heaven. Evangelists in pendentives are sturdily painted, touched by the solidity of Academic art.

Iglesia de Jesús (Parish Church). The small, old Church of Jesus was redecorated in 1942 by a local Popular artist, Pancho Mora, with paintings of fine quality. The cupola is filled with very stylized curtains that disclose only a tiny spot of Heaven expressed by two cherubs and two hearts. Within the drum of this small dome two angels kneel beside a cross accompanied by symbols of the Crucifixion. In wide panels on either side of the church Mora has painted two contrasting subjects: in one, the Last Supper; in the other, the town of Ixmiquilpan against its mountain landscape with paths leading to two local miraculous crosses placed on mountaintops. Pale pinks and tawny browns predominate in the color of these charming paintings.

ACTOPAN, HIDALGO (SITE 17)

Butcher Shop

Near the great decorated monastery of Actopan, a *carnicería*, or butcher shop, advertises itself in a fashion similar to the one in Teotihuacan: an ox is weighing a fully dressed man who hangs from a hook passed through his shoe. The ox is very happy; the man is not (Plate 142).

SAN ANTONIO AMETUSCO, HIDALGO (SITE 18)

Hacienda

A series of paintings in the interior of a pulque hacienda near San Antonio Ametusco picture architectural landscapes with men and horses in the foreground and roads disappearing into the distance. In one of these murals a large number of mounted *campesinos* are amidst monuments that suggest Mexico City; other scenes are of prosperous village life (Plate 143).

142. Satirical Butchering Scene. Butcher Shop, Actopan, Hidalgo.

Photo by Pablo Méndez
Courtesy Fondo Editorial de la Plástica Mexicana, Arte Popular.

143. Street Scene. Panel, Interior of a Pulque Hacienda, San Antonio Ametusco, Hidalgo.

Western Mexico

Western Mexico is a region of artists.

Almost all of the painters who have created Mexico's contemporary mural movement originated in the West, where Mexican Baroque art, kept alive by provincial painters, had continued an informal existence. During the nineteenth century Popular expression in Western Mexico had merged with the more traditional art in both sacred and profane paintings; in the twentieth century this native Mexican element was to vitalize contemporary art.

ATOTONILCO, GUANAJUATO (SITE 19)

Santuario de Jesús Nazareno (Sanctuary). Although described as a unit in the section on the Colonial Period, this site is as much Popular as Colonial in character. It must have served as a school of art for the people of this mining region for the past two hundred years. El Templo del Calvario, in panels of devils, is particularly Popular. Other paintings in this church have a vigor that gives a semi-Popular impression, such as the Miracles of Jesus painted in the vault of El Templo del Calvario.

Large panels near the apse of the main church, painted with the Crucifixion and the Descent from the Cross, are dated 1947 and signed J. Novo. Ornate frames painted around these compositions give a semblance of canvases. This work is semi-Popular in character.

In the portico of the Santuario de Jesús Nazareno are many paintings, in which devils abound, that record the sufferings and fears of the people with drama and vigor.

CADERÉYTA DEL MONTE, QUERÉTARO (SITE 20)

Popular wall paintings in the town of Caderéyta del Monte and in its vicinity are perhaps typical of what can be found throughout this region.

Parroquia. A large painting on the wall of the sacristy of the parish church is formed of angular figures and white lambs in an interesting composition in which a sophisticated American artist found "some of El Greco's emotional feeling." It is possibly contemporary with Tresguerras.

Cathedral. The upper walls of the cathedral show paintings which have the appearance of framed pictures but are actually murals.

Domicilio. A house interior decorated in this same manner, as if with hanging canvases is very charming. Outside walls of some houses have good geometric patterns, as have interior walls, where friezes have often been painted with the use of stencils.

TOLIMÁN, QUERÉTARO (SITE 21)

San Miguel. This small parish church in an Otomí pueblo has been decorated with angels and people, objects and scrolls in the pure style of Popular Art; the style of this decoration in the cupola may be used wherever a wall is made available to a painter of the people. It is as typical as any other expression of Popular art in Mexico.

BERNAL, QUERÉTARO (SITE 22)

Very good paintings are reported to exist in Bernal, a town a short distance from Caderéyta del Monte on the road to Querétaro.

MADELENA, QUERÉTARO (SITE 23)

Maximilian was captured in a chapel on a hill high over Madelena, which is above Caderéyta. In a chapel in Madelena can still be seen crude figures of soldiers, reputedly painted by Maximilian's soldiers.

144. Bacchantes. Hacienda, Parras, Coahuila.

145. Lovers on Horseback. Site not recorded.

HACIENDAS (SCATTERED)

Hacienda Santa Bárbara. An abandoned hacienda near Caderéyta, Querétaro, retains in the porticos primitive paintings which are of interest.

Hacienda. The photograph of infant Greek gods or Bacchantes (Plate 144) was made from a mural in a hacienda in a region near Parrás, Coahuila.

Hacienda. The charming and expert painting of Los Enamorados, or Lovers on Horseback (Plate 145), photographed from a mural painting in an unrecorded site, must have been copied from an engraving or chromo sometime during the nineteenth century, by a painter who extracted the full quality of his model.

Many delightful wall paintings in provincial churches and homes of Western Mexico, including the genre paintings popular during the nineteenth century (such as have been previously described in La Barca), merge with popular expression.

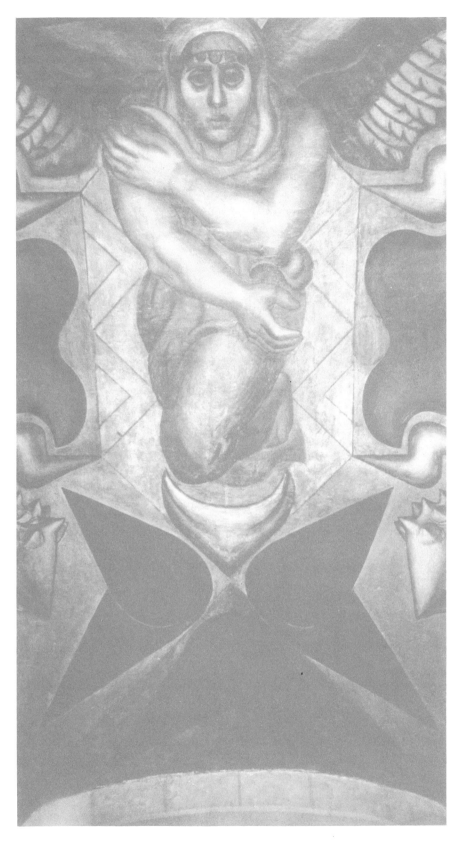

PART FIVE: THE MURAL REVOLUTION
OF THE TWENTIETH CENTURY

Background

Mexico's twentieth-century Revolution was preceded and accompanied by a resurgence of cultural activity; mural painting formed an integral part of this Revolution. For twenty years the mural movement was germinating. At the turn of the century, with the country apparently prosperous and at peace, the government of Porfirio Díaz, in accordance with the tradition of the previous century, financed European study for selected students of the National Academy of San Carlos. Included among these artists were future leaders of the cultural revolt: Gerardo Murillo (better known by his pseudonym, Dr. Atl), Francisco Goitia, Alfredo Ramos Martínez, Roberto Montenegro, and Diego Rivera. During this period of intellectual ferment in Europe the young painters came in contact with the revolutionary technical experiments being made in painting and with a variety of revolutionary political ideals. In Mexico the people were restive under a system of favoritism, dispossession, and ruthless political control. Artists who matured amidst these various tensions at home and abroad served as leaven in the complex Revolution that has followed—national, political, racial, agrarian, social, cultural, educational. Contemporary mural paintings have both anticipated and reflected these various phases of the Revolution, and upon the painted walls of Mexico the muralists brilliantly affirm their country's cultural autonomy.

Mexico's mural movement is inseparable from the changing political scene.

Through the Academy of San Carlos, Mexican artists for a century had been strongly aligned with modern European painting and with the accepted standards of Academic Art. In 1903 a new director, Antonio Fabres, came from Spain to introduce a naturalistic system of teaching based on a photographic standard, which caused some disaffection in the Academy. Diego Rivera, a young student originally from Guanajuato, refused to cooperate and withdrew to work alone.

Gerardo Murillo, or Dr. Atl, a native of Guadalajara, returned early in the century from much study of art and international experience in Europe and Asia. Orozco records that "Dr. Atl carried in his hands the rainbow of the impressionists and all of the audacities of the School of Paris." Freshly impressed by the beauty of his native land, Dr. Atl proclaimed the value of native craftsmanship and of Mexican culture, and at the same time he shared with the art students his enthusiasm for the great Renaissance frescoes of Italy, "which technique had been lost for four hundred years." This magnetic rebel had great influence upon the students. In 1906 he promoted Diego Rivera's first exhibit (shown with a group of Fabres students) and saw him off to Europe with a letter to the Spanish painter Eduardo Chicharro, who became his first European master. In 1907 and 1909 Dr. Atl sponsored exhibits of work with Mexican themes by Jorge Enciso, a young painter recently arrived in Mexico City from Guadalajara. After Fabres had departed from the Academy in 1908 a spirit of experimentation and self-assertion succeeded his exacting disciplines, and the younger artists turned to Mexico for subject matter. Attending Dr. Atl's night classes, mature José Clemente Orozco, a native of Jalisco only recently dedicated to art, and the very youthful David Alfaro Siqueiros, from Querétaro, experienced his liberating and inspiring influence.

For the National Theatre, being built of Italian marble by an Italian architect in Mexico City for the 1910 Centennial celebration of Hidalgo's *Grito de Dolores*, Dr. Atl designed a glass curtain to be made by Tiffany of New York. Characteristically, the subject he chose is of Mexico's most ancient guardians, her snow-capped volcanoes. For many years this curtain, which can still be seen, was the only exhibit in the unfinished Theatre, now El Palacio de Bellas Artes, the center of Mexico's cultural life. When, paradoxically, an exhibition of contemporary Spanish art was imported at great cost in 1910 especially for the Centennial, and Mexican artists were ignored, a group of young painters, under the leadership of Dr. Atl, protested. In September, as a result of this protest, a large number of Mexican artists were enabled to hold a collective exhibit that filled patio, corridors, and unused galleries of the Academy with dynamic drawings and paintings, using Mexican themes and initiating nationalism in art. Inspired by the unexpected success of this hastily assembled exhibit, the artists organized El Centro Artístico for the express purpose of acquiring public walls to paint.

In November, 1910, six artists headed by Dr. Atl were commissioned by the Secretary of Education, Don Justo Sierra, to decorate collectively El Anfiteatro Bolívar, an auditorium newly built in the National Preparatory School, formerly the Jesuit College of San Ildefonso. Included in this group was the future muralist José Clemente Orozco. The subject was the History of Human Evolution. With scaffoldings already in place and designs being made, the political Revolution started under Francisco Madero, and work was suspended. The initiation of public wall painting had coincided with the political revolt, but the mural movement was to bide its time.

The first twentieth-century murals with American subjects were finished by Jorge Enciso just before the flight of Porfirio Díaz. These were friezes painted in oil in two schools (now destroyed) in what was then the disreputable Colonia de la Bolsa. For the Boys' School, Enciso painted "deer, parrots, vultures and volcanoes, owls and branches, quetzals and fig trees, squirrels and mesquite, turkeys and fountains"; for the Girls' School he painted "rabbits and open fields, monkeys and branches, birds and magnolias, spiderwebs and butterflies, eagles and nopales, Mayas modeling and decorating pottery" (Enciso; quoted by Charlot, MS).

In the summer of 1911 art students began a spontaneous strike in protest against continuance of the conservative regime in the Academy, continuing it through the last two years of Madero's tragic Presidency. The strike was terminated during the bloody dictatorship of General Victoriano Huerta, when the students expelled the conservative director and elected as the new director an impressionist painter recently returned from Paris, Alfredo Ramos Martínez. Disdaining academic methods, his first act was to establish in Santa Anita an open-air School of Painting which he named for its French prototype "Barbizon." While revolution raged through the country, the future muralists Siqueiros, Revueltas, Alva de la Canal, Leal, and Cahero were fostered here. When Huerta met military defeat, Ramos Martínez fell in his wake, but the School of Painting he had initiated in Santa Anita was to persist; painting had become a part of the Revolution.

Appointed by First Chief Carranza, as a reward for singlehandedly preventing a French loan to Huerta, Dr. Atl for a short time in 1914 served as director of the Academy. He proposed to change its name to "Workshops." When Mexico City, caught in the conflict between "Liberators," was occupied by Villa's army, Dr. Atl, accompanied by artists Orozco, Goitia, and Guillemín, and by many art students, including Siqueiros, Alva de la Canal, and Cahero, fled to Orizaba, where they entered actively into the Revolution as soldiers, writers, and caricaturists with the Constitutional Army under Obregón. A Mexican Academician, Mateo Herrera, became director of the Academy.

The Agrarian Revolution under Zapata swept the country, and for two months, November, 1914, to January, 1915, kept Eulalio Gutiérrez in office as President and the poet-philosopher José Vasconcelos as Minister of Education. Deserted and wounded, Gutiérrez abdicated, and Vasconcelos from 1915 to 1920 was stranded in the United States, where he had gone to plead for recognition of Gutiérrez. Carranza became Constitutional President in 1917, accepted a liberal constitution, and governed until he was deposed and murdered in 1920. During Carranza's Presidency, in 1919, when the Revolution appeared to be won and Jalisco had for governor the artist José Guadalupe Zuno, a Congress of Soldier-Artists was held in Guadalajara to discuss "the new orientations of art and culture," and Siqueiros, Carlos Orozco Romero, and others were sent abroad by the Revolutionary Government to study art.

Mexico's future muralists in their different ways began to build the foundation for public wall painting that would reflect the time and the people.

José Clemente Orozco in 1916 exhibited in Mexico City his fierce political cartoons, somber paintings of prostitutes, and tender paintings of school girls; all were reviewed with scorn. In 1917 he transferred his candid vision to California. Siqueiros, on his way to Europe in 1919, met with Orozco in New York, where they discussed the marvels of mechanics in relation to art. In Paris, Siqueiros found Rivera; and the sense of art as revolution, developed by Siqueiros during the Mexican struggle, and the formal revolution in plastic art occurring in Europe, in which Rivera was deeply involved, were fused into the revolutionary spark that has animated mural painting in Mexico. The great mural art of Italy profoundly influenced the young artists from Mexico, and they were to return to their country filled with eagerness to paint walls.

Since the surface of Mexico consists of mountain ranges and isolated valleys, numerous distinctive languages, crafts, and customs had developed quite independently; the people on one side of a mountain often knew nothing about the people on the opposite side. The present patchwork of states based on watersheds reflects the influence of these separated valleys, and many indigenous communities still exist unaffected by other communities. Through the Colonial Period and the nineteenth century the people were tied to their land and its labor, although they no longer possessed it. The Revolution that had started in Mexico in 1910 as a political revolt soon upset established patterns and reached into the life of the people. Mountains were crossed, and anxieties and needs were shared. Public mural painting, promoted by liberal intellectuals to dramatize the changing scene, was to wage its own social and cultural revolution and to create its own methods and values. The Mexican people were to become involved emotionally, at different levels of experience, in the Mural Revolution, and this involvement has contributed to the vitality of Mexican art.

The Movement

The contemporary mural movement began after General Alvaro Obregón became President in 1920. José Vasconcelos had returned from exile. First appointed as director of the University, he was soon made Minister of Education, an office suppressed by Carranza and restored through the strenuous efforts of Vasconcelos, who traveled as a "salesman of culture" to the various states for endorsement, assisted, among others, by Roberto Montenegro as "Ambassador of Painting."

Ramos Martínez, again elected director of the Academy, promptly established an open-air Art School in Chimalistac, later moved to Coyoacan. Exhibitions of students' work were held.

A strong nationalist art movement was launched by Dr. Atl, Jorge Enciso, Roberto Montenegro, and Adolfo Best-Maugard. In connection with the Centennial of Independence celebrated by the Revolutionary Government in 1921, these artists organized an exposition of native arts and crafts in Chapultepec Park. The first book on Mexican popular arts, based upon this exhibit, was published in 1921 by Dr. Atl.

Vasconcelos, dreaming of a contemporary art in Mexico springing from her native arts and life, consulted with artists about his ambitious building program for the Ministry of Education and offered them commissions to paint murals. He initiated the mural movement under government patronage by offering "walls, material expenses, artists' salaries, and, most important of all, stylistic freedom." The mural program of Vasconcelos in an ambitious and unfamiliar field, paying only an artisan's wage, did not tempt the established artists, but this opportunity appealed irresistibly to younger painters. Like magnets the walls drew from far and near the gifted and already prepared painters who were to make the Mexican Mural Renaissance.

The first mural commission was given by Vasconcelos for the Revolutionary Government in June, 1920, to Roberto Montenegro, who had recently returned from Majorca, where he had decorated a wall. Montenegro enlisted, for technical advisor, Xavier Guerrero, a painter with much practical experience in decorating walls in Guadalajara, whose native craftsmanship was to smooth the way for other Mexican muralists. In May, 1921, David Alfaro Siqueiros published in Barcelona his famous *Manifiesto a los Plásticos de América,* a manifesto of revolutionary art in which for the first time this art was conceived as monumental mural painting. Diego Rivera, after a long period in France devoted to analytical study of composition and to experiments in cubism and postcubism, returned to Mexico in July, 1921, to paint his first mural. Carlos Mérida arrived in 1920 from Guatemala and Paris, and Jean Charlot in 1921 from his native Paris. In March, 1922, Fernando Leal, Fermín Revueltas, Ramón Alva de la Canal, and Emilio García Cahero were recruited in Mexico City. David Alfaro Siqueiros and Amado de la Cueva were brought home from Europe by Vasconcelos in September, 1922, to paint murals. José Clemente Orozco had returned from the United States in 1920; perhaps because he had been a Carranzista or because he was famed as a caricaturist, Orozco received no mural commission until June, 1923. Emilio Amero, Ramón Alva Guadarrama, Máximo Pacheco, and others were soon painting or helping to paint walls.

From the beginning of public painting the muralists explored the country to study wall paintings from all periods of Mexico's past: fragmentary frescoes from Early Mexico found in ruins, sixteenth-century frescoes uncovered in churches and monasteries, and popular mural paintings adorning *pulquerías*. From all of these sources they enriched their art and their craft. Study, experiment, and hard, exacting work formed the adventure of their days, as with high spirits and tireless labor the muralists in overalls initiated Mexico's revolutionary mural painting. In a short period of experimentation and discovery they brought the Mexican Mural Renaissance into being.

A Syndicate of Revolutionary Painters, Sculptors, and Engravers, organized by the muralists in 1923, published *El Machete*, a brilliantly illustrated organ of propaganda, with Siqueiros, Guerrero, and Rivera as editors and Orozco as contributor. The Syndicate's principles defined and inspired the movement, but as an organization composed of strong personalities, with the mural commissions being awarded individually, it soon fell apart. Under the revolutionary impulse of the Syndicate the gentle nationalist and symbolical beginnings of mural painting soon gave way to powerful social messages and to technical mural solutions that shocked and angered the middle-class Mexicans accustomed to more conservative art. In spite of hostile demonstrations, the artists, supported by Vasconcelos, continued to paint without compromise.

Finally, in June, 1924, students of the Preparatory School violently attacked and defaced Orozco's and Siqueiros' murals. Public pressure grew too great, and Vasconcelos, overwhelmed by the freedom of style and ideology being released on walls, resigned his office as Minister of Education. Most of his artists were dismissed. Champions of modern art, aided by the general tolerance of Mexican people, succeeded in preserving what remained of these first unpopular painted walls. Only Rivera, with Guerrero to assist him, and Montenegro weathered the political storm of 1924. Supported by the new Minister of Education, Dr. Puig Casauranc, Rivera continued to paint public walls—with a pistol in his belt. Orozco in 1925 painted a privately commissioned mural in Mexico; he painted a wall in Orizaba. In 1926 he was permitted to complete his murals in the Preparatoria.

Mural artists being dependent upon commissions, public mural painting has been conditioned constantly by the current political situation. The unsympathetic administration of President Calles from 1924 to 1928 found the unemployed muralists scattered: De la Cueva, Siqueiros, and others went to Guadalajara to paint murals for the state of Jalisco; Charlot began investigations of early Mayan art for the Carnegie Institution of Washington in the ruins of Chichén Itzá; other painters became teachers. In 1927 Orozco returned to New York; Rivera, after completing huge murals, sailed for Russia and Europe; De la Cueva met an accidental death; and Siqueiros became absorbed in Syndicate work that took him far from home. Mural painting for a short time was discontinued. But when the muralists dispersed in 1927 the Mexican Mural Renaissance had already come fully into being, and the great artists who created it had realized the scope of their vision and their powers.

An astonishing amount of work of very high quality was done by Mexican muralists during these first few years of the movement. Technical problems were often confronted cooperatively and resolved in concert. In the early days Rivera, by analyzing great works of art, taught interested fellow artists the harmonic proportional principles of form and composition which had come down from the ancient Greeks through Byzantine painters to artist-architects of the Renaissance. This rediscovered knowledge formed the core of the cubist movement in France, where the composition was built to the squared canvas. When the principles were intelligently applied in painting walls, unity of the painting with the structure of the building was achieved and the integrity of the flat surface of the wall was respected; also, the volume of painted form was controlled so as to be identified visually with the thickness of the wall. With this application mural painting, as distinct from both decoration and easel painting, was reborn.

With few exceptions the first sites decorated were Colonial buildings. The period and the material of construction, the design of the building, and the source of light were taken into consideration in choosing the motif and the medium, in making the composition, and in determining the color. The possible range of vision was carefully studied so that the whole composition or its essential units could be accommodated to the eyes of the observer to be seen conveniently in a single glance. A vaulted and arcaded building constructed of *tezontle* (a violet-red, porous lava stone used extensively in Colonial Mexico) and open to daylight is very different from a modern structure of steel and smooth concrete with controlled sources of light. The artists soon found that each kind of building suggests its own basic solutions and requires an appropriate decoration.

Of great importance in painting a wall is the medium employed. At first this was oil color; then tempera, water color mixed with an agglutinant, was used. Rivera, in his first mural, introduced the medium of encaustic —color dissolved with oil of lavender or other solvent into "copal" (a resin) and wax, then melted with a blowtorch onto the surface of the wall. The technique of fresco painting was soon revived by different artists, notably Charlot, Alva de la Canal, and Guerrero, through experimentation aided by the practical knowledge which Mexican masons have retained from the past. Fresco is pure pigment ground in water and applied to a surface of lime-and-sand plaster while this is still wet. There are variations of fresco technique, as when Orozco has added color to thick limewater, or color has been mixed into the plaster for outside work. Relatively few pigments, largely earth colors, are chemically suited for fresco painting. A wall must be painted from the top down, preplanning being essential, and the limited section of a day's work can usually be distinguished from other areas. Once the plaster is dry it admits of no correction, and great sureness of execution is required. Fresco soon became the medium most generally employed by Mexico's mural painters; this oldest known technique has assured relative permanency to the great mass of contemporary murals.

During this Revolutionary Period, Mexican muralists working in freedom not only revived mural painting but created anew this social art. Through prodigious labor the chief protagonists of the mural movement achieved mastery of the walls. Each muralist among these self-appointed "painters for the people" has presented in his paintings his personal sense of values, and the small group of artists who started the movement, and who for the most part never ceased to paint walls, reveal among them a vast range of ideas and of technical expression, ideas and techniques that blazed trails which have been followed during succeeding developments of the mural movement.

Vasconcelos unwittingly had tapped a vast reservoir of creative energy, releasing a powerful stream which he was unable to control or to stem. The ensuing eager struggle and competition for walls to paint, the surge of ideas taking form in a fluid revolutionary culture, the knowledge of structural composition fortuitously recovered in Europe at this time, and the technical expertness of the artists involved, all of these elements combined to bring forth the Mexican Mural Renaissance and to renew Mexico's long tradition.

The Mural Renaissance: 1920–1927

First Murals Commissioned in Mexico City

In 1920, at the end of ten years of revolutionary civil war, José Vasconcelos, as Minister of Public Education, initiated mural painting in Mexico by enlisting artists to aid in the development of Mexican cultural values. The first sites to be commissioned for decoration were buildings under his Ministry in Mexico City (Site 1), and mural work proceeded more or less concurrently in all. These buildings are treated here individually as units.

San Pedro y San Pablo, San Ildefonso 60 (Annex, National Preparatory School). The first mural commission from the Mexican government was given to Roberto Montenegro to decorate the former Iglesia de San Pedro y San Pablo, adjoining the former Jesuit College of this name. Manuel Toussaint notes (1948, p. 115) that the church was built from 1576 to 1603 and that its cupola is reputed to have been the first one built in New Spain. These convent buildings had most re-

cently been used as a barracks; Vasconcelos gained their possession for his Ministry and had them cleaned and restored, the church building to serve as a lecture hall and the old college again to be a school.

Church: The decoration of this structure is by Montenegro and Xavier Guerrero, with Jorge Enciso acting as advisor. Two stained-glass windows unveiled in 1921 and 1922 were designed by Montenegro with folk motifs: Jarabe Tapatío (a dance of Jalisco) and a Street Scene in Manzanillo. In 1922 Montenegro decorated the apse of the church with an oil painting, the Dance of the Hours, in which an armored knight stands in the center beneath a Tree of Life filled with flowers and birds, and twelve allegorical nymphs are placed symmetrically to the sides; it is painted upon a background of gold.

The nave of the church was decorated in 1921 by Xavier Guerrero in glue tempera—domes, arches, and pillars all being covered with bluebirds and blackbirds and with pomegranates and flowers. In 1922 Guerrero painted the cupola of the side chapel with stylized signs of the zodiac upon a ground of vivid blue. Since this church is now used as a library, much of the wall decoration is covered by shelves.

Patios: The old Colegio de San Pedro y San Pablo, at this time raised from ruin, was decorated by Dr. Atl in the two large patios with nine panels filled with scenes and figures to symbolize turbulent nature: The Beautiful Wrath of the Sea, and other seascapes, Rain, and night landscapes with volcanoes.

These murals painted in "Atl" colors have entirely disappeared. Dr. Atl said in reference to their reception: "Those paintings do not please laymen who do not understand them; they do not please those who commissioned them either; nor do they please artists, who find them dynamic to excess. So I am the only one they please" (quoted by Charlot: 1963, pp. 103-104).

Stairway: Roberto Montenegro, commissioned in 1923 to decorate the walls of the great stairway that opens into the patios of San Pedro y San Pablo, painted in fresco the Festival of the True Cross, in which masons have raised a decorated cross over a newly completed building. With scaffoldings still in place, celebrants of a festival are placed at the different levels of the building and scaffold. This painting was made after the mural movement had got under way and Montenegro departs here from his earlier purely decorative style of work. It was completed in January, 1924.

This first building to be commissioned for decoration was again being painted by Montenegro in this stairway from 1929 to 1931, so that his later paintings belong with the last of the first ten years of mural work.

Escuela Nacional Preparatoria, Justo Sierro 16 (National Preparatory School). Decorations in the ancient buildings of San Pedro y San Pablo had served to introduce the ambitious mural plans of Vasconcelos. The former Jesuit College of San Ildefonso, converted into the National Preparatory School, was his second choice, and artists were sought for this work at home and also among those still abroad. At this time Diego Rivera returned from his long sojourn in Europe and entered into the plan with enthusiasm.

The handsome Colonial building of the Preparatoria covers an entire block. It was built in the eighteenth century of *tezontle* and gray sandstone. The three interior courts or patios are surrounded by three stories of open corridors, and great stairways ascend from the West Patio or Patio Grande and from the East Patio or Patio Chico. Opening from the large West Patio is the Auditorium, newly built for the Preparatory School just before the start of the Revolution, which in 1910 had prevented its decoration by the group under Dr. Atl. In 1921 Diego Rivera was commissioned by the Minister of Education, José Vasconcelos, to decorate this Auditorium.

Anfiteatro Bolívar: Rivera's project for the decoration of the Auditorium originally comprised all paintable surfaces of the architecture, including vaults, arches, and lunettes, the subject being the History of Philosophy from Pythagoras to Marx and Engels. However, only the background of the stage was decorated. The medium chosen was encaustic, and Rivera was assisted by artists Carlos Mérida, Jean Charlot, Xavier Guerrero, and later by Amado de la Cueva, who worked together as craftsmen in preparing all stages of the mural painting in what was truly a workshop.

In the decoration of the stage, symbolizing Creation, Diego Rivera initiated monumental mural art (Plate 146).

The stage includes a background wall, arched to fit a vaulted ceiling, which in its center frames a vaulted recess for an organ. Rivera first painted the large enclosing wall to symbolize the Philosophy of Humanism. In the center of the basket-handle arch of the stage wall, on the background of gold, a half circle shows constellations painted upon deep blue, its center representing Primeval Energy, from which three rays extend to terminate as hands in symbolic gesture: one points down to a great central figure in the vaulted recess; the others point to Angels of Life—Science and Wisdom—suspended on either side as they preside over the principles of Man and Woman, indicated by nude figures seated below, as if upon the earth. Between angels and nudes, symbolic figures rise in tiers: Under Science, Man faces Knowledge, Fable, Erotic Poetry, and Tradition, with Tragedy behind these; above stand Virtues—Prudence, Justice, Strength, and Continence—in halos of gold. Under Wisdom, Woman is accompanied by Dance, Song, and Music, with Comedy above; standing figures in halos represent Faith, Hope, and Charity. Wisdom on Woman's side unites the groups with a gesture that signifies Infinity. This immense mural with figures of about twelve feet, the first painted by Rivera, was influenced by the great Early Italian and Byzantine frescoes that he had seen in Europe.

Very different in character is the painting of the arched recess in the center of the stage, in which Rivera represents the Philosophy of Pythagoras. From a pyra-

146. Diego Rivera. Creation. Teatro Bolívar, Escuela Nacional Preparatoria, México, D.F.

mid of green growth the Tree of Life, that forms the background for the organ, a great figure of the Panto-crator, All-Ruler, rises with arms extended against the sky of gold. This figure is supported by the four symbols of the Logos, First Principle: Lion, Seraph, Eagle, Bull, placed within the green foliage. The warm color and richness of form found within this vaulted recess was painted after Rivera had taken a trip to Tehuante-pec, in the interval between the two murals, and he records here his reaction to the tropical life of his own country. Small animals appear in side spaces.

The impressive decoration of the stage was completed early in 1923. As Rivera was then urged by Vasconcelos to paint in the headquarters of his Ministry, the Secretaría de Educación Pública, completion of the entire project for the Auditorium was suspended indefinitely.

Patio Grande (West Patio): The Auditorium adjoins the West Patio, where in 1922 artists were invited to work. When established painters declined, Fernando Leal was asked to paint and to recommend others for the task. Commissions were then given to five very young artists: Fernando Leal, Jean Charlot, Emilio García Cahero, Ramón Alva de la Canal, and Fermín Revueltas, who were associated with the art school in Coyoacan. With great eagerness these painters, soon nicknamed "Dieguitos," selected walls and began to paint. Given no limitations as to subject or style, each was entirely on his own.

Walls of the upper flights of the great stairway were selected by Fernando Leal and Jean Charlot for their murals. Charlot's panel, the south wall of the stairway, was painted while he was assisting Rivera in the Auditorium, and it was the first of the murals to be completed. Accompanied by general interest and experimentation in fresco technique, his was the first

147. Jean Charlot. Massacre in the Main Temple (detail). Stairway, West Patio, Escuela Nacional Preparatoria, México, D.F.

mural to be painted in fresco. Charlot chose for his subject a scene from the Conquest, Massacre in the Main Temple, in which mounted, armored Conquistadores attack Indians in feathered headdresses engaged in a floral dance. In the midst of the conflict a maiden pierced by a spear (Plate 147) symbolizes the destruction of peace and gentleness. At the upper end of the panel Charlot painted Rivera, Leal, and himself (Plate 148); at the lower end he painted the legend, "This fresco is the first to be done in Mexico since Colonial times. Painted by Jean Charlot and plastered by master mason Luis Escobar." The composition is related to the ascending stairs by oblique thrusts of the long spears, which were painted last in encaustic vermilion; the use of black is conspicuous throughout.

Fernando Leal, on the corresponding wall opposite Charlot's, experimented with fresco but elected to paint in encaustic. Leal has represented a contemporary scene of a ritual dance given in a church, Pilgrimage of Chalma (Plate 149), famed shrine of the people, in

148. Jean Charlot. Massacre in the Main Temple (detail showing Diego Rivera, Fernando Leal, and Charlot). Stairway, West Patio, Escuela Nacional Preparatoria, México, D.F.

which masked and plumed Indians and little girls in white with wreaths of flowers dance for an audience of pilgrims. This panel is painted in brilliant color. The young friends had parted company in choice of subjects and media; they also differed in their approach to painting on a wall, Charlot making structural use of his composition and Leal using a more realistic approach.

In 1924 Jean Charlot painted in fresco four small panels on this stairway landing. Above the decora-

tive window that occupies the wall, he painted shields— of Colonial Mexico, with double-headed eagle, and of the University of Mexico, with a condor; in two narrow panels figures represent Cuauhtemoctzín, the last Aztec Emperor, and Saint Christopher, as symbol of the Conquest.

To the right of the entrance of the stairway an interesting panel was painted in encaustic in 1922 by Emilio García Cahero, representing Friars from the Colonial Period. This painting was destroyed in 1926,

149. Fernando Leal. Dance of Chalma (detail). Stairway, West Patio, Escuela Nacional Preparatoria, México, D.F.

with the artist's permission, to make way for a painting by Orozco, and no photograph was taken.

The main entrance to the Patio (a high vaulted passageway no longer in use) was chosen by Ramón Alva de la Canal and Fermín Revueltas for their murals, these being the largest available walls and also arched. On the east wall Alva de la Canal painted the Raising of the Cross when the Spanish first landed in the New World (Plate 150). After much experimental work, encouraged by the success of Charlot's mural, Alva painted his wall in fresco and helped to ease the way for those who followed.

On the west wall Revueltas painted, in encaustic, Devotion to the Virgin of Guadalupe (Plate 151), the Virgin and two angels being pictured in clouds with Indians kneeling below. This wall painting shows the first use of native costume. At the time Revueltas was but twenty-one years old and his assistant, Máximo Pacheco, was sixteen.

Rivera had worked behind closed doors in the Auditorium, but this work in the Patio was truly public painting and these young muralists were the ones who caught the first brunt of derision and vandalism from the students and the public; barricaded, they kept on painting.

Patio Chico (East Patio): Late in 1922 Vasconcelos had enticed David Alfaro Siqueiros home from Europe especially to paint murals. From then until mid-1924, assisted by Xavier Guerrero, Siqueiros worked on the great walls of the stairway that rises from the small East Patio of the Preparatoria. On a vault of the stairs he painted in encaustic a figure to symbolize the Spirit of the Occident Alighting on Mexico, combined with symbols of the elements (Plate 152). In a panel on the landing of the stairway Siqueiros painted Saint Christopher, the man who crossed over the water, as a symbol of the Conquest. This was his first experiment in fresco and he meant to have replaced it. As he struggled with the new medium and with the art of designing a wall, he did over and over the same stretch, to the dismay of Vasconcelos, who needed something to show for his expenditures.

Upon the high walls of the stair well Siqueiros painted in fresco his first revolutionary murals. In colossal scale he represents: Revolution That Breaks Chains, with Indian figures holding broken bits of chain (Plate 153); Burial of the Dead Workman shows fellow workers carrying a vivid blue coffin; Breaking of Fetiches is of saints and symbols spaced over a wall that included windows. Amidst ceaseless political

Courtesy Jean Charlot

150. Ramón Alva de la Canal. The Raising of the Cross (detail). East Wall, Entrance, West Patio, Escuela Nacional Preparatoria, México, D.F.

activity Siqueiros created these remarkable murals which have never been completed. In 1924 the lower sections of the paintings were destroyed in a riot by students and the artist was dismissed. These remains of huge Indian figures painted in earth colors against a deep ochre express with power the Indianism, the abiding reality, of Mexico and are a most important contribution to the mural movement.

Upon a vault of the stairway and in a panel on the landing Xavier Guerrero painted experimental frescoes of a child and of a woman wrapped in *rebozos*. A *pulquería* painter decorated, in encaustic, the fluted ceiling of the stair well with a strong design in black and red that follows the construction and reinforces it visually.

Patio Grande (West Patio): Meanwhile, in mid-1923, José Clemente Orozco had been commissioned to paint

151. Fermín Revueltas. Devotion to the Virgin of Guadalupe (two details). West Wall, Entrance, West Patio, Escuela Nacional Preparatoria, México, D.F.

153. David Alfaro Siqueiros. Revolution That Breaks Chains. Stair Well, East Patio, Escuela Nacional Preparatoria, México, D.F.

152. David Alfaro Siqueiros. Spirit of the Occident Alighting on Mexico. Stairway, East Patio, Escuela Nacional Preparatoria, México, D.F.

in the Preparatoria, and the principal decorations of this site are his work. The most mature of the muralists, he was the last of them to be given walls to paint. For a year and a half Orozco had been observing the growth of paintings on walls and he came into the mural movement with well-defined ideas as to what mural art should be. Benefiting from the experience that others already had with fresco, he soon mastered this art. In the large West Patio, where the young artists had previously painted the panels described above, Orozco's murals cover walls of all three floors on the north side of the Patio, the entrance to the monumental stairway, and the lower walls and vaults of this stairway. His first period of work in the Preparatoria was from June, 1923, to August, 1924, when the student riot occurred and his work, like Siqueiros', was damaged and when both were dismissed. It was 1926 before Orozco was permitted to finish his mural contract.

The great hands of workers, clasped between hammer and sickle or holding tools of intellectual labor (Plate 154), and painted over arches, belong to his first period of work, as do also parts of the first floor and of the stairway, and the long wall of the second floor. The panels of the series on the first floor, now in striking contrast one to another, were first painted while Orozco wrestled with fresco technique, mural composition, and ideas. As he worked, his conceptions and moods changed and he would redo whole panels. Four of these, partially destroyed in the riot, were repainted when he resumed work in the Preparatoria.

At the right end of the wall, the earliest panel, Maternity (Plate 155), a nude mother and child with attendants hovering above, was not destroyed; it is painted in golden Venetian hues with classic technique and feeling. In the next space, where originally he had painted a Man Struggling with a Gorilla, Orozco substituted, in colder, simpler technique, the Destruction of the Old Order; the central panel underwent transformations: Sunrise, Spring, Death of the Sun, to evolve finally as the Trench, or Man's Struggle against Man (Plate 156); Christ Destroys His Cross, or New Redemption, has given way to the Strike, in which the head of a colossal figure of Christ has been retained above a black-and-red banner held by strikers; two of three figures of Revolution were changed from workers with manual and intellectual tools into figures of despair, a hooded figure of Force remaining unchanged above. The last panel of this wall, The Rich Feast While the Poor Quarrel, was painted with bitter caricature during the first period of work.

154. José Clemente Orozco. Hands of Workers. Arch, West Patio, Escuela Nacional Preparatoria, México, D.F.

155. José Clemente Orozco. Maternity (detail). North Wall, West Patio, Escuela Nacional Preparatoria, México, D.F.

156. José Clemente Orozco. The Trench. First Floor, West Patio, Escuela Nacional Preparatoria, México, D.F.

157. José Clemente Orozco. Franciscan Succoring Indian. Stairway, West Patio, Escuela Nacional Preparatoria, México, D.F.

158. José Clemente Orozco. Ancient Races. Stairway, West Patio, Escuela Nacional Preparatoria, México, D.F.

In the same satirical spirit Orozco decorated the second floor: (from left to right) Justice and the Law in a drunken dance; the Final Judgment and "Father God," a cross-eyed God of the rich and the poor abandoned to devils; Liberty Swinging; Social and Political Junkheap, with buzzards sitting on discarded honors; the Church as Receiver; Reactionary Forces shown as disdainful women. These caricatures were painted swiftly when Vasconcelos, disturbed by the "uglyism" that was occurring on the walls, gave Orozco sixty days in which to complete his contract; they show the artist's haste in execution and record his resentment at the indignity of disapproval. It was just a year after he had started his mural career that the student assault with sticks and stones occurred, but the first paintings on the two floors and the Franciscan side of the stairway had been completely painted at that time.

When Orozco resumed painting his frescoes in the Preparatoria, early in 1926, he related his paintings to Mexico of the Conquest and of the Revolution. His bitterness had passed and pity had taken its place. Upon

159. José Clemente Orozco. Thirsting Men (detail). Entrance to Stairway, West Patio, Escuela Nacional Preparatoria, México, D.F.

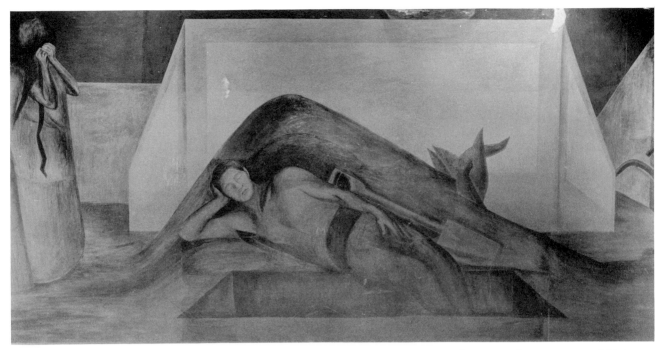

160. José Clemente Orozco. Gravedigger Asleep. Third Floor, West Patio, Escuela Nacional Preparatoria, México, D.F.

161. José Clemente Orozco. Mother's Farewell. Third Floor, West Patio, Escuela Nacional Preparatoria, México, D.F.

walls of the stairway, as companion to Franciscan Succoring Indian (Plate 157), he painted Ancient Races (Plate 158); upon three vaults he painted Cortés and Malinche in the center; Youth, and the Conqueror Builder and Indian Worker are to the sides. Beside the entrance to the stairway he represents Engineers, and Thirsting Men (Plate 159).

In the same tender spirit Orozco painted the third-floor wall as a continuous mural of the Revolution, with incidents shown against a pueblo background: Women of the Workers; the Gravedigger Asleep (Plate 160); the Mother's Benediction; Return to Labor; the Mother's Farewell (Plate 161); Peace; and Return to the Battlefield (Plate 162). The theme of these paintings is sorrow among the people during war.

This series of frescoes in the Preparatoria, decorating the north wall of Patio Grande and the lower walls of the monumental stairway, comprises most of the contribution made by José Clemente Orozco to the rebirth of mural art in Mexico. It was here that he first integrated wall paintings with structure and strove to communicate meaningfully through public painting; in doing so he achieved the stature of a great muralist.

Secretaría de Educación Pública, República Argentina y González Obregón (Ministry of Public Education). The Ministry of Public Education was remodeled from a ruin, originally the convent of La Señora de la Encarnación, that had been partially rebuilt under Díaz

162. José Clemente Orozco. Return to the Battlefield. Third Floor, West Patio, Escuela Nacional Preparatoria, México, D.F.

in neoclassic style, and was now hastily completed by the Minister of Education. This Ministry, popularly called simply la Secretaría, was the third building to be commissioned by Vasconcelos for mural decoration. It is the site most completely decorated, all walls of two large adjacent patios, surrounded by three stories of arcaded corridors, being covered with frescoes painted almost exclusively by Diego Rivera.

Different artists were commissioned to paint in the new offices of the Minister of Education and in the Library:

Offices: The Reception Room of the Minister, on the third floor of the Secretaría, was decorated in 1922 by Roberto Montenegro in encaustic with two scenes that represent historical allegories of Spain in America. At the same time in the adjoining Exhibition Hall, also in encaustic, Carlos Gonzales painted two panels, the Dance of the Old Men, a carnival dance, and Lacquer of Michoacan.

Library: The Library of the Ministry, situated on the first floor at the street corner, was decorated during 1922 and 1923. In the Children's Room, Carlos Mérida painted, in mat oil, Little Red Riding Hood, and in the Periodical Room he made a decoration of Native Women in a Landscape, which suggests his native Guatemala. These first murals by Mérida are not well preserved. In 1920 Carlos Mérida had held in Mexico City an exhibit in which he presented Mayan motifs in modern terms and included two projects for murals. Rivera credited him with having been the first of the painters "to incorporate American picturesqueness into true painting" (Charlot: 1963, p. 72).

In the Main Reading Room of the Library a panel was painted in tempera by Emilio Amero in 1923. As the young painters strove to create a legitimate Mexican art, Rivera had said of this panel that it was the most Mexican of the paintings made up to that time. But the learned Vasconcelos distrusted this native direction, and the unfinished panel was destroyed. Amero has painted no more murals in Mexico.

163. Diego Rivera. Refining Sugar. First Floor, First Patio, Secretaría de Educación Pública, México, D.F.

The Courtyard: The immense courtyard enclosed by the Ministry building is divided unequally by a bridge of passageways, the First or East Patio being smaller than the Second or West Patio. The comprehensive mural decoration by Diego Rivera covers all wall spaces on the three floors of the First Patio, and the elevator vestibule and the monumental stairway that open from it; also, most of the walls of the Second Patio. As all offices of the Secretaría are entered from the open corridors that surround the Patios, these walls are broken by doorways into many relatively small panels. Pilasters of the corridors half hide many of these panels, limiting the range of vision and confounding the problems, but it was in solving these difficulties that Diego Rivera realized his immense capacities as a muralist. He composed the panels into the architecture, incorporating painted form with the wall to sustain and illumine it. With exception of a few groupings, the panels are painted as self-contained units that relate throughout to form a whole.

First Patio: Diego Rivera started painting in the smaller East Patio in March, 1923, designing this as the Patio of Work. On the ground floor he has pictured types of people and of labor from different sections of the Republic. Here Rivera painted his first frescoes, Jean Charlot assisting, as two women of Tehuantepec carrying trays of fruits and flowers on their heads. These panels face the land of the South and flank the entrance to the former elevator shaft, in the vestibule of which he painted typical scenes of tropical life in that region: Women Bathing, Women Washing, the Woman's Costume, where he emphasizes the plastic quality of Mexico and identifies his art with native culture. In the Patio, in the succeeding panels facing south, Rivera, assisted by Xavier Guerrero, has painted industries typical of the south: Weaving, Dyeing, Marketing Tropical Fruit, Cultivating Sugar Cane, and Refining Sugar (Plate 163).

On the side that faces east he represents the industries of the central region: Silver Mining, with panels showing the Descent, and the Return of the Miners (Plate 164); the Embrace of city and country workers; Making Pottery; the cultivation of corn and wheat he shows as Indians Awaiting the Harvest and as a Landlord Weighing the Grain, with a background of mountains passing over arched doorways to unite all panels. In these murals Rivera, assisted by Xavier Guerrero, had used a variation of fresco technique that included nopal juice, which he then abandoned for the usual process.

Rivera painted the panels that face the North to rep-

164. Diego Rivera. Leaving the Mine. First Floor, First Patio, Secretaría de Educación Pública, México, D.F.

resent industries of this region: Iron Mining, Smelting, and Ranching; also, on this side, in relation to great landholdings and heavy industry, Revolution is represented by the Release of a Peon; the New School is being held out-of-doors; a Yaqui Deer Dance makes transition to the Second Patio.

The mezzanine of this First Patio of Work is painted in grisaille, in imitation of low relief, to symbolize the sciences that correspond to the industries on the ground floor.

On the third floor the arts, placed also in relation to

165. Diego Rivera. Burial of a Worker with Furies. Stairway of Climates, Secretaría de Educación Pública, México, D.F.

the industries on the first floor, are painted in grisaille alternated with full-color frescoes that depict Martyrs of Mexican Independence.

The monumental stairway rises from the First Patio opposite the Tehuanas; Rivera has painted this as the Stairway of Climates. A continuous series of landscape compositions climb the stair well to represent the varied climatic conditions from sea level, through life in the tropics, to the industrialized highlands. In this large decoration symbolic figures combine with the ascending Mexican landscapes and types of people to represent: Subterranean Water; the Islands; the Tropics; *Xochipilli*, the Aztec Flower God; a Hacienda; Burial of a Worker with Furies flying overhead (Plate 165); the Industrialized Land; the Trinity of Architect, Sculptor, and Painter, in which Rivera pictured himself as the Architect (Plate 166).

Second Patio: The large Second or West Patio of the Secretaría was first planned as a collective project, as indicated in the Painters' Syndicate program, to depict both Labor and Festivals. In 1923, while Rivera was

166. Diego Rivera. Trinity of Architect, Sculptor, and Painter (detail). Stairway of Climates, Secretaría de Educación Pública, México, D.F.

188

painting the First Patio, the ground floor of the Second Patio was partially decorated with fresco paintings of contemporary Mexico by Amado de la Cueva, Jean Charlot, and Xavier Guerrero. In August, 1923, the work of these younger painters, who also had assisted Rivera, was stopped by him. Two panels painted by Amado de la Cueva—Dance of the Santiagos, and Fireworks—and two by Jean Charlot—Cargadores or Burden Bearers (Plate 167) and Lavanderas or Washer Women—and two panels over doorways painted by Xavier Guerrero are still in place on the north wall. One panel by Charlot, Dance of the Ribbons, was destroyed in 1925 to make way for a painting by Rivera.

The mezzanine of the Second Patio is decorated with a series of shields of the various states of Mexico painted in fresco by Emilio Amero, Jean Charlot, Amado de la Cueva, and Xavier Guerrero. This decoration, especially commissioned by Vasconcelos late in 1923, when criticism of the murals was rife, must have been judged to be a safe subject to present to an indignant public. After Vasconcelos had resigned as Minister, the young muralists, being given no more walls to paint, disbanded and scattered, and their syndicate also was no more.

Lavanderas was the last real mural to be painted in Mexico by Jean Charlot, who, however, through the years has carried the Mural Renaissance into many parts of the United States. Orozco has written with appreciation of the contribution of this young French artist who through his knowledge and sensibility had helped to relate Mexican art to the modern School of Paris: "Charlot, with his equanimity and his culture, often tempered our too hasty youthfulness, and with his clear vision he frequently illumined our problems" (1945, p. 83). Orozco noted the profound influence that Pre-Cortesion art had upon Charlot, "whose work is still saturated with it."

When Calles became President he appointed Dr. Puig Casauranc as the new Minister of Education, and he retained Diego Rivera to complete the decoration of the large inner Patio. Rivera worked here during 1925 and until the latter part of 1927.

Rivera designed this Second Patio as the Patio of Festivals. On the large central section of the wall that faces north, including three panels and the spaces over doors, Rivera has represented Taking Possession of the Land by the Rural Population. To either side of this central painting he shows festivals as celebrated in the country. In two panels he depicts the Harvest Festival; in two he portrays Todos Santos (All Souls' Day) or Feast of the Dead, as celebrated with flowers on graves,

167. Jean Charlot. Burden Bearers. North Wall, First Floor, Second Patio, Secretaría de Educación Pública, México, D. F.

and with candles in a home (Plate 168). In contrast, Rivera has painted the large end panel with Masques of Death, as Todos Santos is celebrated in the city.

In the center of the wall that faces east is shown the Festival of Work or First of May, which includes numerous workers with banners facing a central doorway; above it a red banner is painted with the words, "The true civilization will be the harmony of men with the earth and of men with one another." In large panels to the sides are piñatas of Exploding Judases fashioned as generals, priests, and politicians, which fill one panel, and on the other side, the Festival of Santa Anita, showing barges laden with flowers and fruits to celebrate the generosity of nature.

On the wall that faces south Rivera has represented in the three central panels and over doors the Trianguis, or People's Market, filled with the people, the merchandise, and the many activities that characterize the traditional markets of Mexico. On either side of this large fresco are the two narrow panels painted by Jean Charlot, the two by Amado de la Cueva, and the over-door panels by Guerrero (described above). Beyond these, on the large end panels Rivera has painted on one, a symbolic dance in a church, in which young boys represent the months going around a man dressed in red as the sun, and little girls in white wreaths as stars (Plate 169), and on the other panel he shows the Sandunga, a ritual marriage dance of Oaxaca.

On the third floor of the Patio of Festivals Rivera has festooned the words of two Ballads of Revolution above panels painted to illustrate them. Upon the walls that face east and south, in 1926–1927, he painted—in a series of panels—a song of the Agrarian Revolution of Mexico: Zapata the Leader; the Ballad Singer (Plate 170); Lunch in the Rain (Plate 171) as one of several series of panels to show the life of the agrarian worker. In contrast, he has symbolized in other panels the life of international wealth to be liquidated (Plates 172, 173), after a successful revolution. As worker, soldier, and farmer study together they plan for the coming day (Plate 174).

In this Second Patio, Diego Rivera was ably assisted by Ramón Alva Guadarrama and also by Pablo O'Higgins, a Californian who ever since has been identified with Mexican mural art.

The wall that faces north was left unpainted in 1927, when Rivera departed for Russia, and the Ballad painted there was to begin another period of work. Rivera's entire work in the Secretaría has been estimated as 168 panels, covering over 17,000 square feet.

168. Diego Rivera. All Souls' Day. First Floor, Second Patio, Secretaría de Educación Pública, México, D.F.

169. Diego Rivera. Symbolic Dance. End Panel, First Floor, Second Patio, Secretaría de Educación Pública, México, D.F.

170. Diego Rivera. *Corrido:* The Ballad Singer. Third Floor, Second Patio, Secretaría de Educación Pública, México, D.F.

171. Diego Rivera. *Corrido:* Lunch in the Rain. Third Floor, Second Patio, Secretaría de Educación Pública, México, D.F.

172. Diego Rivera. *Corrido:* Wealthy Financiers. Third Floor, Second Patio, Secretaría de Educación Pública, México, D.F.

173. Diego Rivera. *Corrido:* Fighters of the Revolution and Civilian Debauchers. Third Floor, Second Patio, Secretaría de Educación Pública, México, D.F.

174. Diego Rivera. *Corrido:* Revolutionary Change (detail). Third Floor, Second Patio, Secretaría de Educación Pública, México, D.F.

Biblioteca Iberoamericana, González Obregón (Storage). Adjoining the Secretaría de Educación Pública is the former Templo de la Encarnación. Projected as the Spanish-American Library—but not so realized—it was commissioned by Vasconcelos for mural decoration to Roberto Montenegro, who in 1922 painted figures in tempera to symbolize transplantations of Spain to America. The panel of figures is placed below a large decorative map of Spanish-America.

Decorating walls of the handsome Colonial church are several shields painted in fresco in 1924. One, by Jean Charlot, is the coat of arms of Mexico's ancient University; others are by Ramón Alva Guadarrama.

Estadio Nacional (Murals Destroyed). In 1924 Diego

Rivera decorated the façade of the National Stadium with colossal figures, incised into the cement and painted in encaustic, to symbolize Valor and Foresight standing guard beside the entrance. This was the first exterior mural painted (but one) and the first use of cement for design.

Escuela de Ferrocarrileros (Murals Destroyed). The School of Railroad Engineers was partially decorated by Fermín Revueltas in 1923 with abstract cubistic designs painted in encaustic, but his contract was canceled before he could complete this work. Many years were to pass before purely abstract design again appeared in Mexican murals.

Casa de los Azulejos, Avenida Madero (Sanborn's

175. Xavier Guerrero. Ceiling Detail with Nahuatl Inscription. House of the Director, Escuela Nacional de Agricultura, Chapingo, México.

Restaurant). During the interval that separated José Clemente Orozco from his half-destroyed walls in the National Preparatory School he painted the first mural in Mexico City that was not officially commissioned. The fresco painted on the stairway of the Colonial House of Tiles in Mexico City carries this legend: *"Omniscience,* painted by José Clemente Orozco by order of his great admirer, Francisco Sergie Iturbide, in the year 1925." A central radiant figure, Grace, kneels between two standing figures, Force and Intelligence, her upturned face receiving the light from above.

Escuela de Orientación, near Stadium (High School). In Mexico City during 1926 and 1927, while Orozco was completing his murals in the Preparatoria and Rivera was painting in the Secretaría, Roberto Montenegro decorated the Lincoln Library of the modern Orientation High School, formerly called Centro Benito Juárez. Montenegro made symbolical representations of Mexican History; also, he painted a decoration illustrating Aladdin and the Magic Lantern.

SPREAD OF THE MURAL MOVEMENT

Chapingo, México (Site 24)

Escuela Nacional de Agricultura (Agricultural School). In the Valley of Mexico near the ancient city of Texcoco the former Hacienda de Chapingo, converted

into the National Agricultural School, was the first site outside of Mexico City to be commissioned for mural decoration by the central government. It is usually called simply Chapingo.

Xavier Guerrero in 1923 painted frescoed decorations in the residence of the director of the Agricultural School (Plate 175). At this time he painted also floral panels in the corridors of the School. When Diego Rivera was commissioned to paint in Chapingo, Guerrero was his assistant. From 1924 to 1927 Rivera worked in the entrance hall and on the stairway of the School and, most particularly, on the monumental walls of the former Chapel of the Hacienda, which he decorated elaborately with frescoes that cover all wall spaces. During this most fruitful period he was painting also in the Secretaría de Educación in Mexico City, alternating work in the two sites as he commuted between them.

For this book Diego Rivera has given his own description of the frescoes:

In the vestibule of the Agricultural School are represented the four seasons of the year which rule cultivation of the earth and harvesting. In the hall of the first floor are painted: Country People Taking Possession of the Community Land [Dividing the Land, Plate 176]; and Science and Revolution Uniting City and Country Workers, placed on a background of a cooperative village adjoining it.

"Here we teach exploitation of the earth, not man," is inscribed in the vestibule of the School.

Chapel: Rivera's description of the chapel follows:

In the former chapel, converted into a hall for conferences and student activities, the different stages of the social transformation through Revolution are represented in relation to the architectural style of the building and the subdivision of walls that this style imposes, and in comparison with the successive stages of the transformation of the earth through the geological cataclysms that have prepared the present fertile soil for cultivation by man.

This last stage—germination, flowering, and fruit-bearing—is paired with the Revolutionary stages: preparation through agitation and propaganda as germination, armed struggle as flowering, and organization of production as the fruit of the struggle.

Upon the wall of the vestibule the Earth is represented in its primitive state (Plate 177).

Upon the intermediate wall the Earth is represented as monopolized by Capitalism and its consequences, Clericalism and Militarism.

Upon the arched wall that forms the background of the hall

176. Diego Rivera. Dividing the Land. School Stairway, Escuela Nacional de Agricultura, Chapingo, México.

177. Diego Rivera. The Virgin Earth. Panel, Chapel, Escuela Nacional de Agricultura, Chapingo, México.

178. Diego Rivera. The Fertilized Earth Served by All Elements. Arched Wall, Chapel, Escuela Nacional de Agricultura, Chapingo, México.

is painted the Fertilized Earth with the other elements of nature, Air, Water, and Fire, at the service of the human family through industrialization (Plate 178).

In the series of frescoes, anthropomorphic representations of natural forces are used, on one hand, in accord with the Spanish Baroque style of the building, and, on the other, with the native tradition of Mexico, which since time immemorial in prehistoric civilizations has used the anthropomorphic simile for the representation of natural forces.

The sides of the chapel contain circular windows with the depth painted into the design. On the side that represents the geological preparation of the Earth, Rivera has used nude female figures to symbolize nature's progressive stages from birth to maturity (Plate 179). On the opposite side, above panels that commemorate the Revolution through Dead Heroes of the people (Plate 180) great hands reinforce the meaning of the struggle.

179. Diego Rivera. Life and Earth. Side Wall, Chapel, Escuela Nacional de Agricultura, Chapingo, México.

180. Diego Rivera. Dead Heroes. Side Wall, Chapel, Escuela Nacional de Agricultura, Chapingo, México.

181. Diego Rivera. The Harvest. Vault, Chapel, Escuela Nacional de Agricultura, Chapingo, México.

197

182. José Clemente Orozco. Armed Workers in a Field. Stairway, Escuela Industrial, Orizaba, Veracruz.

Within divisions of the dome Rivera has painted young Indian figures poised with sheaves of ripening grain against a background of blue that binds visually the divisions of the vault. These symbolize the Harvest produced by man's labor in harmony with nature's munificence (Plate 181).

Orizaba, Veracruz (Site 25)

Escuela Industrial (Industrial School). José Clemente Orozco, after painting his great panel in Sanborn's and before resuming his work in the Preparatoria, was commissioned by Dr. Puig Casauranc to paint a wall in the Industrial School in Orizaba. Orozco has recorded that "in two weeks time with only a plasterer's help" he painted in fresco a wall of one hundred square meters above the monumental stairway of this Colonial building. The mural is divided by a large central window on the stairway landing. Across the upper wall Orozco has painted Social Revolution represented as Armed Workers in a Field (Plate 182). In panels to either side

183. José Clemente Orozco. Sorrowing Women (two side panels). Stairway, Escuela Industrial, Orizaba, Veracruz.

of the window he has painted their anxious and Sorrowing Women (Plate 183).

Ten years earlier Orozco had participated in the Revolution under Carranza in this same city of Orizaba.

Guadalajara, Jalisco (Site 26)

Biblioteca del Estado (Mural Destroyed). Carlos Orozco Romero, on his return from studying art in Europe, stopped over in Mexico City long enough to experience the lure of the mural movement. Arriving in his native city of Guadalajara in 1923 he painted the first mural to be made outside of Mexico City during the revival of public painting. Unfortunately, Orozco Romero's encaustic decoration of Potters, painted in the patio of the State Library, has been plastered over, and this interesting artist has painted no more murals.

Palacio de Gobierno (Murals Destroyed). Amado de la Cueva, after having painted two murals in Mexico City, was disappointed at being given no more walls to paint. He returned to his native city of Guadalajara and was soon painting frescoes for the state of Jalisco. During 1924 and 1925 he painted in the State Capitol three large panels. One presented a figure representing Saint Christopher as a symbol of the Christian Conquest, "like the sculptured figure on Santa Mónica Street." In contrast he painted in the other two panels Cortés and Nuño de Guzmán, the brutal conqueror of Western Mexico. All of these panels were whitewashed in 1931.

Ex-Universidad (Workers' Assembly Hall). The former church of the old Jesuit College, later the University of Guadalajara, was decorated from 1925 to 1927 by Amado de la Cueva, with the assistance of

184. Amado de la Cueva. Agriculture. Entrance to Hall, Former University of Guadalajara, Guadalajara, Jalisco.

David Alfaro Siqueiros. The high walls of the building are painted in different tones of earth red; a frieze formed of workers, hammers, sickles, guns, plows, and sprouting seeds is placed along the spring of the vault. Clusters of red five-pointed stars decorate the barrel vault and the cupola, and large hands of workers are clasped in the pendentives. The huge form of a workman surrounded by symbols of Agriculture is painted upon the high, arched, red wall above the entrance to the hall (Plate 184). Figures are painted in different tones of brown outlined in black.

This decoration, the last work of Amado de la Cueva, who was killed in a motorcycle accident on the day the scaffolding was removed, is all that remains from this earliest period of work in Guadalajara.

THE UNEMPLOYED MURALISTS DISPERSE

Since no more mural commissions were in prospect under Calles' Presidency and since the contracts previously given had for the most part been fulfilled, in 1927 the muralists scattered. Many years were to pass before Siqueiros painted another wall in Mexico. Orozco, having completed his commission in the Prepara-

toria, went back to the United States, where he remained for seven years. Jean Charlot, after doing research in Mayan art in Yucatán, was to become a vitalizing influence in the art of the United States. The muralists who remained in Mexico passed the contagion of wall painting to pupils while they waited to re-enter the mural movement.

Diego Rivera had completed his monumental work in Chapingo; in the Secretaría only one wall of panels remained to be done when he was invited to Russia to attend the celebration of the Tenth Anniversary of the October Revolution; he headed the Mexican Delegation. In Russia he was received with much honor as a great mural painter of revolution. One mural, projected for Russia, was postponed, however, indefinitely. When Rivera rather suddenly returned to Mexico he stopped over in Paris, where he was acclaimed a great muralist.

In Mexico City a search for a fresco in progress disclosed a most refreshing project under way by the youngest muralist of them all, Máximo Pacheco, who, until Rivera resumed painting, was for a while the only muralist at work for the Mexican government.

México, D.F. (Site 1)

Escuela Sarmiento, Parque Balbuena (Primary School). An open-air school built as a number of separate units in Balbuena Park, which adjoins a workers' district of Mexico City, is decorated with a series of fresco panels painted by Máximo Pacheco from 1927 to 1929. Interesting exterior murals of Campesinos Plowing made by Pacheco in 1922 on the Entrance have been destroyed. In panels above blackboards at either end of the open rooms, Pacheco has painted the life of children at work and at play and their social problems and possibilities: how to bathe and dress to be healthy; how poor children live and how the rich live; the Greedy Child; happy children playing in water and upon the land; and beautiful images of the country. In twelve panels this very young artist (at this time hardly more than a child himself) has represented the dreams, fears, and hopes of childhood with poignantly contemporary quality, in which mural art has come very close to the people of Mexico. Lunch Time, and Children and Water represent very well the charm of Pacheco's work (Plate 185).

Máximo Pacheco previously had assisted both Revueltas and Rivera.

These first public painted walls began to speak to the people of Mexico in different ways but with unifying force, exerting the life-giving power of art.

185. Máximo Pacheco. (*above*) Lunch Time; (*below*) Children and Water. (half panel)
Panels above Blackboards, Escuela Sarmiento, México, D.F.

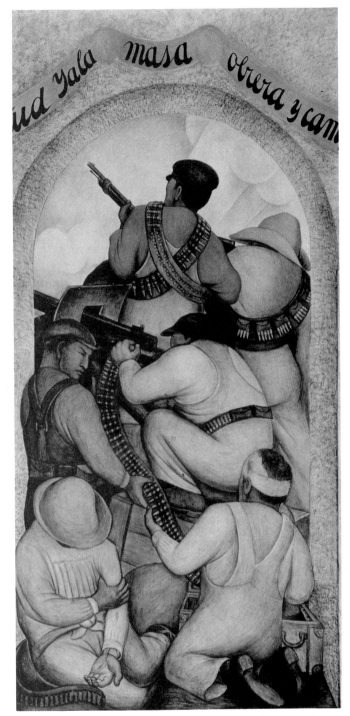

186. Diego Rivera. *Corrido:* Fighters for the Revolution. Third Floor, Patio of Festivals, Secretaría de Educación Pública, México, D.F.

187. Diego Rivera. *Corrido:* Workers United. Third Floor, Patio of Festivals, Secretaría de Educación Pública, México, D.F.

Rivera's Triumphant Return and Departure: 1928–1930

The re-election of Obregón in 1928 had been followed by his assassination and, with Portes Gil as Provisional President, Calles continued to rule. But public painting is everybody's concern, and from the beginning of the mural movement Mexico's painted walls had attracted much attention—amazed admiration as well as violent opposition. When Diego Rivera, after having been acclaimed abroad as a great muralist, returned to Mexico in 1928 he was received with honor. He finished his last wall in the Secretaría and soon was given other impressive mural commissions which launched him into two amazingly productive years. During this period Rivera was elected by the students as director of the Academy of Fine Arts. However, his ambitious plan to educate artist-workers failed to receive cooperation from the architects on his staff and his tenure proved short-lived. During this period, also, he gave lectures on structural composition which were to inspire future muralists and architects.

México, D.F. (Site 1)

Secretaría de Educación Pública. In 1928 Rivera completed the last panels of his contract in the Ministry of Public Education and with this work began the second phase of his mural career.

The Mexican Agrarian Revolution had been the chief theme of his paintings in both the Secretaría and Chapingo. The International Proletarian Revolution is the subject of the song festooned above panels of the wall that faces north on the third floor of the Secretaría's Second Patio. This second Ballad was written by a weaver from Puebla who had gone as a delegate to

188. Diego Rivera. Life. Ceiling, Secretaría de Salubridad, México, D.F.

203

189. Diego Rivera. Hand with Wheat. Secretaría de Salubridad, México, D.F.

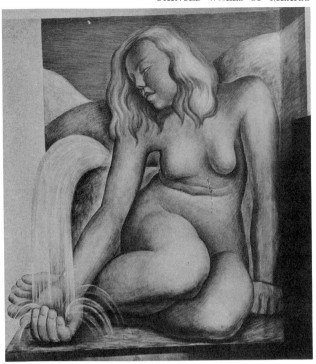

190. Diego Rivera. Purity. Secretaría de Salubridad, México, D.F.

Russia and who upon his return to Mexico wrote this *corrido* to tell his proletarian and agrarian comrades how they could realize the Proletarian Revolution. The illustrative panels are filled with factory workers rather than *campesinos,* or workers of the soil, and activities represented here, in contrast to the first Ballad painted in 1927, are militant. Among the subjects represented are Insurrection, with workers being armed; Fighters for the Revolution (Plate 186); Workers' Committee Takes over Factory; Workers United (Plate 187).

Rivera considered this Ballad of Revolution to crown his work in the Ministry of Public Education, fulfilling its educational Mission to present to the public the unrealized program of the Proletarian Revolution.

Secretaría de Salubridad, Paseo de la Reforma (Ministry of Health). The modern building which houses the Ministry of Health, across from the entrance to Chapultepec Park, was decorated in 1929 by Diego Rivera, who thus described his subject: For the Director's Office, the subject proposed by the architect of the building, Carlos Obregón Santacilia, was appropriate to the painting of six monumental hands, elements all

in harmony with the style and use of the building. The figures on the ceiling represent Life (Plate 188) and Health; those on the walls, alternating with huge hands (Plate 189) represent Fortitude, Continence, Purity (Plate 190), and Science.

Upon the small walls in the vestibule of the Laboratory of Microbiology and Bacteriology is represented the human struggle against pathogenic germs. Realistic representations of Microorganisms, very much enlarged, are attacked by great hands of workmen (Plate 191).

Diego Rivera designed four stained-glass windows for the stairway of Salubridad: The Four Elements are presented through the work of man in relation to each element, and the forces and products useful to human life proceeding from each.

Palacio Nacional (National Palace). The decoration of the Monumental Stairway of the National Palace was commissioned to Diego Rivera in 1929. At that time he projected a series of murals upon which he worked intermittently until 1955—only two years before his death in 1957. During 1929 and 1930, and briefly in the summer of 1931, Rivera painted the greater part of the immense frescoes of the monumental stairway, an epic of the Mexican people. He described the murals (1934) in relation to the architecture of the building:

The monumental stairway has three large walls, naturally of trapezoidal form, ascending from the center to the sides. The composition follows both the form of the wall's surface and the architectural function of the place and of the whole building. Since the National Palace, by its historic tradition, is a center of the life of Mexico, the natural theme to be treated on the stairway, which in turn is the center of the building, is the History of Mexico expressed in plastic condensation and composed dialectically. As the three walls cannot be seen simultaneously without foreshortening of the sides, or through a less direct view of these, upon the central wall is painted the period of history which is better and more objectively known and analyzed, the period from the beginning of the Conquest of Mexico by the Spaniards until the period contemporary with the beginning of the painting in 1929.

Upon the side walls are represented less familiar periods: to the right of the spectator, the distant past of Mexico, with allusion to her first mythological history; upon the stretch of wall to the left, the present moment in Mexican history, dominated by the colossal figure of Marx.

On the wall for Early Mexico, above representations of Indian labor, ceremonies, and sacred wars, presides the floating figure of Quetzalcoatl, "Feathered Serpent," the beneficent Culture God of the Toltecs.

The great central wall, covered by a synthesis of Mexico's history since the Conquest, is unbroken except by five intrinsic arches that divide the upper wall and by ascending stairs on either side below. The sequence of the composition begins at the lower right and swings from one side of the wall to the other, like a pendulum, as it moves upward in long sweeps of time. In the center of the wall an eagle holding a serpent symbolizes Mexico's resistance and self-assertion (Plate 192), which is illustrated by heroes from Cuauhtemoctzín, last Aztec Emperor, shown in Eagle Warrior costume, battling below, to Obregón, victorious general of Mexico's twentieth-century Revolution, placed within the central arch above. The sections under the two adjoining arches indicate conflict between progressive and reactionary elements; these include the Inquisition and Juárez, shown holding his Reform Laws (Plate 193). The outer sections of this wall depict aggressions from without: at the bottom is recorded Colonial conquest and enslavement; the upper wall represents the more recent foreign invasions by France (Plate 194) and by the United States.

Upon this immense wall of the Monumental Stairway

191. Diego Rivera. Microorganisms. Secretaría de Salubridad, México, D.F.

the most significant events of Mexico's history are recorded. In the incidents and in portraits of the makers of this history from the time of the Conquest, through the Colonial Period of conflicting aspirations, through Revolt, Independence, Dictatorships, Invasions, and Reform, culminating in the upper center of the wall in the heroes of the victorious Revolution of the twentieth century, Rivera celebrates Mexico's Nationalist Revolution of freedom from foreign domination. His mural painting is part of this freedom.

The wall to the left, opposite Mexico's Distant Past, Rivera painted some years later as The Present. This fresco and the panels of the upper corridors of the great court of the National Palace, to which the stairway leads, are described with Rivera's later work.

San Pedro y San Pablo (School). From 1929 to 1931

192. Diego Rivera. History of Mexico: Affirmation. Monumental Stairway, Palacio Nacional, México, D.F.

193. Diego Rivera. History of Mexico: Progressive-Reactionary Conflicts. Monumental Stairway, Palacio Nacional, México, D.F.

194. Diego Rivera. History of Mexico: Colonial Enslavement-Foreign Invasion. Monumental Stairway, Palacio Nacional, México, D.F.

Y EN EL LIBRO TU LIBERTAD ~

195. Roberto Montenegro. Education. Stairway, San Pedro y San Pablo, México, D.F.

Roberto Montenegro completed the frescoed decoration which he had begun in 1923 on the walls and vaults of the stair well of the old Colonial building of San Pedro y San Pablo. During this later period he filled remaining high walls with architectural compositions representing Reconstruction. Lower panels, above the dado, he painted in grisaille with Mexican popular arts and with figures in relation to the earth and to the Revolution. In one of his last panels, a boy reading in a cornfield, "y en el libro tu libertad," Montenegro places his hope in Education (Plate 195). Montenegro's paintings in San Pedro y San Pablo span ten years of intermittent work and make transition from symbolical decorative painting to structural compositions related to Mexico.

Cuernavaca, Morelos (Site 8)

Palacio de Cortés (State Capitol). The series of frescoes painted by Diego Rivera in 1929 and 1930 in the Palace of Cortés in Cuernavaca was commissioned as a gift to the state of Morelos by the late Honorable Dwight W. Morrow, who at the time was ambassador to Mexico from the United States. "Since the walls proposed for the frescoes form the loggia of the palace which Cortés, captain general of the Conquerors, had forced the enslaved natives to construct, it seemed logical and appropriate to use as subjects for the murals incidents from the Conquest of Mexico, particularized in relation to Hernando Cortés and Cuernavaca. The painting includes aspects of the Revolution, as historic

196. Diego Rivera. Defense of Cuernavaca. Palacio de Cortés, Cuernavaca, Morelos.

corollary of the Conquest, the Valley of Morelos having been a principal theatre of revolt" (Rivera).

The decoration covers the two end walls and the long connecting wall of an upper open gallery which looks out over the valley to the volcanoes in the east. The sequence moves from right to left; it begins at the far end and passes through successive high panels separated by arched windows. The Defense of Cuernavaca, depicting the battle preceding the capture of the city, covers the end wall, broken by a low arched doorway (Plate 196), and is continued onto the contiguous side panel to fill the corner. Above the doorway is painted a pyramidal temple where a human sacrifice is being offered; in the accompanying battle, Rivera contrasts the culture of masked Indians with weapons of stone and that of armored Spaniards with firearms (Plate 197); a mounted white horse, representing technical domination, seems to have leapt the corner in the relentless advance of the war. In the succeeding panel, Passing over the Ravine, he has painted a tree felled to form a bridge (Plate 198) across the protective gorge, over which a detachment of Spaniards and their Tlaxcalan allies are passing to attack the city from the rear. The third panel, the Taking of Cuernavaca, shows Cortés and his men consolidating their victory by branding slaves. In a narrow panel past the central arch that spans the corridor, a Cross which Cortés quarters with his sword is being carried in procession; an Indian stands immediately beneath it. Building the Palace (Plate 199), and Harvesting Sugar Cane (Plate 200) follow; Religion fills the corner and is represented by a tree under which are contrasted the good and the evil which occur beneath its branches. Over the arched door of this end wall, as counterpart to the Human Sacrifice of the Aztecs, Rivera has painted the Inquisition (Plate 201). Revolt fills this last panel, symbolized by the agrarian leader Zapata holding the reins of the white horse, or power.

The plastic quality of this series of frescoes was dictated by its actual architectural location, the character and period of the building, and the fact that the murals are placed in full light before the landscape, so very rich in form and color, of the southern valleys of Cuernavaca and Cuautla. Rivera's landscape, continued through the upper section of the walls of the loggia and passing over the windows, is painted to unite the murals to one another and to the land.

In small panels, painted in grisaille on the high dado

197. Diego Rivera. Defense of Cuernavaca: Tiger Knight (detail). Palacio de Cortés, Cuernavaca, Morelos.

below the frescoes, Rivera has represented incidents from the larger Conquest of Mexico, to which the Conquest of Cuernavaca is related as a branch is to a tree.

The central arch across the loggia represents the Bridge of Revolution. It is supported on the inner and outer sides by figures of Mexican revolutionary leaders: on the inner side, José María Morelos, the most heroic figure of the Revolt of 1810, looks east toward the field of his action, while Emiliano Zapata, beloved chief of the Agrarian Revolution of 1910, appears against the valley, truly related since this is the same field that saw both revolutionary struggles for power and for land. The keystone of the arch, a sheaf of corn, is flanked by half-reclining figures of an Indian man and woman. On the far side the figures represent the Revolt of 1810; on the near side, the Revolution of 1910, with the banner of Revolution, "Tierra y Libertad," land and liberty, for which the Indian has struggled.

Rivera planned, but did not execute, a series of murals for the front corridor of the Palace of Cortés, in which the white horse as symbol of power was to have been plowing for the people of Mexico.

When late in 1930 Diego Rivera was invited to paint murals in San Francisco his public painting in Mexico was again temporarily suspended.

198. Diego Rivera. The Bridge. Palacio de Cortés, Cuernavaca, Morelos.

199. Diego Rivera. Building the Palace. Palacio de Cortés, Cuernavaca, Morelos.

200. Diego Rivera. Harvesting Sugar Cane. Palacio de Cortés, Cuernavaca, Morelos.

201. Diego Rivera. The Inquisition: Freedom. Palacio de Cortés, Cuernavaca, Morelos.

The Young Muralists: 1930–1936

During the early thirties both José Clemente Orozco and Diego Rivera were painting important frescoes in the United States; Orozco made a short visit to Europe; David Alfaro Siqueiros painted open-air murals in experimental techniques in Los Angeles; Xavier Guerrero for ten years traveled through eastern Europe and western Asia. In Mexico government-sponsored mural painting for a short time was in abeyance; however, the Mural Renaissance was by no means abandoned.

Immense walls had been painted during the first ten years of the mural movement, and young artists who had had some mural experience or were eager to experiment with mural techniques longed for the prize of a wall to paint. A few painters served their apprenticeship as muralists by painting in *pulquerías* or other popular gathering places. Fortunately, the great depression of this period was partially solved in Mexico, as in the United States, by a public works program. During the Presidency of Abelardo Rodríguez, from 1932 to 1934, while Narciso Bassols was Minister of Education, a number of functional schools designed by the artist-architect Juan O'Gorman were built, old schools and civic centers were remodeled, and artists were commissioned to decorate many of these public buildings. At this time also cultural missions, sent by the government into rural communities throughout the country, spread the mural movement and brought many young painters into contact with village life. Local artists frequently assisted in the decoration of open-air theatres and other community centers, and popular mural painting was thus given a fresh impulse, so that almost anywhere in Mexico a public wall was considered a mural possibility. These visiting artists from cities were in turn influenced by the intimate personal quality, the vigor, and the originality of the local painters of the people.

Each muralist learns his art by painting walls. With materials and walls and a small wage supplied by the government, many young painters were enabled to try themselves out as muralists; thus a fresh wave of experimental public painting arose in Mexico. A few young artists from the United States identified themselves with the movement. Working singly or in groups, the painters often pooled their technical and compositional knowledge; some excellent work was produced. Because of the previous distinguished accomplishments of Mexico's muralists, the painters were aware of the limitations and possibilities of a wall, and most wall paintings in Mexico have mural quality. Some of the young artists who used this opportunity freely to dedicate themselves to mural painting during the thirties have emerged as Mexico's new generation of muralists.

During this phase of the mural movement, some writers and artists organized themselves as the Liga de Escritores y Artistas Revolucionarios (Union of Revolutionary Writers and Artists—LEAR), and from 1933 to 1937 gave direction to mural work of emerging artists.

Mexico City and Environs (Site 1)

From 1930 to 1936 many young artists were commissioned by the government to paint murals in schools and other public buildings in the Federal District. Only a few of these painted walls are recorded here; principally, these are murals of which photographs have been secured and of which descriptions were given the author. Also noted are a few sites decorated by artists who have continued to paint murals. Many of these paintings have not been preserved.

Museo Nacional de Antropología e Historia, Calle de Moneda 13 (now Museum of International Archeology). In 1930 Rufino Tamayo began his first fresco in the old National Museum of Anthropology and History. The mural, on the right-hand side at the rear of the entrance hall, consists of two panels divided by a door, above which are painted toppling columns, and in each panel is a figure. The version painted first but not completed showed a figure like a centaur (as a mounted Spaniard first appeared to the Indians) spearing dark figures that calmly faced it; also, a dark suspended figure enveloped in light. The fresco was largely repainted in 1938, when the figures to the sides of the doorway became revolutionary soldiers striking down figures in the foreground, seen from behind in hat and coat; on the left side the soldier uses the butt of a rifle, on the right a hammer.

On an arch over the hall on the inner side are painted two hands, one chained and clenched, the other open.

Escuela de Cuauhtémoc, Colonia Morelos (Primary School). After completing the series of panels in Escuela Sarmiento, Máximo Pacheco continued through the

202. Fernando Leal. Exaltation of Bolívar. Foyer, Anfiteatro Bolívar, Escuela Nacional Preparatoria, México, D.F.

years to decorate public walls, working either alone or with a group, his skill as a fresco painter being much in demand. The School of Cuauhtémoc, named for the last Aztec Emperor, is in a workers' district of Mexico City, the same area where the brave leader had made his last stand against the Conquerors. Pacheco decorated this school in fresco in 1930.

Delegación de Atzcapotzalco (Primary School). The district offices of Atzcapotzalco were decorated in 1931 by Juan O'Gorman and Máximo Pacheco, working together in fresco. Wide friezes, formed of rocky landscapes laced with industrial units and enlivened with workers, encircle the upper walls of two small adjoining rooms now used as a primary school.

Anfiteatro Bolívar, Justo Sierrra 16 (School Theatre). The foyer of Bolívar Theatre of the National Preparatory School was decorated in encaustic by Fernando Leal, from 1931 to 1935, with a series of symbolic representations of incidents from the Life of Simón Bolívar, the great South American Liberator for whom this hall is named. The painting, Exaltation of Bolívar (Plate 202), which shows Bolívar leading in battle, is dominated above by floating, symbolic figures.

Edificio El Nacional (Building Destroyed). Fermín Revueltas in 1932 painted a series of frescoes in the press building of *El Nacional*, organ of the Revolutionary Government. In six small panels, placed high on walls of an inner hall, symbols of Revolution and of

203. Rufino Tamayo. Music. Stair Well, Former Conservatoria Nacional de Música, México, D.F.

Capitalist Control were alternated with hugh hands and with blazing suns; floating figures, representing Freedom and Slavery, filled the arched end panels.

Conservatorio Nacional de Música, Moneda 12 (Government Offices). Rufino Tamayo in 1933 painted a symbolic composition in fresco upon the stair well of an old Colonial building, which at the time served as the National Conservatory of Music.

The central standing figure of an Indian woman represents Music [Plate 203]. A nude figure on the left side is Intuition, this being a gift from nature, whereas the figure of Intelligence, above the head of Music, is clothed as being a form of labor. Intuition and Intelligence raise right arms with clenched fists to indicate force. Low in the panel a seated woman symbolizes Humanity.

The panel on the left side represents simply Song; on the right, Instrumental Music. Instruments painted upon lower walls of the stairway symbolize String, Wind, and Percussion Music (Tamayo: 1934).

This fresco of Musical Motifs painted in somber hues is intensely Mexican in feeling.

Banco Nacional Hipotecario, Avenida Madero 32 (Bank.) The National Mortgage Bank was decorated by Fermín Revueltas in 1933 with a long panel that forms the background of the Bank. This fresco symbolizes Man in Control of the Forces of Nature through Machinery. This was the last mural to be painted by Revueltas, who died in 1935 on the eve of beginning the important mural commission of decorating the monument to Alvaro Obregón, the murdered President-elect.

Escuela Industrial de Mujeres (Destroyed). Alfredo Zalce in 1933 painted his first murals in the vestibule of the Women's Industrial School in Mexico City in praise of woman's work, textile work, Women Dyeing Cloth (Plate 204), figures working together. "I wished to re-create the moment of their best postures."

The decoration covered the whole vestibule—all walls and the ceiling. "What interested me was the composition of the whole rather than the details. In each wall there is a door. My greatest difficulty was to compose the spaces above these doors so as to unite them with the ceiling covered with geometric forms" (Zalce, personal report, 1934).

Escuela Pro-Hogar, Avenida Central, Colonia Pro-Hogar (Primary School). Ramón Alva Guadarrama decorated a new school in a workers' district with social aspects of the life of children in the city and in the country.

To the left of the entrance the City is represented by Vice with a pulque shop in the rear; in the center beside the door

204. Alfredo Zalce. Women Dyeing Cloth. Vestibule, Escuela Industrial de Mujeres, México, D.F.

Persuasion through Reading is illustrated by a teacher showing a boy his lesson.

To the right of the entrance, the Country is represented by a school teacher with children; an overseer and a laborer indicate the Revolution; Agriculture is symbolized by ears of corn; above, a plan of study is brought to a *campesino* plowing with animals.

On the stairway an Open-Air School is in session under a spreading tree [Plate 205]; on one side a mother is bringing her son to school; on the other, a whole family is listening to the class.

In the assembly room on the second floor, panels are painted around the room: Studying the Lesson; the Teacher Is Sick; the Day Ends and the Night Begins; the Day Comes

205. Ramón Alva Guadarrama. Open-Air School. Stairway, Escuela Pro-Hogar, México, D.F.

and the Sun Awakens the *Campesino;* Children Enter School; and the Examination. (Alva Guadarrama: 1934)

Escuela Melchor Ocampo, Coyoacan (Primary School). Julio Castellanos completed only a part of his projected decoration for the Melchor Ocampo Primary School. The principal panel is on the stairway landing.

According to the understanding of little children, I have taken a subject from the past: how heaven and hell were used to terrify people and to control them. I have used the invention of the devil together with the author of this invention. The children of the school, not believing in the devil (in this falsehood), do a childish thing; they toss the two in the blanket [Plate 206]. Technically there are great defects as it is the first time I have painted in fresco and I am paying for inexperience. The lack of form and strength comes from insufficient use of color so that the wall shows through. If covered too thickly it lacks brilliancy. There are one large wall and many small ones that improve as I go on (Castellanos: 1934).

Two smaller panels represent the Game of the Little Fish and, partly over a door, Children with a Pony (Plate 207).

Escuela Emiliano Zapata, Villa Madero (Primary School). A modern primary school in a workers' district

of Guadalupe, or Villa Madero, contains the first murals painted by Pablo O'Higgins. In two panels he represents children under different compulsions: Compulsion of Belief is illustrated by the priest Zumarraga in the early days of the Conquest blindfolding an Indian child from his cultural past; Compulsion of Work is represented by Child Glass Blowers (Plate 208) at work in a glass factory of today (1934). A third panel is Liberation of Children through Education.

Escuela Gabriela Mistral, Calle de Peralvillo (Primary School). Julio Castellanos and Juan O'Gorman, working in collaboration, decorated the portico and the entrance hall of a Colonial school building with a series of frescoes representing Life and Death. Castellanos painted the portico: On the north half he represented Death among plants, vegetables, and trees, and among Mexico's poor. Life he represented on the south side, where a mother teaches her son botany; two men rest from plowing the land; and birth occurs in a simple home. O'Gorman decorated the passageway to the patio with architectural forms to express Death and Life, Death being sham construction and imitations, such as hollow Greek columns; Life, the techniques of today. Opposite a castle and a church he

206. Julio Castellanos, Children Tossing the Devil. Stairway Landing, Escuela Melchor Ocampo, Coyoacán, México, D.F.

207. Julio Castellanos. Children with Pony. Escuela Melchor Ocampo, Coyoacán, México, D.F.

208. Pablo O'Higgins. Child Glass Blowers. Escuela Emiliano Zapata, Villa Madero, México, D.F.

209. Jesús Guerrero Galván. School Activities. Escuela Colonia Portales, México, D.F.

placed a factory and a school. These murals were never finished.

Escuela Colonia de los Alamos (Primary School). Jesús Guerrero Galván decorated a new school with frescoes representing School Activities and showing children at work and at play (Plate 209).

Escuela San Simón, Delegación de General Anaya (Primary School). Roberto Reyes Pérez painted frescoes of large figures to represent the Worker in this workers' district.

Other Primary Schools. In addition to individual commissions, as indicated above, a number of primary schools, being newly built or restored in or near Mexico City, were commissioned to be decorated collectively by groups of young artists. Most of these schools were decorated by Máximo Pacheco, Jesús Guerrero Galván, Roberto Reyes Pérez, Juan Manuel Anaya, José Chávez Morado, and Raul Anguiano, working as teams in different combinations. Sometimes the artists painted separate panels; sometimes they worked in collaboration on the same area. Practically no murals have been preserved in primary schools.

Centro Vasco de Quiroga, Avenida del Trabajo (Workers' School). The lecture hall of this workers' night school was decorated by Máximo Pacheco, working alone, with five panels painted in encaustic to represent the Evolution of Mechanical Science.

Instituto Politécnico, Colonia Argentina (Technical School). Increasingly, the mural commissions were given to groups. Five panels representing Forces of History were painted in the loggia of the Technical Institute by Roberto Reyes Pérez, Máximo Pacheco, Raul Anguiano, Jesús Guerrero Galván and Francisco Gutiérrez, working in collaboration. Gutiérrez continued to teach the experimental use of new mural materials in this modern technical school, experiments which were to influence future mural art.

Escuela Nacional de Maestros (Destroyed). The Theatre of the National Teachers' School was decorated by Roberto Montenegro. The school walls were painted collectively by Raul Anguiano, Máximo Pacheco, and Jesús Guerrero Galván. The building has been razed and replaced by the fine new National Normal School.

Mercado Abelardo Rodríguez, República de Venezuela (Market). The Rodríguez Market, remodeled from the Colonial Convent of San Gregorio, was decorated during 1934 and 1935 by a group of young painters, the chosen general subject being the Production and Distribution of Food, and the related subjects of Nutrition and Disease. Entrance halls, stairways, and an interior

210. Pablo O'Higgins. Grain (detail). Patio, Mercado Abelardo Rodríguez, México, D.F.

patio were assigned to different painters, each of whom worked independently.

The southeast entrance, decorated by Ramón Alva Guadarrama in fresco and encaustic, represents Production of Food by Workers in the Country; the vault is decorated with symbols of the sun, moon, and stars on a bright blue ground. This tender painting was the last work by Alva Guadarrama before his death.

Painted in fresco by Marion Greenwood, a visiting American artist, the high walls of the south stair well picture Food and Its Marketing on the Viga Canal, in the vicinity of Mexico City, presenting a scene of colorful abundance.

On a similar stairway at the east end of the market Grace Greenwood her sister, painted a fresco representing Gold, Its Mining, Minting, and Distribution, based on careful study of these activities.

Reached by these two stairways, a long wall on the second floor is interestingly decorated in colored cement, with landscape and human forms modeled in high relief by the Japanese-American artist Isamu Noguchi.

A south entrance shows highly characterized street types painted in tempera by Pedro Rendón.

The main entrance to the market building is through a vaulted hall decorated with frescoes by Antonio Pujol. In the intersected vaults he pictures the beauty of healthy growth in plants and the deformity of disease. Upon an end wall of the hall Pujol has painted Miners and their conditions of work.

Adjoining this entrance, the main stairway ceiling is decorated in tempera by Ángel Bracho with huge human forms, showing the nerves and blood vessels that sustain life. This mural was unfinished.

The ceiling of a second large stairway is designed with large historical figures painted in tempera by Miguel Tzab. It also was unfinished.

A small central patio, preserved from the Convent cloister, was selected for decoration by Pablo O'Higgins, the leader of the group. The distribution of various cereals and their relation to human life forms the subject of this minutely painted decoration of the walls and vaults of the open corridors (Plate 210). However, these frescoed walls were but half-completed when the project was cancelled.

Centro Escolar de la Revolución, Arcos de Belem y Balderas (School Center). A modern educational center for children has replaced the formidable Colonial prison, Carcel de Belem. The wide portico of the school displays a series of frescoed panels painted in 1936 by young artists: Aurora Reyes, Raul Anguiano, Gonzalo de la Paz Pérez, Ignacio Gómez Faramillo, and Evarardo Ramírez. A giant figure fills each panel to symbolize different forms of Social Strife.

Fermín Revueltas previously had designed large, brilliantly colored stained-glass windows for two libraries that are entered from the ends of this portico, the Children's Library and the General Library.

Talleres Gráficos de la Nación, Tolsa y E. Martínez (National Publishing House). The stairway of the National Publishing House was decorated collectively in 1936–1937 by a group of young painters, Pablo O'Higgins, Leopoldo Méndez, Fernando Gamboa, and Alfredo Zalce. Upon the wall of a stair landing, against a background painting of the print shop, O'Higgins, with some assistance from Gamboa, painted a worker calling to his companions to organize themselves. Zalce decorated a vault under the ascending stairs with a large figure of a Worker Demanding Unity. On the companion vault Méndez painted Gassed, a monumental figure of despair (Plate 211).

211. Leopoldo Méndez. Gassed. Stairway, Talleres Gráficos de la Nación, México, D.F.

MORELIA, MICHOACAN (SITE 27)

Biblioteca del Estado (Murals Destroyed). Antonio Silva in 1930 decorated the State Library with frescoes in two panels and two lunettes, to represent the theme that the Earth Belongs to the Workers. The murals were soon covered over.

Universidad de Michoacán (State University). In the patio of the former Colegio de San Nicolás, now the State University, Marion Greenwood in 1933 painted in fresco long panels that picture various activities of native Tarascans in this high lake country. These murals are a young American painter's appreciative interpretation of Indian life.

Museo Michoacana (Murals Destroyed). Frescoes painted at this time in the fine old Colonial Museum by the American artists Grace Greenwood and Ryah Ludins have not been saved. More recently other American painters experimented upon these walls.

CULTURAL MISSIONS

Programs of Cultural Missions, sent during this period into different parts of the country by the Minister of Public Education, included the mural decoration of centers, new schools, and out-door theatres under construction in pueblos throughout the country. Only a few of the many can be noted here.

Morelia, Michoacan

Casa del Obrero (Murals Destroyed). The Agrarian Committee Headquarters, housed in an old school back of the market of Morelia, was decorated rapidly by young artists working as a Cultural Mission. Here Leopoldo Méndez painted his first mural in a lunette over a doorway with a figure of Lenin as Leader; Alfredo Zalce painted a panel with a figure of Juárez helping an Indian; Raul Anguiano painted a lunette with a worker calling to a soldier and a *campesino*.

This was hasty experimental work for all and not coordinated; it was not preserved.

Ayotla, Tlaxcala (Site 28)

Escuela de Ayotla. In 1932 exterior decorations were painted by Alfredo Zalce and Isabel Villaseñor on the façade of a school as it was being completed in the town of Ayotla. With this decoration the mural movement was extended past cities into the countryside of the region of Tlaxcala, where Colonial painting had originally begun soon after the Conquest.

Axochio, Veracruz (Site 29)

Escuela. Miguel Covarrubias reported finding most interesting murals painted in the school of the town of Axochio, where the artist Ramón Cano had taken Mexico's Mural Renaissance to the eastern coastal region of the state of Veracruz.

Uruapan, Michoacan (Site 31)

Escuelas. As director of the Division of Cultural Missions, Alfredo Zalce painted various schools in Michoacan. In Uruapan most interesting designs in colored plaster decorate façades of adjoining schools for boys and girls.

Other Cultural Missions Projects

Francisco Dosamantes, while working for Cultural Missions, made many murals in tempera and in oils for rural schools in the states of Oaxaca, Guerrero, Michoacan, Colima, Coahuila, and Chihuahua. Fernando Castro Pacheco decorated various schools in his native Yucatán.

ART SCHOOLS

Schools of art opened in different places by young artists sometimes included mural techniques. For example:

Taxco, Guerrero (Site 32)

Escuela del Arte. A cultural mission, under direction of the Japanese artist Tamiji Kitagawa, offered classes in fresco technique and mural composition to young artists in the beautiful town of Taxco.

Coyoacan, D.F. (Site 33)

Escuela del Arte. Frida Kahlo, as her contribution, taught young artists mural composition and guided their fresco paintings in Jardín de Niños, Calzado de Coyoacan. Also, they painted with her a store front in Coyoacan, with the name La Rosita, in which the figure of a girl painted in a medallion amidst scrolls made the wall look like a lovely valentine. The paintings have not been saved.

Through these various kinds of mural activity the movement spread and grew strong in the consciousness of the Mexican people as well as upon their walls.

212. Diego Rivera. Man at the Crossroads. Upper Gallery, Foyer, Palacio de Bellas Artes, México, D.F.

The Second Surge of Mural Art Begins: 1934–1940

Muralists Return to Mexico.

Meanwhile, another great surge of mural painting arose under the principal originators of the movement.

General Lazaro Cárdenas, elected President in 1934, continued in office under the changed electoral law until 1940. Very soon Cárdenas asserted his independence of Calles, whom he despatched into exile in the United States. The nationalist character of the new administration is reflected in murals. However, since at this time the emphasis was on social measures, mural commissions were given by departments of government, or by states, and not by the central government.

Coincident with Cárdenas' accession to power, Diego Rivera and José Clemente Orozco returned to Mexico with prestige enhanced by the important murals each had painted in the United States. These two muralists, "Los Dos Grandes," were invited by the Minister of Education, Antonio Castro Leal, to paint walls in the National Palace of Fine Arts (Bellas Artes), into which the unfinished National Theatre from Díaz' time was being transformed. The mural movement was given fresh impetus with these paintings.

David Alfaro Siqueiros, having also returned to Mexico at this time, debated publicly with Diego Rivera as to the nature and function of revolutionary art. Technically, Siqueiros demanded the use of new materials and methods derived from modern industry; compositionally, he insisted on an art that takes into consideration a progressive point of view by the observer, movement related to the cinema, with involvement of a time element, so that the means may be as revolutionary as the content. Rivera conceived of mural art as a partner of architecture, identified with it as a reinforcement of its public function.

Siqueiros' participation in the Spanish Civil War was to delay for some years his mural experiments, but Rivera and Orozco resumed work immediately, painting first the murals in the Palace of Fine Arts. With their works in Bellas Artes each entered upon his second great series of Mexican murals. Rivera resumed work on the monumental stairway of the National Palace, for which Mexico's history—past, present, and future—was his theme. Orozco began to paint immense murals

in Guadalajara for his native state of Jalisco. Cárdenas' home state of Michoacan also commissioned murals at this time. Some new muralists were given walls to paint.

México, D.F. (Site 1)

Palacio de Bellas Artes (Palace of Fine Arts). Diego Rivera and José Clemente Orozco were given corresponding walls at either end of the upper gallery that surrounds the large foyer of Bellas Artes.

Rivera's mural faces east. He explained (1934) that his Man at the Crossroads represents the scientific industrial worker in control of natural forces by means of the machine. With Technical Knowledge he could look toward a better future, which would evolve from the present bitter conflict of social forces—"The Capitalist disorder and the Socialist Order." The sides of the frescoes represent the Liquidation of Religion and Its Superstitions, through knowledge of the forces that rule evolution, and the Liquidation of Capitalist Power by the productive classes when they apply knowledge of historic laws to revolutionary action.

Rivera reproduced here his mural that had been destroyed in Rockefeller Center. He illustrates the given theme, Man at the Crossroads Looking toward a Better Future, by a central figure of a workman whose hands control a dynamo. Below the Worker a huge hand clasps a sphere marked with molecular symbols of atomic structure; from it radiate shafts of light, painted with symbols of the natural forces of germs and electrons, which form diagonals of the wall. The Worker is flanked by broken statuary, representative of old beliefs, and by people, including Lenin, representative of new ideas. Plants that sustain human life form the foreground. For Rivera science and mechanics point the way to the future under Marx, and the necessary revolution is primarily social and scientific (Plates 212, 213, 214).

Orozco's fresco, facing west, represents a colossal struggle. Against a background of mechanized war, two huge figures of men fight to the death above grinning, bejeweled, nude harlots (Plates 215, 216 [color, p. 232]). Orozco called this fresco the Catharsis. Aristotle described tragedy as effecting a catharsis of pity and fear

213. Diego Rivera. Man at the Crossroads (left-end section). Upper Gallery, Foyer, Palacio de Bellas Artes, México, D.F.

214. Diego Rivera. Man at the Crossroads (right-end section). Upper Gallery, Foyer, Palacio de Bellas Artes, México, D.F.

through creating these emotions. Painted in gradations of red and black, the color of this mural is as violent as the action in the composition, which is swung on great diagonals. For Orozco, Humanity is dehumanized in a mechanical world and purification lies in showing realistically the lurking evil: the Revolution is against spiritual death.

In Bellas Artes these two very different mural revolutions are presented. The years spent painting in the United States had affected the work of each artist—but differently. Rivera, for the poetry of his earlier Mexican frescoes, substituted a carefully scientific attitude with exact knowledge and reasoned theory. Orozco's mural,

on the contrary, is a highly emotional work based on intuition and on moral concern, his former compassion disappearing as he accuses mankind of stupid brutality. This divergence became more pronounced in both subject and treatment in the subsequent work of these two artists, each painter, as the mural conflict continued, perhaps acting as a whetstone to the other in their stupendous undertakings.

Palacio Nacional, Zócalo (National Palace). After finishing his wall in Bellas Artes, Rivera resumed painting his great fresco on the monumental stairway of the National Palace.

In 1935, upon the stairway wall facing north and op-

215. José Clemente Orozco. Catharsis. Upper Gallery, Foyer, Palacio de Bellas, México, D.F.

posite his mural of Mexico's Distant Past, Rivera painted his conception of the Present in Mexican history. This large wall is dominated by a colossal figure of Marx, who holds a tablet to instruct armed workers and points to the Future, typified in the upper left as controlled production (Plate 217).

Below the painting of Marx the wall is divided into rectangular spaces to frame groups: Officer, Banker, and Priest; Demagogues; Vices of Rulers. Propaganda, Agitation, and Conflict reign on the right side of the wall. Labor in country and city is symbolized in figures that ascend the stairs at lower levels. In this wall of the Present, Rivera related Mexico to the World Revolution of Communism (Plates 218, 219, 220). He had

planned to elaborate the Future in the adjacent panels of the upper corridors. However, his contract having been fulfilled, his work was discontinued here.

When Rivera again painted in the National Palace in 1943 he worked on the other side of the monumental stairway on corridor panels adjacent to Mexico's Distant Past.

Orozco Paints in Guadalajara

Orozco, after completing his great wall in Bellas Artes, went to Guadalajara, where from 1936 to 1940 he created immense murals for his native state of Jalisco. During this period he worked more or less concurrently on three buildings—the University of

217. Diego Rivera. The Present: Marx (detail). Monumental Stairway, Palacio Nacional, México, D.F.

218. Diego Rivera. The Present: Conflict (detail). Monumental Stairway, Palacio Nacional, México, D.F.

219. Diego Rivera. The Present: Conflict (detail). Monumental Stairway, Palacio Nacional, México, D.F.

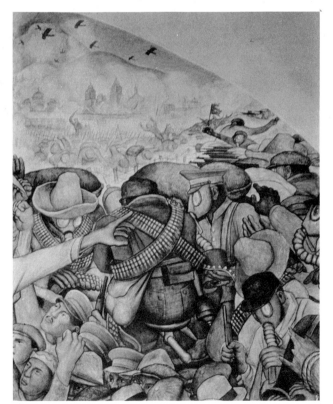

220. Diego Rivera. The Present: Propaganda (detail). Monumental Stairway, Palacio Nacional, México, D.F.

Guadalajara, the Capitol, and the Guadalajara Orphanage.

Guadalajara, Jalisco (Site 26)

Universidad de Guadalajara, Avenida Enrique Díaz de León (University of Guadalajara). The Lecture Hall (Paraninfo) of the University Medical School, a twentieth-century building lighted from a large, low dome, is one of three buildings in Guadalajara decorated at this time by Orozco. Upon the small stage of the hall he represents Workers and Soldiers illumined against a dark background by the fire of Life and Conscience; to the sides are False Leaders and the suffering Victims who react against them.

The principal decoration of the hall fills the cupola, in which Orozco symbolizes the Progress of Science in four figures arranged around the lantern: Superstition with a rope around his neck plunges downward on one side of the dome next to the upright figure of Mechanics; Breaking Down the Archaic System of Science

221. José Clemente Orozco. Progress of Science. Lecture Hall, Universidad de Guadalajara, Guadalajara, Jalisco.

by Thought is represented by five heads that superimpose as one on a single body, whose hands hold geometric instruments before geometric symbols; a cadaver lies below. Man the Creator with upraised hand dominates the dome and assures scientific progress (Plate 221).

Palacio de Gobierno, Plaza de Armas (State Capitol). In a great vault that curves up over the monumental stairway of this early Colonial building Orozco has painted an immense figure of Father Miguel Hidalgo (Plate 222), the rebel priest who in this region in 1910 initiated the revolt of Latin America from Spain and was repaid with excommunication and execution. Hidalgo's figure rises high into the vault with one clenched hand

uplifted, while the other holds a flaming sword over the forces of Darkness, painted beneath him on the central wall of the stairway as battling cruelly (Plate 223). On the left ascending wall knives and snakes pour from symbols of military and clergy. Contemporary Circus is Orozco's name for the panel on the right, in which he presents a Carnival of Idealogies, where *payasos* (clowns) play with political symbols and with their victims.

Hospicio Cabañas (Orphanage). A complex of neoclassic buildings designed by Tolsa was erected at the beginning of the nineteenth century by Bishop Cabañas y Crespo as an orphanage, which it still is.

In the center of the Hospicio Cabañas stands a

216. José Clemente Orozco. Catharsis (detail). Upper Gallery, Foyer, Palacio de Bellas Artes, México, D.F.

222. José Clemente Orozco. Miguel Hidalgo. Stairway, Palacio de Gobierno, Guadalajara, Jalisco.

223. José Clemente Orozco. Miguel Hidalgo (detail). Stairway, Palacio de Gobierno, Guadalajara, Jalisco.

vaulted cruciform chapel with short arms open to front and rear, and long closed arms to the sides. A small dome is placed high over the intersection. The long barrel vaults at the sides are divided each into three arched sections, with corresponding wall panels below and lunettes at extremities. Every part of this chapel has been painted by Orozco with symbols of the might and pride of the Spanish Empire in the New World and with the aftermath of desolation.

Figures symbolical of Spain and of the Conquest (Plate 224) fill the vaulted sections to right and left of the cupola. In opposing wall panels that correspond to these sections are contrasted symbols of the present world. On the left under Conquest are the Unknown and the Conquered, the Scientific and the Religious, the Ridiculous and the Tragic. On the right under Empire are Charity and Despotism, Suffering Humanity and Military Might, Demagogues and Dictators.

Seated figures of Cervantes and El Greco in lunettes at one end symbolize Western Culture; Mechanical Warriors (Plate 225) are at the other end.

Orozco has painted the short vaults of the chapel with Religions of America in one, and Huichilobos, bestial God of War, in the other; in panels under these he represents Human Warriors and Missionaries. In twin lunettes over entrances ships sail out of darkness.

In the pendentives of the dome masculine figures struggle upward (Plate 226). The dome rests upon a high drum in which sixteen activities of the human race are represented by symbols. Within the small, high cupola Fire rises aflame, a youthful figure surrounded by dark reclining figures of Earth, Air, Water. Or are these different attributes of Man? Is the figure that falters the same as the flaming one? And as the one who reaches a helping hand? Justino Fernández suggests that it is.

224. José Clemente Orozco. The Conqueror. Vault, Chapel, Hospicio Cabañas, Guadalajara, Jalisco.

225. José Clemente Orozco. Mechanical Warrior. Chapel, Hospicio Cabañas, Guadalajara, Jalisco.

Murals Painted in Michoacan

Isla de Janitzio, Lago de Patzcuaro, Michoacan (Site 34)

Monumento de Morelos (Monument). A huge figure, built of cement blocks to represent the revolutionary hero José María Morelos, surmounts the conical island-town of Janitzio. The interior of the Monument, divided into five tiers or stories, was decorated by Ramón Alva de la Canal in 1938. Successive panels depict incidents from the life of the rebel priest Morelos, friend and disciple of Father Hidalgo and the greatest leader in the 1810–1820 War of Independence.

Jiquilpan, Michoacan (Site 35)

Biblioteca Gabino Ortiz (Public Library). Following his work in Guadalajara, José Clemente Orozco in 1940 went to Jiquilpan (Cárdenas' native city) to decorate a Colonial chapel converted into a public library.

The vaulted apse, painted in rich fresco color, shows la Madre Patria, Mother Mexico herself (Plate 227), wrapped in a *reboso* and serenely seated upon Ancient Ignorance, symbolized by a fierce jaguar; she is traveling over difficulties represented by thorny *nopales*, or prickly-pear cactus. Foreign Ignorance, another jaguar, leaps into the picture. Against the red, white, and green of a huge Mexican flag that fills the background of the vault, the Eagle of Freedom is being choked by the Serpent of Greed. Ill-armed and unheeding custodians of Mexico's liberties stand guard.

Eight large panels of the side walls, painted only in black onto the white surface, picture horses, or Brute Force, and men, whose heads are only mouths, who fight fiercely and die. One side relates to the Agrarian Revolution of Mexico, and another, to War in general (Plate 228).

Above the entrance to this library Orozco has painted False Leaders who deceive the people, pictured as dancing figures that embrace jaguars, which gaily climb tall *nopales* on either side of the doorway. Above, a dancer holds a serpent by its tail.

Patzcuaro, Michoacan (Site 36)

Biblioteca Gertrudis Bocanegra (Public Library). Juan O'Gorman painted a large mural in the Public Library of Patzcuaro in 1941 and 1942. The library is named for Gertrudis Bocanegra, a heroine of Patzcuaro who in 1817 sacrificed herself and her family in Mexico's War of Independence. In the decoration of a huge arched end wall of the vaulted Colonial building O'Gorman has symbolized the history of the Tarascan, or Purehpecha, Indians of this high lake region of Michoacan (Plate 229).

The upper part of the wall, presided over by the Indian Gods of the Sun and the Moon, represents the creation of this volcanic country and its settlement by the race that still inhabits it.

Erendira, the Indian princess who on horseback sought to warn her people of deception (Plate 230), stands in opposition to devastation of the land and humiliation of the people by the Conquerors under Nuño de Guzmán. The roots of a cut tree signify the Indian culture after the Conquest. At a lower level reconstruction of the country takes place under the leadership of an Augustinian missionary, Fray Juan Batista, and of Don Vasco de Quiroga, who as governor of Michoacan tried to redress the wrongs done to the Indians. Using Sir Thomas More's *Utopia* as his guide, Quiroga organized various pueblos as craft centers, introducing new tools and techniques. The re-

226. José Clemente Orozco. Dome and Pendentive Decorations. Chapel, Hospicio Cabañas, Guadalajara, Jalisco.

227. José Clemente Orozco. Mother Mexico. Apse, Biblioteca Gabino Ortiz, Jiquilpan, Michoacan.

228. José Clemente Orozco. War. Two side panels, Biblioteca Gabino Ortiz, Jiquilpan, Michoacan.

229. Juan O'Gorman. History of the Tarascan Indians. Arched Wall, Biblioteca Gertrudis Bocanegra, Patzcuaro, Michoacan.

sults of this development still distinguish Michoacan craftsmanship.

In the lower right-hand section Doña Gertrudis Bocanegra is being executed; above her stand Morelos, the liberator, and also Zapata, beloved leader of the People's Revolution of a century later. At the far right side stand Tarascans of today armed with tools, and on the other side stands a figure of the artist O'Gorman, holding a plaque which promises that, in spite of the Conquest and the centuries of exploitation, "from the latent force of the undefeated Indian race there will arise an extraordinary art and culture."

OTHER MURALS PAINTED DURING CÁRDENAS' ADMINISTRATION

Puebla, Puebla (Site 37)

Instituto Normal de Puebla (Normal School). Alfredo Zalce during 1938–1939 decorated the principal wall of the dark stairway of the Puebla Normal School to represent the conflict of the time between the government, represented by school teachers, and factions among the people who objected to government policy. The press is represented as loose sheets of paper rising endlessly; tear gas and machine guns menace workers; a teacher is hanged from a tree, and a school is destroyed.

Jalapa, Veracruz (Site 38)

Escuela Normal de Jalapa (Mural Destroyed). In 1938 frescoes were painted in the Normal School of Jalapa by José Chávez Morado, which have not been preserved.

México, D.F. (Site 1)

Escuela Estado de Michoacan, Colonia Michoacan (Technical High School). The Expropriation of Oil Property by the Cárdenas Government is the subject of frescoes painted by Pablo O'Higgins in 1938–1939 to dramatize that Cárdenas had support from all classes in Mexico. These paintings are in the assembly hall of a new technical high school.

Sindicato de Electricistas (Union Headquarters). David Alfonso Siqueiros returned to Mexico for a short visit in 1939, when he painted his first Mexican murals in "duco," in the Headquarters of the Union of Electricians in Mexico City; these cover three walls of a stairway in a tightly woven design of symbols of fascism, in which machinery devours humans while an orator directs through a microphone. Working with

230. Juan O'Gorman. Erendira (detail, History of the Tarascan Indians). Arched Wall, Biblioteca Gertrudis Bocanegra, Patzcuaro, Michoacan.

Siqueiros were Luis Arenal, Antonio Pujol, José Renau, Miguel Prieto, and others.

Guadalajara, Jalisco (Site 26)

Sindicato Único de Trabajadores Automobilistos (Automobile Workers' Union Headquarters). The return of Xavier Guerrero to Mexico in 1939 was registered in a series of frescoed panels painted in the Headquarters of the Automobile Workers' Union in Guadalajara to depict the history of the revolutionary movement.

231. José Clemente Orozco. Injustice among the People (detail). Foyer, Palacio de Justicia de la Nación, México, D.F.

232. José Clemente Orozco. Injustice in the Court (detail). Foyer, Palacio de Justicia de la Nación, México, D.F.

The Muralists Work in Mexico City: 1941–1947

Manuel Avila Camacho, a reserved, temperate general who had served as trouble shooter for Cárdenas, was chosen to succeed him and his "bloodless revolution." However, this election was strongly contested by counterrevolutionary forces, including those influenced by Falange and Pro-Axis elements. With the Second World War beginning in Europe, Avila Camacho allied Mexico with the United States; Mexican influence effectively aligned Latin America with the Allied cause, and Lázaro Cárdenas became Mexico's Minister of Defense. The war years saw feverish activity in Mexico. Under pressure of events and of new wealth much change took place and Mexico's Revolution receded, but not so all revolutions on her walls.

During the middle-of-the-road Presidency of Avila Camacho, murals were again sponsored by the central government, and the muralists painted in Mexico City. While war raged, Orozco, working in the foyer of the Supreme Court, made his comments on human justice, and in the church of the Hospital de Jesús he painted an apocalyptic vision. Rivera pictured Mexican archeology, history, and medical science in greatest detail. Siqueiros returned in 1944 from painting immense murals in Chile to be acclaimed the third great muralist in Mexico and to paint murals in Bellas Artes and elsewhere in imperishable Duco color. Commissions were given to a few younger painters, making this a period of continuous mural painting in the City of Mexico.

OROZCO

Palacio de Justicia de la Nación, S.E. of Zócalo (Supreme Court). The Supreme Court occupies a modern building south of the National Palace. At the beginning of the administration of Manuel Avila Camacho, in 1941, Orozco was commissioned to decorate the foyers of the Appellate Courts.

The paintings by Orozco in the upper foyer refer to the rights of the people as assured by the Constitution of Mexico. This liberal constitution, first accepted in 1917, is constantly being reformed and supplemented.

High over the stairway a large panel represents Artículo 123, labor legislation assuring protection of workers as to hours of work, remuneration, holidays, health care, right to unionize and to strike, and all that gives dignity to human labor. However, the painting suggests that in the House of Labor the worker does not stand upright; workmen stoop immobilized; a reclining figure in the foreground hides his head behind a red banner; confusion reigns beyond the door at rear.

Opposite this panel on the main wall of the foyer Orozco presents Mexico's subterranean wealth, which Artículo 27 consigns to the Nation. Gold, Silver, Copper, and especially Petroleum lie as symbols in strata across the wall; these are surmounted by a spotted beast, a *Tigre* (Jaguar) all teeth and claws, which leaps fiercely under the Mexican flag as defender of this wealth. Petroleum, a dark eyeless beast in the center, has fangs of pipelines.

On side walls of the foyer Angels of Justice strike with diagonal rays over doors leading to the Courts. On the right side is shown Injustice among the People, with Justice asleep on her throne while busy masked thieves are struck by a flaming bolt held by a figure of wrath (Plate 231); on the left, Injustice in the Court shows Justice and her throne lying beneath a table where conspirators huddle as a vengeful figure strikes through the doorway (Plate 232) and the angel aims his flaming sword.

These panels in Justicia, suggesting laws in the breach rather than in the observance, were not popular with government officials, and Orozco was not permitted to finish his mural contract in Justicia.

In 1945 George Biddle, a painter from the United States, was invited to paint in the street-floor lobby of the Supreme Court Building. His two large panels are filled with symbolical figures that float in the air.

Templo de Jesús Nazareno, Rep. Salvador y Piño Suárez (Church). The former church of the Hospital of Jesus was selected by José Clemente Orozco as the site in which to continue his unfinished contract for painting murals in the Supreme Court Building. This church, built with Cortés' endowment and erected on the spot where he and Montezuma first met, is where Cortés' bones were found concealed. From 1942 to 1944, while the Second World War raged, Orozco painted a series of apocalyptic frescoes that cover the

233. José Clemente Orozco. The Devil Bound (detail). Templo de Jesús Nazareno, México, D.F.

234. José Clemente Orozco. Apocalypse (detail). Vault, Templo de Jesús Nazareno, México, D.F.

high vault and upper walls of the front half of the church of Jesús Nazareno.

In the center of the vault above the choir loft Divinity is represented by a radiant house surrounded by angelic figures. On side walls of this section the Devil Bound by Angels (Plate 233) presents a huge struggling devil with claws, who is being tied to a post by a most determined angel (Allegory of the Mystery of Life), and the Devil Freed (or Babylon), a scene of destruction.

Tremendous apocalyptic horses plunge in the vault in front of the choir. Three in number, they are accompanied by an apocalyptic beast or *Tigre* upon which rides a fat blond courtesan in a liberty cap. She holds a glass for a toast (Plate 234). On the side walls of this section the heads of great horses disintegrate; from one head come fluttering papers; from the other, a great tangle of barbed wire or mechanical forms.

Because there was no inclusive contract, only the front half of the church walls were painted at this time. Orozco's death in 1949 has precluded the completion of this great complex of murals. The church is again used for religious services. The frescoes, although darkened by smoke, are protected from destruction by the Mexican government.

RIVERA

Instituto Nacional de Biología Aplicada or Cardiología, Avenida Cuauhtémoc y Dr. Márquez (Research Hospital). The Cardiac Research Hospital, popularly called Cardiología as cardiac science is the specialty here, was decorated by Diego Rivera in 1943.

Upon the two high side walls of the vestibule Rivera has painted the detailed history of the development of medical knowledge of the human heart. Portraits of great medical scientists are arranged in ascending com-

235. Diego Rivera. Early Medical Researchers. Vestibule, Instituto Nacional de Biología Aplicada, México, D.F.

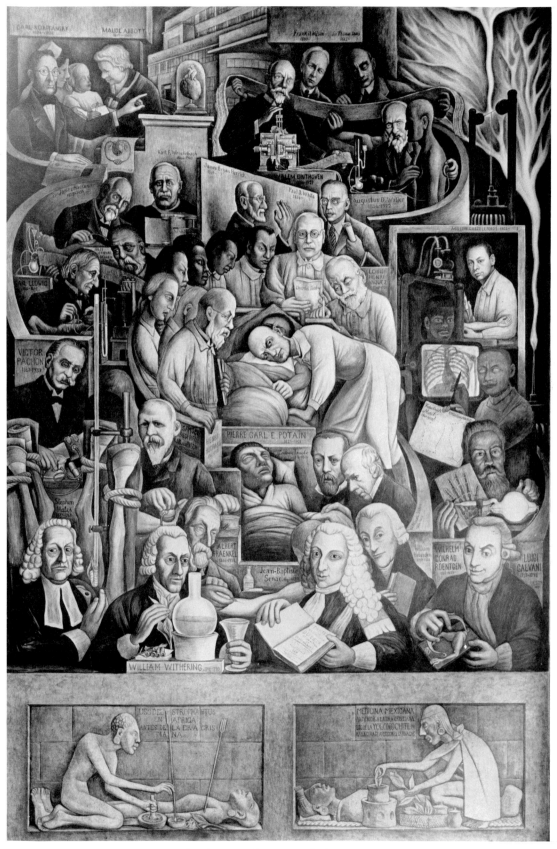

236. Diego Rivera. Recent Medical Researchers. Vestibule, Instituto Nacional de Biología Aplicada, México, D.F.

237. Diego Rivera. Mexico before the Conquest: Tlatelolco Market (half panel). Upper Corridor of Main Court, Palacio Nacional, México, D.F.

positions. Upon the left wall he shows the first contributors to this science from early in the Christian Era to the beginning of cardiac specialization in 1839. Alongside the learned doctors rises a red flame of ignorance and superstition, shown consuming Michel Servet in 1553 (Plate 235). Upon the right wall Rivera depicts more recent research methods in this science through portraying the great contributors with their instruments. A white flame of illumination rises here into the future (Plate 236).

There are two grisaille panels on each dado below the murals. In each panel a doctor attends a patient: on the left side he represents Greece and China; on the right, Africa and Mexico, indicating in legends that methods for the treatment of heart disease existed in these lands prior to the Christian Era. Rivera in Cardiología shows a phase of high development reached by

medical science in Early Mexico; also, he celebrates techniques of modern medical science in which Mexico shares.

Palacio Nacional, Zócalo (National Palace). In 1943 Diego Rivera began again to paint his comprehensive historic murals in the National Palace.

The walls of the monumental stairway he had previously painted to span Mexico's history from the Distant Past to the Present Moment. This stairway leads to an upper open corridor that passes around the main court of the Palace. On the long wall that faces south and extends from the Distant Past of Mexico, Rivera intermittently painted a series of panels in which he elaborated the Indian way of life before the Conquest.

Upon backgrounds formed of reconstructions of Tenochtitlan (Mexico City) and of the forests and lakes that then filled the Valley of Mexico, Rivera represents

244. Diego Rivera. Revolution Comes to the Alameda (detail). Hotel del Prado, México, D.F.

238. Diego Rivera. Tlatelolco Market (detail). Upper Corridor of Main Court, Palacio Nacional México, D.F.

Markets, Industries, and Arts of the Aztecs. Scientifically re-created from Rivera's wide knowledge of Indian arts and traditions, these panels are of great historic value.

One long panel presents the Tlatelolco Market (Plate 237), where recent excavation has revealed early constructions in what was a rival city to Tenochtitlan, shown in the background with its waterways and lakes and snow-capped mountains. In the market scene every detail is of anthropological interest (Plate 238). A priest is seated in a cubicle in the center of the long panel.

Another panel is a closer view of the island city Tenochtitlan. Its pyramidal temples rise where churches stand today, and its waterways and causeways replace present streets. In the foreground are brilliantly costumed Aztecs.

On the succeeding panels Rivera has represented the Arts of Mexico—Pottery, Dyeing, Painting, Weaving, Feather Mosaic, Rubber Extraction—in which he pictures the land and the people, the customs and the occupations native to Mexico. These highly colored panels are filled with the sensory quality of the land (Plates 239, 240, 241).

Below all of the brilliantly colored panels, in small compositions, Rivera painted in grisaille details of various activities of the Aztecs—agriculture, building, arts, crafts, and the merging of processes to emphasize the creativity of man as all of his faculties come together in the work of his hands (Plate 242).

Beside the doorway that leads from this corridor Rivera has painted panels with fruits and vegetables and healing herbs as he also lists what is native to Mexico.

On the side of the court opposite the monumental stairway, on the wall that faces west, Rivera subsequently painted the corridor panels to represent Cortés and his men as ugly intruders into this country. The series dealing with the Conquest of Tenochtitlan had not been completed by Rivera at the time of his death.

In these immense frescoes of the National Palace, Diego Rivera has synthesized his concept of the peoples and the happenings that have created contemporary Mexico.

Hotel Del Prado, Avenida Juárez (Hotel). Changing Mexico is the theme of a long frescoed wall painted by Diego Rivera in 1946–1947 in the elaborate new Hotel Del Prado, a building sponsored by the Mexican government.

The mural reproduces Alameda Park, which the hotel faces. The park shows through the windows as

239. Diego Rivera. Arts of Early Mexico: Dyeing. Upper Corridor of Main Court, Palacio Nacional, México, D.F.

240. Diego Rivera. Arts of Early Mexico: Feather Art. Upper Corridor of Main Court, Palacio Nacional, México, D.F.

241. Diego Rivera. Arts of Early Mexico: Feather Art (detail). Upper Corridor of Main Court, Palacio Nacional, México, D.F.

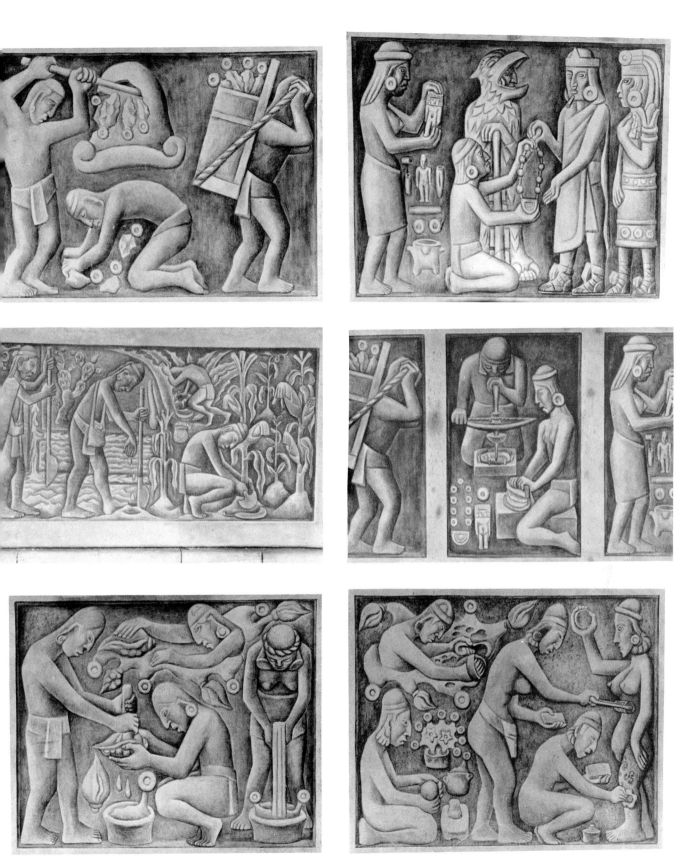

242. Diego Rivera. Arts of Early Mexico: Six Grisaille Panels from Lower Frieze. Upper Corridor of Main Court, Palacio Nacional, México, D.F.

243. Diego Rivera. Sunday Promenade in the Alameda. Hotel del Prado, México, D.F.

245. David Alfaro Siqueiros. Democracy Freeing Herself. Upper Gallery, Palacio de Bellas Artes, México, D.F.

if in continuation of this painting. Originally painted in the restaurant, this wall was later moved to the entrance lobby of Del Prado Hotel.

From left to right a sequence of incidents moves in a continuous composition that synthesizes eras, from the time of the Inquisition to the beginning of the twentieth-century Revolution. The wall originally was divided visually by unattached pillars into three sections. The first section spans the nineteenth century and is dominated by the figure of Benito Juárez holding the Reform Laws. The central section (Plate 243) shows a Sunday Promenade in the Alameda at the turn of the century; the artist of the people, José Guadalupe Posada, walks with a stylish Calavera, one of Posada's famed skeleton creations; Rivera shows himself as a half-grown boy holding her other hand; Frida, his wife, follows him. The last section illustrates the exclusion of Indians from the Alameda and the Advent of Revolution on horseback (Plate 244, color, p. 248).

In the first section, beside the figure of Juárez, Rivera painted a philosopher of that period in Mexico holding a tablet with the words *Diós no existe*. So great

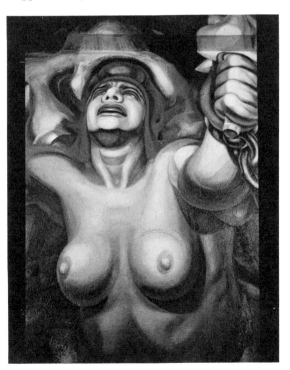

246. David Alfaro Siqueiros. Democracy Freeing Herself (detail). Upper Gallery, Palacio de Bellas Artes, México, D.F.

247. David Alfaro Siqueiros. Torture of Cuauhtémoc (detail). Upper Gallery, Palacio de Bellas Artes, México, D.F.

was the opposition to this motto that the whole wall was curtained off for several years until Rivera was willing to erase the words.

This brilliantly colored fresco appears to represent early personal impressions of the artist.

Miguel Covarrubias painted two immense pictured maps in the rear lobby of Hotel Del Prado. Designed as decorations, these glorified maps represent two different Mexicos: In Old Mexico are pictured the natural assets and the historic points of interest in this fascinating land. Against the enduring mountains and valleys, which everywhere corrugate the land, Covarrubias has placed principal structures that survive from Early Mexico and from the Colonial Period. Indians in regional costumes of the country mingle with animals, birds, trees, and flowering plants that are also indigenous in the various sections of the land. Covarrubias illustrates Mexico of the Present with Modern Cities tied together by highways and railways, airways being suggested apart. In the two maps the enveloping Ocean and Gulf are painted with the lasting and transient values. Mexico is here easily seen and understood.

Decorative paintings in the cocktail lounges and the breakfast room of Hotel del Prado are by Roberto Montenegro and Gabriel Fernández Ledesma.

SIQUEIROS

Palacio de Bellas Artes (Palace of Fine Arts). In 1945 David Alfaro Siqueiros was invited to paint in the

Palace of Fine Arts, where Rivera and Orozco were already represented by the large panels painted in 1934 in the upper gallery of the foyer. These three artists were then acclaimed "Los Tres Grandes."

At this time Siqueiros painted in the upper gallery on walls that face south between the paintings of the other two muralists. His three panels, much smaller than the end panels, are done in pyroxylin. These represent Democracy Freeing Herself flanked by two Slaves. Democracy is a monumental nude half figure in a red liberty cap with weighted chains on outstretched hands, in one of which she holds a torch, in the other a flower (Plates 245, 246). In the smaller panels the two prostrate bound figures represent Victims of War and of Fascism.

In 1950 Siqueiros again painted in Bellas Artes. Opposite his first panels he painted three panels on the wall facing north: the Torture of Cuauhtémoc, last Aztec Emperor, and of the Lord of Tacuba by the Spanish Conquerors trying to extract the secret of hidden treasures (Plate 247); Cuauhtémoc Alive in shining armor defeating the Spanish centaur; a faceless figure with outstretched, empty hands whom the artist named the Man of our Epoch.

Tesorería de Gobierno del D.F., Rep. Brazil #31 (Government Building). During 1946–1947 Siqueiros was painting the monumental stairway of a Baroque palace. Formerly used as the Customs House, it was at that time the Treasury for the Federal District.

The open stairway separates two large courts with approaches from each in the center; it then rises to east and west and divides again to north and south, so that the end walls are V-shaped. The vault is arched both in length and in breadth, the whole offering a complicated field for experimentation.

The height of the vault is great, but it is raised even higher visually, by a strong design, as of wheels within wheels like a gyroscope, which reaches from end to end of this great width and propels the huge figures of the Old Order Descending on one end wall and the New Order Ascending on the other. In this complicated composition figures fall headlong, pushed by demonic spirits around a central axis. Painted in pyroxylin, the color is not applied directly to the wall but to a false surface suitable to the material. This mural was never completed.

OTHER ARTISTS

Aerodromo Central de México (Airport). Two frescoes painted by Juan O'Gorman in the Airport in 1937 were destroyed during remodeling of the large waiting room. These were satirical fantasies, as elaborately executed as Early Dutch paintings but contemporary in feeling and meaning.

In 1943 O'Gorman painted a much larger removable panel for the Aerodromo, placed high within the station. In this mural O'Gorman presents a detailed history of the development of air travel from the first hot-air balloons to modern aviation. He portrays a large number of distinguished inventors and flyers, and these he skillfully incorporates with the landscape background. Everything in this long panel is painted in great detail.

Hospital de Maternidad, Avenida Gabriel Mancera (Murals Destroyed during Remodeling). Pablo O'Higgins and Leopoldo Méndez, working in collaboration during 1946–1947, decorated the vestibule of this modern Maternity Hospital built by Social Security. On the first panel, that reaches from the floor to the ceiling, was painted the skeleton figure of a woman. Placed

above and to the sides of the arched entrance to the corridors, the large fresco illustrated on one side the negative, the witchcraft of primitive methods; on the other, the positive, modern scientific care given to women and to babies in this institution. The whole composition of successive incidents was bound together by abstract symbols of life and growth.

Escuela Estado de Hidalgo, Avenida Ferrocarrileros, Colonia Anahuac (School). In 1946 and 1947 José Chávez Morado painted a series of panels in tempera in this primary school in a workers' district of Mexico City. In one panel a large feminine figure representing Mexico is painted one half as a sculptured form from Early Mexico and the other half as a living Indian woman with a sleeping child in her arms. A pick and shovel placed beside half-excavated walls suggest that much digging into Mexico's past remains to be done.

Orozco Creates His Last Murals: 1947–1949

México, D.F. (Site 1)

Escuela Normal Superior, Calzada de Tacuba (Normal School). José Clemente Orozco in 1947 decorated the National Normal School, designed by architect Mario Pani. It is sometimes called the UNESCO Building, as here the United Nations held cultural conferences when the building was first completed.

Orozco's murals are upon the great stage of the Open-Air Theatre and upon side walls of the main entrance to the complex of buildings that forms the National Normal School.

Teatro Lauro Aguirre: The Open-Air Theatre has for its background a high curved wall placed between two similar, four-storied buildings that converge to enclose the Theatre. Orozco has covered the huge wall with symbols of Mexico incised and painted into the cement. This Historic Synthesis shows Mexico represented by an eagle's claw that grasps a snake, of turquoise color and with drooping head, placed above the central doorway and its door from the old National University building. The constructive hand of man is indicated in geometric architectural forms that fill side spaces, while at one end an immense human figure climbs stairs out of the panel, his head rising beyond its dimensions into the sky (Plate 248).

The scale of the decoration of this wall of 380 square meters is adapted to the surrounding architecture and is visually united with it in design and color. Materials incorporated with the concrete of the wall include silicates and metals mixed with the colors for protection from the weather and for variety in texture, the effect often being like enamel. Marble dust varies values of the basic cement color. The incised lines of the design are pitted to give greater tactile quality. The shadowed line and the unequal lighting of the curved wall give richness to the immense geometric design (Plate 249).

This is the only mural by Orozco which he did not make with his own hands; a crew of seven young artists worked under his guidance: Alfonso Ayala, Armando López Carmona, Ramón Sánchez, Guillermo Monroy, Juan Franco, Arturo Estrada, Fermín G. Chávez.

With this great parabolic wall of the Lauro Aguirre, Open-Air Theatre, Orozco initiated the Technological Revolution in mural art.

Vestibule: At the entrance to this large and impressive complex of Normal School buildings Orozco painted, on one side, frescoed figures of Mexico's poorest, most ragged, and most ignorant people facing toward the marbled lobby (Plate 250); upon the other,

248. José Clemente Orozco. Historic Synthesis. Stage, Open-Air Theatre, Escuela Normal Superior, México, D.F.

249. José Clemente Orozco. Historic Synthesis (detail of lower right-hand corner). Stage, Open-Air Theatre, Escuela Normal Superior, México, D.F.

250. José Clemente Orozco. The Poor of Mexico. Entrance, Escuela Normal Superior, México, D.F.

he shows two boys in a window pointing to the school (Plate 251). Orozco indicates that a wide gap exists between Mexico's deepest needs and this elaborate building; also, that the answer lies in the education of Mexican youth for the Defeat and Death of Ignorance.

Museo Nacional de Historia, Castillo de Chapultepec (Historical Museum). José Clemente Orozco in 1948 painted a fresco in La Sala de La Reforma of the National Museum of History in Chapultepec Castle. Allegorically, Orozco represents in one panel the history of the Reform Period under Benito Juárez and of the Empire of Maximilian.

The wall is dominated by a colossal portrait of Juárez painted on a background of fire. At one side a soldier holds in one hand a torch and in the other a chain with which he binds hands and feet of an archbishop, pictured as a vulture. Armed revolutionists are grouped on the other side under the Mexican flag, adorned with the eagle in control of the serpent.

251. José Clemente Orozco. Youth and Education. Entrance, Escuela Normal Superior, México, D.F.

Courtesy Fondo Editorial de la Plástica Mexicana

252. José Clemente Orozco. Juárez and Independent Mexico. Panel, Sala de México Independiente, Museo de Historia, México, D.F.

Across the bottom of the panel the mummy of Maximilian is being carried by his partisans (Plate 252).

This mural was the first of a series to be painted in Chapultepec Castle by different artists to symbolize successive periods of Mexican History.

Guadalajara, Jalisco (Site 26)

Cámara de Diputados, Palacio de Gobierno (State Capitol). In the dome of the Legislative Chamber of the State Capitol of Jalisco, Orozco has recorded the Great Legislation of the Mexican Revolution. Finished in 1949, the year of his death, this was the last of the great frescoes painted by Orozco.

Liberty and the Slaves he has illustrated by a figure of Father Hidalgo, who had led the Revolt from Spain in 1810, surrounded by chained slaves in agonized positions. Hidalgo writes the word *Libertad* as he gives the decree abolishing slavery, an act which occurred in Guadalajara in 1811.

The figure of José María Morelos, friend and disciple

of Hidalgo and the most important leader in the War of Independence, holds symbols of the Agrarian Laws.

Benito Juárez is shown with his Reform Laws of 1857, dispossessing the Church.

First Chief Carranza presents the Mexican Constitution of 1917, the first constitution to contain guarantees of workers' rights. This liberal constitution has been changed and added to through the years, because it is alive to the nation's needs, but essential articles are jealously guarded. Traditionally, Mexicans have been governed by law and have been inhospitable to personal rule. Orozco affirms here that the Mexican Revolution rests securely on Law.

México, D.F. (Site 1)

Multifamiliar Miguel Alemán, Avenida Coyoacán y Félix Cuevas (Federal Housing Project). In September, 1949, José Clemente Orozco had begun to draw a mural design upon a wall in the entrance court of the large Housing Project named for President Miguel Alemán, when death intervened. Orozco's design for Springtime shows a reclining female figure surrounded by other slightly drawn festive figures, which may be mythological. Spring had been among the first mural subjects essayed by Orozco.

A bronze memorial plaque with a death mask is placed beside this last work done by José Clemente Orozco.

Orozco has stated of mural painting: "It is the highest, the most logical, the purest, and the strongest form of painting. It is, furthermore, the most aloof, since it cannot become a source of personal wealth, nor can it be hidden for the sake of the privileged few. It is for the people. It is for *all*" (Quoted, Rodríguez: 1954, p. 139).

New Uses and New Materials Are Found for Murals: 1946–1964

The Second World War had found Mexico reclaiming her great natural resources and entering rapidly into the Technological Revolution of the twentieth century, to be won through education. The continuing mural development dramatizes the changing aspirations of the Mexican nation. Much important new construction undertaken by the government during Miguel Alemán's administration was designed to include murals, notably in buildings for Public Works, for services of Social Security, on exterior walls of the great complex of University City, and for Federal Housing Projects. With this planned development a whole new era of mural art has been initiated.

Because some frescoes of the contemporary mural movement had deteriorated from exposure to the weather and to the public, more permanent techniques were being developed. Various impervious materials have been used experimentally in the Instituto Politécnico, under direction of Francisco Gutiérrez. David Alfaro Siqueiros had long used modern commercial products, and he and other muralists collaborated with Gutiérrez in developing new plastic media for mural painting; these have caused a technical revolution. Orozco at this time created the great mural in the Open-Air Theatre of the National Normal School (described above), in which he initiated exterior mural decoration in new materials and techniques. Mosaic, at first used sparingly, has gradually been substituted by many muralists for painting, so as almost to outmode fresco. As exterior murals have been executed in durable materials, the decorations have grown to architectural dimensions. Especially is this true where mosaic of colored stone or of glass has been used, as in University City, the new home of Universidad Nacional Autónoma de México (UNAM), the oldest university in the New World.

ADORNMENT OF PUBLIC-SERVICE BUILDINGS

Public works, undertaken on a grand scale during the Presidency of Miguel Alemán, include mural decoration. The sites recorded here indicate various kinds of new media employed by Mexican muralists as they move into the Technological Age, which is creating its own art.

México, D.F. (Site 1)

Salto de los Aguas de Lerma, Parque de Chapultepec (Water Basin). Water, the chief concern of the people of Mexico through the ages, has been brought to the Valley of Mexico from beyond the western mountains by diversion of the Lerma River, to help meet the soaring needs of the City of Mexico. Diego Rivera was commissioned to decorate the receptacle for this water, which now pours with great force into the large basin sunk into the earth and enclosed by a chapel-like structure with a low vault.

The water enters the basin through a tunnel, above which Rivera painted two immense hands spilling water, as if to join the flowing stream. In great detail Rivera painted the floor of the receiving basin with currents of water bearing symbols of life in water: chemical forms, plant life, crustacea, vertebrates. A great circle in the center of the basin depicted a process of evolution. Around the margins of the reservoir Rivera painted various forms of plant and animal life, including most especially reptiles.

253. Diego Rivera. Woman. Salto de los Aguas de Lerma, México, D.F.

On the surrounding walls of the enclosure Rivera painted on one side a Negro Man with speech scrolls formed as question marks, on the other, a Mongolian Woman with Child (Plate 253), as being the original races. They rise from blue waves. Primitive people, animals, and a great variety of plant life bear witness to Earth's fecundity where there is water, and to suffering where there is drought. Miners appear to loosen rocks to enlarge the tunnel.

Rivera, in painting this receptacle for the life-giving water, used polystyrin as the medium upon an especially prepared cement surface. When the water from the Lerma River was released into the great basin, prepared with such care for its reception, the current proved too strong and the designs on the floor have dimmed. Frogs, turtles, crabs, and snakes escaped around edges to survive in full color with the paintings above the water line. Rivera painted the vault with rain clouds, storm, and lightning.

In a clearing before the structure that receives water from the Lerma River, Rivera designed a fountain with an immense cement figure of Tlaloc, the Rain God, sprawled in a shallow pool as if he had plunged from on high. Spare use of design in blue mosaic relieves the gray cement of the figure and of the convolutions of the pool's margins.

Atarasquillo, México (Site 39)

Escuela de Santa María (School). It is interesting to record that, as a form of payment for the water taken from the Lerma River, the Mexican government built new schools in Atarasquillo, near Toluca, for the villagers most affected. True to form, muralists Pablo O'Higgins and Ignacio Aguirre were commissioned to decorate these schools. In a fresco for the school of Santa María, O'Higgins shows figures of Hidalgo, Morelos, and Juárez towering above a school in this mountain landscape. Aguirre's fresco upstairs illustrates the Principle of Reforestation.

Escuela de San Mateo. In the school of San Mateo, O'Higgins painted symbols of Earth, Water, and the Harvest.

México, D.F. (Site 1)

Instituto Mexicano de Seguro Social, Paseo de la Reforma (Administration). Mural painting has accompanied the expansion of Social Security services in Mexico. In the wide loggia of the handsome, modern Social Security Administration Building a long panel over the centrally placed elevator shafts was designed for mural decoration. Jorge González Camarena has painted this panel; on one end he represents the Smelting of Precious Metals; on the other he shows reclining figures of an Aztec Warrior and a Spanish Conqueror being fused one into the other, also by fire, to produce Mexico Today.

For the entrance to Seguro Social, González Camarena designed polychrome sculptured figures.

On the tenth floor of this large building Federico Cantú painted two panels; in one of them Quetzalcoatl, Toltec God of Culture, presents gifts to the people of Mexico; in the other Maternity is the subject.

CREATION OF ARCHITECTURAL MURALS

Ciudad Universitaria (University City), D.F. (Site 40)

Through collaboration of many eminent Mexican architects, engineers, and artists, University City has grown from Mexican cultural roots into the Technological Age, modern materials and design meeting here with Early Mexican architectural and pictorial influences. Built solidly upon the volcanic rock of the Pedregal, this extensive arrangement of buildings for the National University, "daring in conception and brilliant in execution," was planned and built during the Presidency of Miguel Alemán. University City covers many acres, its buildings being spaced around recreation fields which were planned for spectacular performance, and which also afford long vistas. Mexico's mural art has become externalized in University City and achieves colossal dimensions, "as if addressed to the surrounding mountains." The decoration of these buildings initiates extensive use of mosaic and sculptured design, as this dramatically self-assertive environment has been created for Mexico's leaders of tomorrow.

Biblioteca Central. The Central Library of the University, an example of fully incorporated material, was designed by the artist-architect Juan O'Gorman. The four unbroken walls of this rectangular building are filled with designs in mosaic of stone and tile and colored cement, so as to appear like pages from a gigantic Aztec Codex; these symbolize Mexican Culture. The north and south walls are much less wide than the side walls. The north wall, built around the eagle and serpent, represents Mexico's Indigenous Past; the south wall, centered by the shield of Carlos V, symbolizes the Colonial Past; on the long west wall the shield of the National University stands for the Present; on the east wall the Atom, as symbol for the Future, is paired with Fire for Freedom of the Spirit. Seen from any direction the Library rises like ancient picture writings to dominate University City.

Instituto de Ciencias. José Chávez Morado has designed two mosaic decorations of brilliantly colored glass for buildings of the Science Institute. On a long wall of the School of Science, against a pyramidal background, he depicts the Return of Quetzalcoatl: In a boat formed of serpents, like the fabled raft on which he had departed, Quetzalcoatl-Ehecatl, God of Wind, is accompanied by figures that represent the cultural influences from Europe, Asia, and Africa, including a monk and an angel. All extend hands to produce the clear light of culture, that which survives on earth from human life. For the Science Auditorium the panel of the façade symbolizes the Conquest of Energy; the discovery of fire and its uses is shown as a tree of flame from which the *tigre*, as symbol of Mexico, leaps toward the Atom Star; human figures, male and female, carry torches to indicate the continuity of culture.

Instituto de Medicina. Francisco Eppens Helguera designed exterior murals in semisculptured, colored-stone mosaic for the Medical Institute. A head with three masks, to represent Indian, Spanish, and mestizo elements, accompanied by symbols of Mesoamerican gods, to symbolize Life and Death, decorates the west wall of the School of Medicine. The façade of the School of Dentistry shows other symbolic stone reliefs.

Estadio. Diego Rivera designed figures in gigantic scale around the base of the great flaring oval bowl of the University's Stadium, as if upholding it. Sculptured and incised and decorated with colored-stone mosaic, these forms symbolize Sports of Mexico through the Ages, including the great International Contests of the Present.

Rectorio. David Alfaro Siqueiros was the only artist who painted his mural in University City. It is upon a large wall of the Administrative Building, which can be seen from the freeway that encircles the Campus. Monumental figures in the foreground are boldly modeled; a crowd of students with banners fills the background as they struggle toward some common goal. The figures in this painting are designed to change for the passing observer. Siqueiros calls his mural, the People for the University and the University for the People. It was not completed.

México, D.F. (Site 1)

Multifamiliar Presidente Benito Juárez, Avenida Anza y Córdoba (Cooperative Housing Project). From

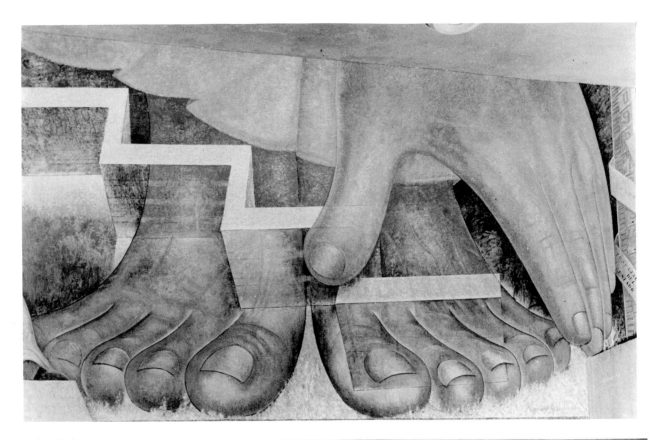

254. Xavier Guerrero. Construction of Public Housing (panel and detail). Vestibule, Central Building, Multifamiliar Benito Juárez, México, D.F.

1949 to 1952, while the decorations of University City were in progress, Carlos Mérida was making interesting exterior wall designs for a government-sponsored housing center, a cooperative for Civil Service employees named for the President of La Reforma, Benito Juárez.

Edificios tipo "C": Incorporated into façades of a group of related tall buildings in this great urban center, and spaced between series of windows, are relief-block panels of cement designed by Mérida. Each large square panel is filled by one or more highly stylized white figures that stand against backgrounds of vivid blue, yellow, red, or green. In semiabstract pattern Carlos Mérida represents gods, goddesses, and legends from Mayan and Aztec civilizations. Three-dimensional designs are built also into the exterior stair wells and columns of these units. Similar subjects from Meso-

264. David Alfaro Siqueiros. Díaz (The "Mural of the Hats"). Fifth Gallery, Museo Nacional de Historia (Castillo de Chapultepec), México, D.F.

american mythology decorate the large, well-lighted tunnel that connects the buildings.

Jardín de Niños: In the Children's Garden, Mérida has covered a large wall with concrete blocks painted in gay vinylite colors and arranged in abstract design.

Edificio Central: In 1953 Xavier Guerrero painted a mural panel above elevators in the vestibule of the Central Building of this large housing project. Guerrero's mural pictures the Construction of Public Housing (Plate 254). The white zigzag line that runs through the long panel is a "statistical curve" which shows the ups and downs of housing development in Mexico. But in spite of all efforts to house the people there are still those without shoes, pictured on the right side of the panel as huge bare feet standing in the midst of emerging walls, the body presumably that of Mother Mexico rising through the entire structure, with a helpful hand reaching downward. The middle section illustrates workers from the country helping in the construction of housing, which they themselves will receive later.

While Guerrero was painting this middle section two poor women were watching him. One asked the other the meaning of the painting, to which the barefoot woman replied, "Es un paisaje de trabajo" (It is a landscape of work).

This mural is executed in colored cement and pyroxylin.

Comisión Federal de Electricidad, Calle Ródano 14 (Federal Commission for Electricity). In 1952 Jesús Guerrero Galván painted a long wall in the Administration Building of the Electric Power Commission, a department which was nationalized in 1961. In this mural Guerrero Galván shows the conversion of natural forces into controlled electric power; he pictures, also, the many uses for electricity in modern life.

Commission buildings built elsewhere are being designed for mural decoration.

Mosaic Art Flourishes

Mexican murals have always been made where people pass or congregate. As government-sponsored mural art moved out of doors to decorate exterior walls, this public development proved to be contagious, and soon gaily colored decorations began to appear upon façades of theatres, banks, office buildings, hotels, restaurants, and homes, to enliven the appearance of streets in the City of Mexico.

Diego Rivera in 1953 designed the immense façade of El Teatro de los Insurgentes, executed in brilliant colored-glass mosaic, to dramatize the successive eras of Mexico's theatre, shown here in relation to the in-

Courtesy of Carlos Mérida. Photo by Alfonso Soto Soria.

255. Carlos Mérida. Detail of Mural in Venetian Mosaic. Hall, Reaseguras Alianza, México, D.F.

surgent leaders for whom the great Avenida Insurgentes is named.

In Mexico City the spread of federal services is most especially celebrated in the decoration of exterior walls of new administration buildings. An impressive use of polychrome stone mosaic for architectural decoration can be seen upon the walls of the modern Secretaría de Comunicaciones y Obras Públicas (Ministry of Communication and Public Works), where muralists Juan O'Gorman and José Chávez Morado have each covered three huge unbroken walls of this complex ten-story building with historic allegories. These are expressed in design derived from Mexican archeology, a convention of design to which mosaic lends itself with grace. The walls spread out like an opened codex to be read by passers-by. In Comunicaciones, as on other mosaic walls, incidents and heroes from Mexico's colorful history are related to the special services of the department in Mexico today, appearing here as different modes of communication.

Numerous artists have participated in the development of mosaic art in Mexico; many have contributed also to the invention of variations of mural techniques.

Carlos Mérida has created semiabstract and abstract mural decorations in various public and private buildings in Mexico City, Acapulco, and Guatemala City. These are executed either in mosaic (Plate 255), or Mérida has used silicate color on carved stone or cement for both exterior and interior mural design.

Xavier Guerrero, working with luminous color on designs of large figures incised into the high cement walls of Cine Ermita, has created most original interior decorations for this cinema theatre in Mexico City.

All over the country, as new buildings are constructed for the proliferating public services, mural decoration is an integral part of the design. In Nuevo Laredo one side of the new Water Works building displays the history of the development of potable water, including the individuals most responsible, executed in mosaic of brilliant color. A great fountain plays before this building to advertise its service.

Mural painters have been the creators also of Mexico's mosaic and sculptured decorations; however, these are not "painted walls" but constitute a subject apart from this monograph. As mural art has become architectural decoration, it is not the deeply personal voice that has waged the mural revolution of the twentieth century, but serves rather to celebrate and to consolidate the victories of the past.

Mural Painting Is Reaffirmed: 1950–1964

TAMAYO PAINTS IN MEXICO

In the meantime Rufino Tamayo had returned to Mexico after having achieved a reputation abroad as a modern muralist of distinction; he was acclaimed the fourth great Mexican muralist, now "Los Cuatro Grandes," and was invited to paint in Bellas Artes.

Tamayo deplored the technical rut into which he judged Mexican mural painting to be caught; also, he rejected mosaic art as an adequate medium of expression. "Tattooed buildings" he called these. He proposed that mural painting change with the changing time and begin to reaffirm its high office. Tamayo was recognized as the torch bearer for a new Mexican Mural Revolution, and he and Siqueiros were to dominate in mural painting, as Rivera and Orozco had done before.

México, D. F. (Site 1)

Palacio de Bellas Artes (Palace of Fine Arts). Rufino Tamayo painted two large movable panels for Bellas Artes, which were installed in 1951 and 1952. At this time the walls of the upper gallery that surrounds the high foyer of the Palace of Fine Arts had all been covered with mural paintings by Orozco, Rivera, and Siqueiros. At first Tamayo's panels were suspended over the foyer to face east and west between the painted walls; later, these were placed on the mezzanine walls directly below the murals by Rivera and Orozco.

Tamayo calls his semiabstract paintings Birth of Nationality (Plate 256) and Mexico Today (Plate 257). These murals have a life independent of the structure of the building; they create a new space of their own. Vinylite is the medium used.

Rufino Tamayo has written of the character of his work:

My painting is realistic because it tries to reduce forms to their essence. Those forms do not remain geometrical; they are forms of concrete objects and people. I do not want to reproduce the tree or the man but to "re-create" them. For me this is the function of art. And this "re-creation" is made by means of poetry. (Mural Painting of the Mexican Revolution, p. 260).

SIQUEIROS EXPERIMENTS WITH SPACE

México, D.F. (Site 1)

Hospital de la Raza, Jacarandas y Calzada Vallejo (Medical Institute). Far north in the city of Mexico, near Insurgentes Norte, this Social Security Medical Center, Hospital de la Raza, contains murals painted by David Alfaro Siqueiros in 1952, works in which he reaches a climax in visual experiment.

256. Rufino Tamayo. Birth of Nationality (detail). Panel, Palacio de Bellas Artes, México, D.F.

257. Rufino Tamayo. Mexico Today (detail). Panel, Palacio de Bellas Artes, México, D.F.

Courtesy Fondo Editorial de la Plástica Mexicana

258. David Alfaro Siqueiros. Women Workers (detail of wall). Foyer, Hospital de la Raza, México, D.F.

Courtesy Fondo Editorial de la Plástica Mexicana

259. David Alfaro Siqueiros. Hazards of Industry (detail). Foyer, Hospital de la Raza, México, D.F.

Upon the large curved wall of the foyer of Hospital de la Raza Siqueiros painted his theme, Victory of Science over Cancer, as an allegory of public health. Columns of joyous workers, one of women (Plate 258) and the other of men, proclaim the New Society, while Industrial Hazards are indicated by a dead workman conveyed on an assembly line (Plate 259). In this huge mural the perspective penetrates the wall and also projects into the space before it and above it; the design changes as the spectator moves. It has been described as "a shell binding the space it holds, and rather frightening" (Honingsberger: p. 114).

In this treatment of space Siqueiros carries farther his concept of mural painting that creates a physical world of its own. His treatment of a wall is entirely different from the classical respect for its integrity. As in previous work, Siqueiros has painted this mural in pyroxylin.

RIVERA PAINTS HIS LAST FRESCO

México, D.F. (Site 1)

Hospital de la Raza. After Siqueiros had created the disturbing mural in Hospital de la Raza, described above, Diego Rivera in 1953–1955 painted his last fresco on a movable wall in this same Medical Center. While still working here Rivera's health deteriorated and he knew that his time was limited; with waning strength he kept on painting. (Diego Rivera's death occurred in 1957).

In this mural Rivera represents the History of Medicine in Mexico. In the center of the large wall he has painted a stone idol of Tlazolteotl as Goddess of Medicine. Plumes decorate her head, and her skirt is covered with designs from the Codex Badiano, a book of medicinal herbs illustrated by an Aztec Scholar in 1542, the first book of pharmacy produced in the New World.

A blue sky across the panel shows a hot sun on the side of native medicine and a new moon on the side of modern medical science. The right side, as Aztec Medical Practice, is illustrated with many incidents: Childbirth, where a woman sings to the new-born babe and the conscious mother extends a hand; the Temazcal (native steam bath); Massage; also, more strenuous methods of treatment (Plate 260). Quetzalcoatl, Creator God, or his priest presides here, adorned with a huge headdress of paper (potent magic).

On the side of Modern Medicine a great crystal of cobalt is prominently displayed in the service of man, a source of help that was to fail Rivera. In successive divisions of the wall space medical technicians are pictured at work; in the upper level people of all ages group about a doctor and an administrator for attention; in the center a young girl holds a dove as symbol of peace, "without which there can be neither health nor progress." High trees frame the sides of the wall, their roots growing from Serpents of Earth which meet below the stone goddess in one human head, divided so as to symbolize both Life and Death.

DIFFERENT MEDIA USED

México, D.F. (Site 1)

Centro Médico, Avenida Cuauhtémoc y Central (Hospital and Laboratories). Called "The City of Health," this Social Security Medical Center, a complex of hospital and laboratory buildings, contains mural decorations both within and without.

David Alfaro Siqueiros, in the building dedicated to the study and treatment of cancer, in 1954 decorated the lobby with paintings that portray incidents of mankind's struggle against this disease (Plate 261). He depicts the Future Victory of Medical Science over Cancer parallel with social and political measures.

Luis Nishizawa, in the vestibule of the Surgical Hospital and on its principal staircase, painted frescoes to symbolize the need for air and water: Ehecatl, God of Air, and Tlaloc, God of Water, preside upon the stairway wall; Fruits of the Earth, Fire, and Medicine he portrays as ministering to Man.

José Chávez Morado, in sculptured colored stone, has covered the façades of the Pedagogy and Dormitory Buildings with designs to symbolize the History of Medicine in Mexico from early times until the present. Working nine horizontal panels in both high and low relief, Chávez Morado has covered immense areas of space, as well as of time and of human experience, with interpretations of the slow evolution of Medical Science.

REGIONAL MURAL PAINTINGS SPREAD

History has continued to be recorded in paintings not only in federal buildings but also in many state capitols, museums, and educational centers, where events are dramatized to remind the people of hard-won vic-

Courtesy Fondo Editorial de la Plástica Mexicana

260. Diego Rivera. Ancient Medicine (detail). Wall, Foyer, Hospital de la Raza, México, D.F.

tories of the past; also, to celebrate the local contributions to the history of Mexico.

Morelia, Michoacan (Site 27)

Universidad de Michoacan (State University). In 1953 David Alfaro Siqueiros painted a mural in the State University (formerly de San Nicolás) to commemorate the Bicentennial of the Birth of Miguel Hidalgo y Castillo, the Father of his Country. This is a ten-foot-square wall which Siqueiros painted in "luminous, three dimensional effect." It shows the Death of Father Hidalgo in 1811, as, standing before the firing

261. David Alfaro Siqueiros. Medical Science and Cancer (detail). Lobby, Centro Médico, México, D.F.

squad, he is being executed before his accuser, a bishop holding a standard topped by a cross. Below a Spanish Crown are printed these words:

Excommunication and death penalty for Miguel Hidalgo for professing and spreading exotic ideas partisan to the democratic French Revolution. For Social dissolution and trying to make Mexico independent of the Spanish Empire. In consequence, a traitor to his country.

Museo Regional (Museum). In 1952 Alfredo Zalce painted frescoes in the Regional Museum of Morelos to represent Defenders of National Integrity, in which Juárez and other heroes of modern Mexico are pictured amidst the people. A symbolic figure of Atomic Death rises in a panel that includes people from different parts of the Earth.

Federico Cantú and other artists have also painted in this Museum.

Palacio de Gobierno (State Capitol). From 1955 to 1957 Alfredo Zalce painted in the state Capitol of his native Michoacan, where he decorated the monumental stairway with frescoes to represent Liberators of Mexico. On this large wall the rebel priests, Hidalgo and Morelos, stand with swords in hand before massed workmen armed with spears and swords, while the bulwark of privilege is being set afire by a heroic figure protected only by a stone tied on his back. Also, continuing resistance to the Dictatorships of Santa Anna, the Empire of Maximilian, and of Porfirio Díaz is symbolized here.

For the Legislative Hall, Zalce has decorated the cupola with figures to indicate the Present Time in Mexico, as an intellectual and a worker clasp hands in fraternity.

Chilpancingo, Guerrero (Site 41)

Palacio de Gobierno (State Capitol). The four walls around the courtyard of the state Capitol of Guerrero have been painted by artists Luis Arenal, Roberto Cueva del Rio, and Gilberto Aceves Navarro, working in collaboration; in these murals the region's history is related symbolically to significant events in the history of Mexico.

Guanajuato, Guanajuato (Site 42)

Alhóndiga de Granaditas (National Monument). José Chávez Morado, native of Guanajuato, has painted a fresco in the Alhóndiga de Granaditas, a Baroque structure like a fort or castle, regarded as the Altar of Mexican Liberty, as here from the four corners of the high, forbidding walls were hung cages exposing the

heads of executed rebels, including Hidalgo, in order to intimidate insurgents.

Chávez Morado has painted the walls of one of the two stairways that rise from the large enclosed patio. Hidalgo, Father of his Country, Liberating the Slaves dominates the main wall; the Rebellion follows, as dark figures armed with sticks and tools shown against radiating light; the Colonial World is symbolized by a figure running with a broken sword; Present Dangers are represented as toppling structures and sweeping flames. The decoration extends over cupola and arches with figures that symbolize the continuity of Mexican History.

Poza Rica, Veracruz (Site 43)

Palacio Municipal (City Hall). Pablo O'Higgins in 1957 painted three large exterior murals for the new Municipal Palace in Poza Rica (Rich Well), the "petroleum capitol" of Mexico, situated in northern Veracruz.

The History of the Region begins here with the Ancient Totonacs and culminates with Nationalization of the Poza Rica Properties in 1938.

A new mural technique was used for these walls by Pablo O'Higgins. He painted the designs onto tiles which were fired in Monterrey and then shipped to Poza Rica for installation. This is a very different process from either painting directly on the wall, or from making a design to be executed by other hands.

As all walls measure about twenty feet in height and together these extend about one hundred forty feet in length, this mural is on a gigantic scale.

Other Cities

In recent years murals have been painted in various other state capitols throughout the country, a few among these being in Aguascalientes (Site 44) by Osvaldo Barra; in Campeche (Site 45) by José Chávez Morado; in Chihuahua (Site 46) by Manuel Piña Mora. In Dolores Hidalgo, Guanajuato (Site 47), the artist Jorge González Camarena has painted murals for an immense Monument to Mexico's Heroes of the Revolt from Spanish Rule.

The sites recorded are but examples of the voluminous mural painting that continues to flourish throughout Mexico under government patronage, its expression changing with moods and events of the time, as the walls continue to project the ideas and the values of the artists who paint them. Mexicans seem to believe that ideas can take their place in the common competitive market, and that artists can produce work of real value to the nation only if they are free in their expression. The contemporary movement had started in this spirit of valuing creative art for its own sake.

Through the years talented youths have been recognized and fostered, and succeeding administrations have kept these young artists supplied with small salaries. In return they dedicate themselves to creative work; also, they give some hours each week to awakening the talent latent in children of the schools. So this is an endlessly growing tale.

Murals in National Museums

México, D.F. (Site 1)

Museo de Artes e Industrias Populares (Museum of Popular Arts). Miguel Covarrubias, in his inimitable style, painted a mural for the Museum of Popular Arts as a design that shows the Geography of Mexican Popular Arts. High in an arched panel is painted a map of the land of Mexico, with the people of the various regions and their distinctive costumes and wares. Covarrubias shows a land teeming with the native life of today, not unlike a cornucopia of picturesque creative living. Above the land and against the area of the Gulf, toys from the various regions are painted to appear large—like *piñatas* hanging above the festive land.

Museo Nacional de Historia, Parque Chapultepec (Historical Museum). Historic Chapultepec Castle crowns "Grasshopper Hill" and overlooks the great surrounding forest and the City of Mexico. This Hill has seen the city grow from an island stronghold, traversed by canals in a great expanse of lakes, into a vast city that fills the valley almost as far as the eye can reach, while the lakes have disappeared. The storied Castle has become the National Museum of History. It has been called an open book for the people of Mexico. Objects of use, documents, graphic arts, sculptures, and paintings from the successive periods of Mexican history are shown in a series of galleries, recording the spirit and the style of the historic periods; these are augmented by mural paintings that record principal events from these eras.

Sala de la Conquista: The first gallery indicates the two great civilizations that have formed Mexico. A great map of Mesoamerica, with symbols of the indigenous cultures placed geographically, has been painted by José Reyes Mesa on one wall; a similar map of Spain at the time of the Conquest has been painted by Pedro Bosch Gimpera on another wall. A large mural painting by Jorge González Camarena expresses the violence of the clash between these two races as they came together in Mexico during the Conquest, and the fusion of the races that has followed.

Sala de México en la Colonia: Dedicated to Colonial Mexico, this gallery is decorated with a map of the City of Mexico as it existed at the end of the seventeenth century.

Sala de la Independencia: A circular wall, originally designed by Juan O'Gorman for Diego Rivera, following Rivera's death was painted by O'Gorman himself with a synthesis of history preceding the period of the Revolt, climaxed in the figure of Father Miguel Hidalgo. He carries the torch of freedom as he urges forward the various peoples of Mexico, represented in ascending tiers against a background of Mexican landscape. Birth of Mexican Nationality is the title of this mural.

Sala de México Independiente: This gallery dedicated to Mexico as an independent country contains the fresco by José Clemente Orozco (the first painted and described above), in which a huge head of Benito Juárez painted as if against fire and shown above the cadaver of Maximilian, symbolizes the Reform Period (Plate 248).

Sala de la Revolución Mexicana: The Gallery of the Mexican Revolution was assigned to David Alfaro Siqueiros, who had been a part of this Revolution almost from its inception. This mural was begun in 1957 and left unfinished in 1960, when Siqueiros was imprisoned for political activities.

266. Rufino Tamayo. Serpent and Jaguar (detail). Museo Nacional de Antropologia y Etnografía, México, D.F.

262. David Alfaro Siqueiros. Strike of Miners in Cananea. Fifth Gallery, Museo Nacional de Historia (Castillo de Chapultepec), México, D.F.

263. David Alfaro Siqueiros. Leaders of the Revolution (detail). Fifth Gallery, Museo Nacional de Historia (Castillo de Chapultepec), México, D.F.

265. Rufino Tamayo. Serpent and Jaguar. Panel, Museo Nacional de Antropología, México, D.F.

Entitled the Revolution against the Porfirio Díaz Dictatorship, the mural by Siqueiros is designed upon four panels placed at right angles to one another. The first section had not been painted at all but is marked with the basic lines of the composition. Another panel shows figures of soldiers and workers, to represent the Strike of Cananea, which was suppressed in 1906 by the Díaz regime (Plates 262, 263): this was the first of a succession of uprisings that initiated the Mexican Revolution of the twentieth century.

Seated in the center of the next panel, austere President Porfirio Díaz is surrounded by other gentlemen in top hats who bid for his attention. Women in large hats fill the foreground. Because of the great variety of kinds and shapes and colors of the hats shown here, this has been called the Panel of the Hats (Plate 264, color, p. 272).

Siqueiros was working on the fourth panel at the time of his arrest. Here he has painted portraits of nineteenth-century socialists.

The Gallery of the Mexican Revolution features the portraits of the men most responsible for the social and agrarian ideas of this Revolution.

Museo Nacional de Antropología, Parque de Chapultepec (Anthropological Museum). Below the Castle of Chapultepec, in which the National Museum of History is established, the great National Museum of Anthropology is newly built in Chapultepec Park to house the fabulous wealth of indigenous art that is constantly being recovered from archeological sites throughout Mexico. This Museum was built during the Presidency of Adolfo López Mateos, and it was opened in September of 1964 just before his term of office ended.

Various muralists were commissioned to paint panels distributed throughout the Museum's numerous galleries; of these only a few are noted here.

Foyer: Rufino Tamayo has painted a long panel in the foyer of the Museum in which he presents the Serpent and the Jaguar, or Tigre, ancient symbols of Mexico, fiercely battling (Plate 265). The oldest and the newest of Mexico come together in this brilliantly colored painting by Tamayo. Using vinylite as his medium, he has painted one end of the panel with an orange sun and a looped, green-feathered serpent upon a muted red background; upon the other end a rampant orange jaguar with spots and a yellow half-moon are shown contrasted against vivid blue. The confrontation in the center shows the jaguar grasping the serpent's head, as these snarling symbolic figures struggle with vicious fangs in this painting of today expressed in terms of Mexico's distant past. Color intensities exceed even those that have graced the ancient cities of Mesoamerica (Plate 266, color, p. 272).

Is this Science that is engaged with Tradition in such fiercely beautiful combat? Or is it Greed fighting with Ignorance, as symbolized by Orozco in Jiquilpan?

267. Pablo O'Higgins. Marriage Day of an Indian Girl. Panel, Tarascan Gallery, Museo Nacional de Antropología y Etnografía, México, D.F.

Or do these struggling figures symbolize Thought and Emotion trying to come to terms? Consulting our archeologist we are told that this mural represents the battle between the highland culture and the lowland culture: the Snake against the Jaguar.

Galleries: Pablo O'Higgins has painted three panels in the Museum, two for galleries devoted to the arts of Michoacan, and one for the gallery of the Tarahumaras of Chihuahua. As these exhibits represent both past and present cultural expression, O'Higgins has painted, in one panel for Cycles of Life, the Marriage Day of an Indian Girl in a Tarascan village (Plate 267), to record customs and crafts still extant among the people of this volcanic region.

One series of panels, painted by Leonora Carrington, pictures El Mundo Mágico de los Mayas ("The Magic World of the Mayas"). This has been reproduced in book form by the National Institute of Anthropology and History (INAH), the book containing also the preliminary studies for the panels. The paintings suggest the Mayas of the mountainous region of Chiapas accompanied by animals and other symbols of their past in an atmosphere of phantasy.

Alfredo Zalce and other artists have painted panels for this beautiful Museum in which Mexico celebrates her indigenous cultures. Each artist in his own way records some phase of Mexico's many-faceted heritage. Large or small in size, old or new in content, these panels are painted in great variety, with techniques to suit all tastes, but all express something of the enigma that is Mexico's cultural heritage.

What Next?

Posthumously, the murals painted for the Mexican government by José Clemente Orozco and Diego Rivera have been officially declared to be Mexico's National Heritage, thus insuring the preservation of this immense legacy of mural art for the nation.

The river of public art flows on, being constantly renewed as it draws into its current more lives and fresh talents and purposes. The mainstream persists in the new generation of muralists who have matured to paint in Mexico. The esthetic revolution of Rufino Tamayo continues. David Alfaro Siqueiros, using industrial materials and techniques, paints again.

As this story of Mexico's painted walls concludes, announcement comes from Mexico City that David Alfaro Siqueiros has been commissioned to paint "the largest mural ever attempted." It is planned to cover 18,500 square feet of space, or "ten times the area of the Sistine Chapel." Siqueiros' mural, to be painted in a building constructed especially for it adjacent to the hotel Casino de la Selva in Cuernavaca, has been commissioned by the industrialist Manuel Suárez. It will depict the artist's prophetic vision of the History of Mankind from the present through the foreseeable future. Siqueiros has established what he calls "the first mural factory" in Cuernavaca, with an assembly line for piece-by-piece execution of murals which are then lifted into place on the wall.

This record of Mexico's Mural Revolution of the Twentieth Century obviously must stop before the Mural Revolution is ended.

BIBLIOGRAPHY

EARLY MEXICO

The Period

Armillas, Pedro
1946 "Los Olmeca-Xicalanca y los sitios arqueológicos del suroeste de Tlaxcala." *Revista mexicana de estudios arqueológicos,* VIII, 137–146.
1948 "Fortalezas mexicanas," *Cuadernos americanos,* VIII, número 5, 143–163.
1950 "Visita a Copán," *Cuadernos americanos,* IX, número 4, 143–152.
1951 "Mesoamerican Fortifications," *Antiquities,* XXV, 77–86.

Benitez, José R.
1934 "Arqueología de Oaxaca, Morelia, y Zacatecas," *Monografías mexicanas.*

Bernal, Ignacio
1962 *Bibliografía de arqueología y etnografía: Mesoamerica y norte de México, 1514–1960* México, Instituto Nacional de Antropología e Historia.

Bliss, Robert Woods
1957 *Pre-Columbian Art.* New York, Phaidon Publisher.

Blom, Franz
1924 "Notes from the Maya Area," *American Anthropologist.*
1936 *The Conquest of Yucatán.* Boston, New York, Houghton Mifflin Company.

Burgoa, Friar
1934 *Geográfica descripción.* México, Talleres Gráficos
[1674] de la Nación.

Carnegie Institution of Washington
1927 *Bulletin,* I, No. 2.

Charlot, Jean
1939 *Art From the Mayas to Disney.* London, Sheed and Ward.
1940 "Twenty Centuries of Mexican Art," *Magazine of Art* (July), 398–405.
1945– "Prehistoric Quota in Mexican Murals," *Kenyon*
1946 *Review,* Kenyon College.
1950 *Art Making from Mexico to China.* New York, Sheed and Ward.

Covarrubias, Miguel
1946 *Mexico South: The Isthmus of Tehuantepec.* Knopf, New York.
1957 *Indian Art of Mexico and Central America.* New York.

Cummings, Byron C.
1923 "Cuicuilco, The Oldest Temple Discovered in North America," *Art and Archeology,* vol. 16, nos. 1–2.

Dutton, Bertha P.
1952 *The Toltecs and Their Influence on the Culture of Chichén Itzá.* Ann Arbor, University of Michigan Microfilms.

Ekholm, Gordon F.
1942 *Mayas y Olmecas. Parentesco del lenguaje de la Huasteca con la familia Mayance.* México, Sociedad mexicana de antropología.
1950 "Is American Indian Culture Asiatic?" *Natural History Magazine* (October), 344–351, 382.

Enciso, Jorge
1947 *Sellos del antiguo Mexico.* México, La Imprenta Policolor.

Fernández, Justino
1954 *Coatlicue: estética del arte indígena antigua.* México, Instituto de Investigaciones Estéticas, Universidad Nacional Autónoma de México.

Gann, Thomas
1925 *Mystery Cities: Exploration and Adventure in Labaantun.* London, Duckworth.

Guzmán, Eulalia
1933 *Carácteres esenciales del arte antiguo mexicano: su sentido fundamental.* México, University of Mexico.
1939 "The Art of Map Making among the Ancient Mexicans." *Imago Mundi,* III.

Jiménez Moreno, Wigberto
1954– "Síntesis de la historia pre-colonial del Valle de
1955 Mexico," *Revista mexicana de estudios antropológicos,* XIV, número 1, 219–236.
1959 *Esplendor del México Antiguo: Síntesis de la Historia Pretolteca de Mesoamérica.* Centro de Investigaciones Antropológicas de México. (Maps).

Joyce, Thomas A.
1927 *Mayan and Mexican Art.* London, "The Studio," Ltd.
1929 "The Art of the Maya," *Bulletin, Carnegie Institution of Washington,* I, No. 36.

Martí, Samuel
1961 *Canto, danza y música precortesianos.* México, Fondo de Cultura Económica.

Morley, Sylvanus Griswold
1911 "Ancient Temples and Cities of the New World: Chichén Itzá, Uxmal, Copán, Quiriguà, Tuloom," *Bulletin, Pan American Union,* XXXII.

Müller Jacobs, Florencia,
1962 "Exploración Arqueológica en Huapalcalco: Quinta Temporada, 1959," *Anales del I.N.A.H.,* Tomo XV, pp. 75–97.
1963 Reprint.

Museum of Modern Art, New York
1940 *Twenty Centuries of Mexican Art.* New York.

Paddock, John
1959 "Tomorrow in Ancient Mesoamerica," *The Texas Quarterly,* II, No. 1, 78–98.

Peñafiel, Antonio
1885   *Nombres Geográficos de México: de los nombres de lugar pertineciente al idioma Nahuatl.* México, Secretaría de Fomento.

Pijoán, José
1946   "Sumna artes: historia general del arte," *Arte precolombino mexicano y maya.* X.

Piña Chan, Ramón
1955   *Las culturas preclásicas de la cuenca de México.* México, Fondo de Cultura Económica.

Sejourné, Laurette
1954   "El mensaje de Quetzalcoatl," *Cuadernos americanos,* LXXVII, número 5 (septiembre–octubre), 159–172.
1959   *Un palacio en la ciudad de los dioses: Teotihuacán.* México.

Stirling, Matthew W.
1947   "On the Trail of La Venta Man," *National Geographic Magazine,* XCI (February), 137–172.

Vaillant, George C.
1941   *Aztecs of Mexico: Origin, Rise and Fall of the Aztec Nation.* Garden City, New York, Doran Company.

Westheim, Paul
1950   *Arte antiguo de Mexico.* México, Fondo de Cultura Económica.
1957   *Ideas fundamentales del arte prehispánico en Mexico.* México, Fondo de Cultura Económica.

Wolf, Eric
1959   *Sons of the Shaking Earth.* Chicago, University of Chicago Press.

Chronicles

Acosta, José de
1940   *Historia natural y moral de las índias.* México, Fondo de Cultura Económica.

Alva Ixtlilxochitl, Fernando de
1952   *Obras históricas.* México, Editorial Nacional, 2 volumes.

Barlow, Robert
1945   "La crónica 'X'," *Revista mexicana de estudios antropológicos,* VII, números 1, 2, 3.

Durán, Fray Diego
1867– *Historia de las indias de Nueva España e Islas*
1880   *de Tierra Firme.* México, Imprenta de J. M. Andrade y F. Escalante.
1964   *The Aztecs: The History of the Indies of New Spain.* Ignacio Bernal (introd.), Doris Heyden and Fernando Horcasitas (eds. and transs.).

Fondo de Cultura Económica
1947   *Popol Vuh.* México, Editorial de Adrián Recinos.

Kingsborough, Viscount Edward
1830– *Antiquities of Mexico.* London, A. Aglio, 9 vol-
1848   umes.

Landa, Diego de
1938   *Relación de las cosas de Yucatán.* México, Editorial P. Robredo.

Motolinía (Fray Toribio de Benavente)
1951   *Historia de los indios en la Nueva España.* México, Editorial Chávez Hayhoe.
1951   *Motolinía's History of the Indians of New Spain.* Washington, D.C., Academy of American Franciscan History.

Ramírez, Códice
1944   *Relación del origin de los indios que habitan esta Nueva España, según sus historias.* México, Editorial Leyenda.

Sahagún, Fray Bernadino de
1956   *Historia general de las cosas de Nueva España.* México, Editorial Porrúa, 4 volumenes.
1950– *Florentine Codex.* Santa Fe, School of American
1963   Research.

Tezozómoc, Fernando Alvarez
1944   *Crónica mexicana.* México, Editorial Leyenda.
1949   *Crónica Mexicoyotl.* México, Universidad Nacional Autónoma de México.

Torquemada, Juan de (1613)
1723   *Primera, segunda, tercera, parte de los viente i un libros rituales i monarchía indiana.* Madrid, N. Rodríguez Franco.

Tovar, Juan de
"Historia de la venida de los indios." (Códice Ramírez).

The Paintings

Acosta, Jorge R.
1945   "La cuarta y quinta temporadas de exploraciones arqueológicas en Tula, Hidalgo: 1943–1944," *Revista mexicana de estudios antropológicos,* VII, 23–65.
1960   "Técnica actual usada en la era prehispánica," *Boletín: Instituto Nacional de Antropología e Historia* (October).

Armillas, Pedro
1947   "La serpiente emplumada, Quetzalcoatl y Tlaloc," *Cuadernos americanos,* XXXI (enero–febrero), 161–178.

Batres, Leopoldo
1906   *Teotihuacán; ó la ciudad sagrada de los Tolteca.* México, Imprenta de Hull.

Bernal, Ignacio
1950   "Compendio de arte mesoamericana," *Enciclopedia mexicana de arte,* No. 7.
1958   "Introducción," *México: Pinturas prehispánicas,* 11–21. UNESCO World Art Series X, New York Graphics Society. Large colored photographs from Bonampak.
1963   "Mexican Wall Paintings of the Maya and Aztec Periods." Mentor-UNESCO Art Book, New

American Library of World Literature. Small colored photographs.
1963 *Teotihuacán: Descubrimientos, Reconstrucciones.* Instituto Nacional de Antropología e Historia, México.

Beyer, Hermann
1922 "La ligadura de los Tunes: Notas acerca de las pinturas murales de Santa Rita, Honduras Británica," *Sociedad científica de "Antonio Alzate," México: Memorias,* XXXIX, Nos. 9–12, 519–525.

Bliss, Robert Woods
1947 *Indigenous Art of the Americas: Collection of Robert Woods Bliss.* Washington, D.C., National Gallery of Art.

Blom, Frans and Oliver LaFarge
1926 *Tribes and Temples: A Record of the Expedition to Middle America Conducted by the Tulane University of Louisiana in 1925.* New Orleans, The Tulane University of Louisiana.

Breton, Adela C.
1911 "The Wall Paintings at Chichén Itzá." Quebec Congress of Americanists, 1906. Reprinted in *Man, Journal of Royal Anthropological Institute.*
1912 "Paintings and Sculpture in Mexico and Central America," *Actas del XVII Congreso Internacional de Americanistas,* pp. 245–247.

Caso, Alfonso
1927 "Las ruinas de Tizatlán, Tlaxcala," *Revista mexicana de estudios históricos,* I, número 4, 1927.
1928 "Los jeroglíficos de Tenayuca, México," *Revista mexicana de estudios históricos,* II, número 5, 141–162.
1932 "Monte Albán, Richest Archeological Find in America," *National Geographic,* CXII (October).
1936 *La religión de los Aztecas.* México, Imprenta Mundial.
1938 *Exploraciones en Oaxaca: quinta y sexta temporadas, 1936–1937* (Instituto Panamericano de Geografía e Historia, Publicación número 34), México, Impreso en la Editorial Cultura.
1940 "Pre-Spanish Art," *Twenty Centuries of Mexican Art,* 23–30. Museum of Modern Art, New York.
1942 "El paraíso terrenal en Teotihuacán," *Cuadernos americanos,* VI, número 6 (noviembre-diciembre), 127–136.
1958 *The Aztecs: People of the Sun.* Norman, University of Oklahoma Press.

Castro Leal, Antonio
1940 "Introduction," *Twenty Centuries of Mexican Art,* 14–20. Museum of Modern Art, New York.

Catherwood, Frederick
1844 *Views of Ancient Monuments in Central America, Chiapas and Yucatán.* New York, Bartlett and Welford.

Charlot, Jean
1928 "Nota sobre la pintura mural de los Mayas," *Forma,* número 5.
1935 "Maya Art," *American Magazine of Art* (July).

1938 "A XII Century Mayan Mural," *American Magazine of Art* (November), 624–629.

Du Solier, Wilfrido
1939 "Una representación pictórica de Quetzalcoatl en una cueva," *Revista mexicana de estudios antropológicos,* III, número 2 (mayo-agosto), 129–141.
1946 "Primer fresco mural huasteco," *Cuadernos americanos,* XXX, número 6, 151–159.

Fernández, Miguel Angel
1935 "Estudio de la pintura en la pirámide de Tenayuca," *Tenayuca* (*Buletin,* Secretaría de Educación Pública), pp. 103–105.
1945 "Las ruinas de Tulum II," *Anales del Instituto Nacional de Antropología e Historia,* I, 95–106.

Gamio, Manuel
1922 "La población del valle de Teotihuacán," *Ethnos: Revista dedicada al estudio y mejoría de la población indígena de México,* II, número 2, 78–85.

Gamio y Marquina, I.
1926 "Teotihuacán y casa de barrios." México, Secretaría de Educación Pública.

Gann, Thomas
1901 *Mounds in Northern Honduras.* Washington, D.C., Bureau of American Ethnology.

García Payón, José
1946 "Los monumentos arqueológicos de Malinalco, Estado de México," *Revista mexicana de estudios antropológicos,* VIII, números 1–3 (enero-diciembre), 5–63.

"Historia Tolteca-Chichimeca" or "Anales de Cuahtinchán." (Codex, 1544)
1937 Konrad Preuss und Ernest Mengin (German edition).
1947 Heinrich Berlin y Silvia Rendon (Spanish edition).
1947 Porrua e Hijos (Mexican edition).

Jiménez Moreno, Wigberto
Códice de Yanhuitlán. México, Secretaría de Educación Pública.

Kelemen, Pal
1943 *Medieval American Art.* New York, 2 volumes.

Lehman, Walter
1922 *The History of Ancient Mexican Art.* New York, Brentanos.
1941 *Una elegía tolteca.* México, Sociedad Alejandro Humboldt.

LePlongeon, Augustus
1886 *Sacred Mysteries among the Mayas and the Quiches 11,500 Years Ago . . .* New York, R. Macoy.
1896 *Queen Moo and the Egyptian Sphinx.* New York, The Author.

Linné, Sigvald
1942 *Mexican Highland Cultures.* Stockholm, The

Ethnographical Museum of Sweden (Publication number 7).

Lizardi Ramos, Cesar
1945 "Tetitla," *Excelsior.*
1960 "La pintura mural en mesoamerica," *Excelsior,* September 4, 1960.
1963 "La Pintura Teotihuacana," *Excelsior,* Sección de rotograbado, 24 de noviembre.

Lothrop, Samuel
1903 *Paintings of Uaxactún.* Cambridge, Peabody Museum of American Archaeology and Ethnology.
1924 *Tulum:An Archeological Study of the East Coast of Yucatán.* Washington, D.C., Carnegie Institute of Washington (Publication No. 335).

Maler, Teobert
1901– *Researches in the Central Portion of the Usumat-*
1911 *sintla Valley: Report of Explorations for the Museum, 1898–1900.* Cambridge, Peabody Museum of American Archaeology and Ethnology.

Margain, Carlos R.
1950 "Los Mayas ayer y hoy: Bonampak," *México en el arte,* IX, 36–54.
1952 ———. Edition speciale en Français, México, Talleres Gráficos de la Nación.

Marquina, Ignacio
1928 *Estudio arquitectónico comparativo de los monumentos arqueológicos de México.* México, Instituto Nacional de Antropología e Historia.
1934 *Cholula.* XVIII Congreso de Americanistas.
1951 *Arquitectura prehispánica.* México, Instituto Nacional de Antropología e Historia.

Mason, Gregory
1927 *Silver Cities of Yucatán.* New York, G. P. Putnam's Sons.

Maudslay, Alfred P.
1889– *Biología centrali-americana: or Contributions to*
1892 *the Knowledge of the Fauna and Flora of Mexico and Central America.* London.
"Peabody Copy of Tiger's 'Battle' Chichén Itzá, Color Decorations in Copan."

Morley, Sylvanus Griswold
1917 "The Ruins of Tuloom," *American Museum Journal,* XVII, No. 3, 190–204.
1946– *The Ancient Maya.* Palo Alto, California, Stan-
1947 ford University Press. México, Talleres de Gráfica Panamericana.

Morris, Ann, Earl Morris and Jean Charlot
1931 *The Temple of the Warriors at Chichén Itzá.* Washington, D.C., Carnegie Institution of Washington.

Noguera, Eduardo
1934 "Xochicalco," *Guía Morelos.* México, Instituto Nacional de Antropología e Historia.
1936 "El arte de la pintura maya y azteca," *México del día* 15 de octubre, México.
1939 "Memorias del XXVII Congreso Internacional de Americanistas," II, 214.

1945 "Exploraciones en Xochicalco," *Cuadernos americanos,* XIX, número 1 (enero-febrero), 119–157.

Pach, Walter
1924 "Greatest American Artists: Work of Aztecs, Toltecs, and Mayas," *Harper's Magazine* (January).
1926 "L'Art au Mexique," *L'Amour de l'Art* (September).

Péñafiel, Antonio
1890 *Monumentos del arte mexicano antiguo; ornamentación, mitología, tributos y monumentos.* Berlin.
1900 *Teotihuacán: estudio histórico y arqueológico.* México.

Ruz Lhuillier, Alberto
1945 *Guía arqueológica de Tula.* México, Ateneo Nacional de Ciencias y Artes de Mexico.

San Francisco, Fray Bernardo de (author and trans.)
1891 *Historia de los mexicanos por sus pinturas.* (Codex, 1547) J. García Icazbalceta (ed.). *Nueva colección de documentos para la historia de México,* III.

Séjourné, Laurette
1954 "El mensaje de Quetzalcoatl," *Cuadernos americanos,* LXXVII, número 5 (septiembre–octubre), 159–172.
1959 *Un palacio en la ciudad de los dioses: Teotihuacán.* México.
1963 "Exploración de Tetitla, Febrero–Octubre, 1963," *Teotihuacán.* Instituto Nacional de Antropología e Historia, México.

Seler, Eduard
1902 *Gesammelte Abhandlungen zur Amerikanischen Sprach-und Alterthumskunde.* Berlin, A. Asher and Company.
1904 *Wall Painting in Mitla: A Mexican Picture Writing in Fresco.* Bulletin 28, Bureau of American Ethnology, Washington, D.C.
1913 "Similarity of Design of Some Teotihuacán Frescos and Certain Mexican Pottery Objects," *International Congress of Americanists: Proceedings of the XVIII Session,* 194–202.

Spence, Lewis
1922 *The Gods of Mexico.* London, T. F. Unwin, Ltd.

Spinden, Herbert J.
1913 *A Study of Mayan Art: Its Subject Matter and Historical Development.* Cambridge, Peabody Museum of American Archaeology and Ethnology, Volume VI.
1931 *Indian Symbolism.* New York, American Museum of Natural History.
1957 *Mayan Art and Civilization.* Indian Hill, Colorado, Falcon's Wing Press.

Stephens, John L.
1841 *Incidents of Travel in Central America, Chiapas, and Yucatán.* New York, Harper and Brothers.
1843 *Incidents of Travel in Yucatán.* New York, Harper and Brothers.

Thompson, Edward H.
1904   *Archaeological Research in Yucatán.* Cambridge, Memoirs of the Peabody Museum of American Archaeology and Ethnology.
1905   "The Mural Paintings of Yucatán," *International Congress of Americanists XIII Session in New York in 1902,* XIII, 189–192.

Thompson, J. Eric S.
1934   *Sky Bearers, Colors and Directions in Maya and Mexican Religions.* Publication No. 436, Washington, D.C., Carnegie Institute of Washington.

Toscano, Salvador
1940   "La pintura mural precolombino de México," *Boletín bibliográfico de antropología americana,* I, número 4.
1944   *Arte precolombino de Mexico y de la América Central.* México, Universidad Nacional Autónoma de México, Instituto de Investigaciones Estéticas.
1946   "La pintura mural," *Mexico prehispánico,* Editorial Emma Hurtado, 552–575.
1946   "Arte precolombino del occidente de Mexico," *El arte y la historia del occidente de México,* 9–33.
1954   "Los murales prehispánicos," *Artes de Mexico,* número 3.

Totten, George Oakley
1926   *Maya Architecture.* Washington, D.C., The Maya Press.

Tozzer, Alfred M.
1910   "Maya and Toltec Figures at Chichén Itzá," *Congrés Internacional des Américanistes,* XXIII, 155.

UNESCO World Art Series, X
1958   *Mexico: Pre-Hispanic Painting.* New York, New York Graphic Society. (Bonampak Paintings in color.)

Vaillant, George C.
1928   "The Native Arts of Middle America," *Natural History,* XXVIII, 562–576.
1935   *Artists and Craftsmen of Ancient Central America.* New York, American Museum of Natural History.
1939   "By Their Arts You Shall Know Them," *Natural History,* XLIII, 268–277.

Villagra Caleti, Agustín
1949   *Bonampak, la ciudad de los muros pintados.* México, Instituto Nacional de Antropología e Historia.
1951   "Las pinturas de Atetelco en Teotihuacán," *Cuadernos Americanos,* LV, número 1 (enero-febrero), 153–162.
1952   "Teotihuacán, sus pinturas murales," *Anales del Instituto Nacional de Antropología e Historia,* V, 67–74.
1954   "Las pinturas de Tetitla, Atetelco e Ixtapantongo" in "La pintura mural en México," *Artes de México,* III (marzo y abril), 39–45.
1954   "Pinturas Rupestres 'Matéo H. Saldaña' Ixtapantongo, Estado de México," *Caminos,* IX, 6–10.
1961   "Los murales de Atetelco, pórtico 3." México,

Boletín del Instituto Nacional de Antropología e Historia.

Von Hagen, Victor W.
1946   "F. Catherwood, Architect," *Historical Society Quarterly* (January), 17–29.

Weittaner, Roberto J.
1947   "Exploración arqueológica en Guerrero," *Cuarto Reunion de Mesa Redonda. El occidente de México.* pp. 77–85.

Willard, Theodore A.
1926   *The City of the Sacred Well . . .* New York and London, The Century Company.

COLONIAL MEXICO

The Period

Casas, Fray Bartolomé de las
1909   *Apologética historia de las Indias.* Madrid, vide
[1561]   McNutt.

Clavijero, Abate Francisco Xavier
1844   *Historia antigua de Mexico.* México, Imprenta de Lara.

García Icazbalceta, Joaquín
1881   *Fray Juan de Zumárraga, primer obispo y arzobispo de México.* México, Buenos Aires, Espasa-Calpa, Argentina, S.A.

Gómara, Francisco López de
1870   *Conquista de México.* México, Imprenta de I. Escalente y ca.

Grijalva, Juan de
1624   *Crónica de la orden de N. P. San Agustín en las provincias de la Nueva España en cuatro edades desde el año 1533–1592.* México, En el religiosisimo convento de San Agustín, y imprenta de Ioan Ruyz, 1924 (2nd ed.), México, Imprenta Victoria.

Keen, Benjamin
1955   *Readings in Latin-American Civilization: 1492 to the Present.* Boston, Houghton Mifflin.

McNutt, Francis
1908   *Fernando Cortés: The Five Letters of Relation to the Emperor Charles V.* New York, 2 volumes.
1909   *Bartholomew de las Casas: His Life, His Apostolate, and His Writings.* New York, G. P. Putnam's Sons.

Mendietta, Gerónimo de
1870   *Historia eclesiástica indiana.* México, Editorial
1945   García Icazbalceta, México, Editorial S. Chávez
(2nd ed.) Hayhoe.

Prescott, William H.
1911–   *The Conquest of Mexico.* New York, E. P. Dutton and Company, 2 volumes.
1913

Torquemada, Juan de
1943– *Monarquía indiana.* México, S. Chávez Hayhoe,
1944   3 volumes.

Wolfe, Eric
1959   *Sons of the Shaking Earth.* Chicago, University of
Chicago Press.

Zavala, Silvio
1937   *La "Utopia" de Tomas Moro en la Nueva España.*
México, J. Porrúa e hijos.
1941   *Ideario de Vasco de Quiroga.* México, El Colegio
de Mexico.

The Paintings

Angulo Iniguez, Diego
1945   *Historia de arte hispanoamericana.* Barcelona,
Salvat Editores, S.A., Volume I.

Atl, Dr.   see Murillo, Gerardo

Azcue Mancera, Luis
1940   *Catálogo de edificios coloniales de Hidalgo.* México, Apuntes geográficos e históricos.

Barlow, Robert W.
1945   "Una pintura de la conquista en el templo de Santiago Tlatelolco," *Tlatelolco a través de los tiempos,* VI, 54–60.
1949   *The Extent of the Empire of the Culhua-Mexica.*
Berkeley, University of California Press.

Baxter, Sylvester.
1901   *Spanish-Colonial Architecture in Mexico.* Boston,
J. B. Millet.

Blom, Franz
1936   *The Conquest of Yucatán.* Boston, Houghton Mifflin Company.

Calders, P.
1945   *Acolman, un convento agostino del siglo XVI.*
México, Editorial Atlante.

Carrillo y Gariel, Abelardo
1944   *Las galerías de pintura de la academia de San
Carlos.* México, Imprenta Universitaria.
1946   *Técnica de la pintura colonial.* México, Imprenta
Universitaria.

Charlot, Jean
1945   "El San Cristóbal de Santiago Tlatelolco, pa-
limpsesto plástico," *Memorias de la Academia de
la Historia,* IV, número 3.
1945   Reprint: *Tlatelolco a través de los tiempos,* V.
1950   *Art Making From Mexico to China.* New York,
Sheed and Ward.

Chávez, Fr. Fidel
1946   *Tlatelolco.* México.

*Chimalpopoca Códice, Anales de Cuauhtitlán, y leyenda de
los soles.* Traducción directa de Nahuatl: Primo
Feliciano Velasquez. Universidad Nacional Autónoma de Mexico, Instituto de Historia. México.

Cortés, Antonio
1922   Chapter II, "Acolman," *La población del Valle de
Teotihuacán.* México.

Cóuto, José Bernardo
1889   *Diálogo sobre la historia de la pintura en México.*
México, Oficina tipográfica de la Secretaría de
Fomento.

Cuevas, Mariano
1921   *Historia de la iglesia en México.* Tlalpan, D.F.,
México, Imprenta del asilo "Patricio Sanz."

Del Barrio Lorenzot, Francisco
1921   *Compendio de las ordinanzas de gremios de la
Nueva España, 1557.* México, Talleres Gráficos
de la Nación.

Del Paso y Troncoso, Francisco
1891   "Notas de pinturas indígenas." México, Paz, *In-
(2nd ed.) formación . . . culto de Nuestra Señora de Guadalupe: sermón que predicó Fr. Francisco de Busta-
mante.

Díaz Barroso, José
1921   *El arte en la Nueva España.* México.

Díaz del Castillo, Bernal
*Historia verdadera de la conquista de la Nueva
España.*
1568   (Archives of Guatemala).
1632   Madrid, Imprenta del Reyno.
1800   London. Maurice Keatings (trans.).
1908   London, A. P. Maudslay.
1956   New York.

Enciso, Jorge
1938   "El convento de Actopan," *Archivo español de
arte y arqueología,* XI, número 35 (enero-abril),
67–71.
1939   *Edificios coloniales, artísticos e históricos de la
República de Mexico que han sido declarados
monumentos.* Universidad Nacional Autónoma de
México, Instituto de Investigaciones Estéticas.

Estrada, Género
1935   *Algunos papeles para la historia de las bellas
artes en Mexico.* México.

Fernández, Justino
1940   *Catálogo de-construcciones religiosas del Estado
de Hidalgo.* México, Secretaría de Hacienda, Talleres Gráficos de la Nación.

García Granados Códice
El señorio de Atzcapotzalco. México, Muséo Nacional de Arqueología.

García Granados, Rafael and Luis McGregor
1934   *Huejotzingo: la ciudad y el convento franciscano.*
México, Talleres Gráficos de la Nación.
1935   "Capillas de indios en Nueva España, 1530–
1605," *Archivo español de arte y arqueología,* XI,
número 35 (enero–abril), 3–29.
1939   "Nómina de los santos conventos franciscanos,"
Investigaciones históricas, I, número 2, 170–176.

BIBLIOGRAPHY

Gates, William (ed. and trans.)
1937 *Yucatán before and after the Conquest.* Baltimore, The Maya Society, Publication 20, 2 volumes.

Gómez de Orozco, Federico
1927 "Monasterios de la Orden de San Agustín en Nueva España," *Revista mexicana de estudios históricos,* I, número 1 (enero–febrero), 40–54.

Gorbea Trueba, José
1960 "Las pinturas murales de Ixmiquilpan." México, Instituto Nacional de Antropología e Historia.
1961 "Los frescoes de la catedral de Cuernavaca," *Boletin, Instituto Nacional de Antropología e Historia,* (abril).
1961 "Culhuacán." México, Instituto Nacional de Antropología e Historia.

Instituto de Investigaciones Estéticas, Universidad Nacional Autónoma de Mexico.
1938 "Planos de la ciudad de México, siglos XVI y XVII," *Estudios históricos.* Collab. M. Toussaint, F. Gómez Orozco, J. Fernández.

Islas García, Luís
1946 *Las pinturas al fresco del Valle de Oaxaca.* México, Editorial Clásica.
1962 "Las murales de Cuernavaca," *Excelsior* (febrero 12).

Jiménez Moreno, Wigberto
1940 "Códice de Yanhuitlán." México, Museo Nacional de México.

Kubler, George
1948 *Mexican Architecture of the Sixteenth Century.* New Haven, Yale University Press, 2 volumes.

Linné, Sigvald
1948 *El Valle de México en 1550. Un estudio del mapa de Upsala, Sweden.* Stockholm, Esselte.

Marquina, Ignacio and Antonio Cortés
1925 Iglesia y convento de San Juan Acolman. México.

McGregor, Luis and García Granados
1934 *Huejotzingo: la ciudad y el convento franciscano.* México, Talleres Gráficos de la Nación.
1947 *Monografía de Actopan.* México, Universidad Nacional Autónoma de México, Instituto Nacional de Investigaciones Estéticas.

Mercadío-Miranda, P. José
1950 *Historia del Santuario de Atotonilco, Guanajuato.* México, privately published.

Moyssén, Xavier
1964 "Tecamachalco y el Pintor Indígena, Juan Gersón," *Anales del Instituto de Investigaciones Estéticas,* No. 33 (Illustrated). Universidad Nacional Autónoma de México, México. 23–39.

Murillo, Gerardo (Dr. Atl)
1924 *Iglesias de México.* México, Publicaciones de la Secretaría de Hacienda.

Pérez Salazar, Francisco
1923 *Algunos datos sobre la pintura en Puebla en la época colonial.* México, Talleres Gráficos de la Nación.
1939 "Algunos datos para la historia de la pintura en Puebla," *Memorias de la Sociedad Científica 'Antonio Alzate,'* XXXXI, números 5, 6.

Revilla, Manuel G.
1893 *El arte en Mexico en la época antigua y durante el gobierno virreinal.* México, Oficina tipográfica de la Secretaría de Fomento.
1923 ———. México, Porrúa Hermanos.

Ricard, Robert
1933 *La "Conquete Spirituelle" du Mexique.* Paris, Institut d'ethnologie.
1947 *La conquista espiritual de Mexico: 1523–1572.* México, Editorial Jus. Angel María Garibay, translator.

Romero de Torreros, Manuel
1922 *Historia sintética del arte colonial de México.* México, Porrúa Hermanos.

Salado Alvarez, Ana
1961 "Cuernavaca cathedral," *Excelsior* (febrero 20).

Sotomayor, Arturo
1962 "Culhuacan," *Novedades* (gravure section).
1962 "Tlayacapan," *Novedades* (gravure section).

Steck, Francis B.
1936 "The First College in America, Santa Cruz de Tlatelolco," *The Catholic Educational Review* (October, gravure section).
1944 *El primer colegio de América, Santa Cruz de Tlatelolco.* México, Centro de Estudios Franciscanos.

Tablada, José Juan
1927 *Historia del arte en México.* México, Compañia Nacional Editora "Aguilas," S.A.

Toussaint, Manuel
1927 "Pintura colonial; notas sobre Andrés de la Concha," *Revista mexicana de estudios históricos,* I, número 1 (enero-febrero), 26–39.
1927 *Arquitectura religiosa de la Nueva España durante el siglo XVI.* México.
1927 "Un templo cristiano sobre el palacio de Xicotencatl," *Revista mexicana de estudios históricos,* I, número 4 (julio–agosto), 173–180.
1932 "Pinturas coloniales en Tecamachalco," *Revista de revistas,* XXII, número 1168 (9 octubre).
1934 *Catálogo de pinturas, Muséo Nacional de Artes Plásticos.* Sección colonial.
1936 *La pintura en México durante el siglo XVI.* México, Imprenta Mundial.
1938 *Planos de la ciudad de México: siglos XVI y XVII.* México, Impreso en los talleres de la editorial Cultura.
1949 *Arte colonial en Mexico.* México, Universidad Nacional Autónoma de Mexico, Instituto de Investigaciones Estéticas.

Velázquez Chávez, Agustín
1939 *Tres siglos de pintura colonial mexicana.* México, Editorial Polis.

Von Wuttenau, Felix
1940 *Tepozotlán*. México, privately published.

Weismann, Elizabeth Wilder
1950 *Mexico in Sculpture, 1521–1821*. Cambridge, Harvard University Press.
1950 "Stone Sculpture in Colonial Mexico," *Magazine of Art*, (March).

ACADEMIC ART

Alamán, Lucas
1942 *Disertaciones sobre la historia de la República mexicana*. México, Editorial Jus, 3 volúmenes.

Arnaiz y Freg, Antonio
1938 "Noticias sobre la Academia de San Carlos," *Anales del Instituto de Investigaciónes Estéticas*, I, número 2, 21–43.

Baxter, Sylvester
1901 *Spanish-colonial Architecture in Mexico*. Boston, J. B. Millet.

Calderon de la Barca, Frances Erskine
1843 *Life in Mexico*. London.
1940 E.P. Dutton and Company, New York.
(2nd ed.)

Carillo y Gariel, Abelardo
1939 "El arte en México de 1781 a 1863," *Datos sobre la Academia de San Carlos*. México, Instituto Nacional de Antropología e Historia.

Charlot, Jean
1945 "Juan Cordero, muralista mexicana," *Hoy*, número 442 (agosto 11).
1946 "Juan Cordero, a Nineteenth-Century Mexican Muralist," *The Art Bulletin*, XXVIII, número 4.
1962 *Mexican Art and the Academy of San Carlos: 1785–1915*. Texas Pan-American Series. Austin, University of Texas Press.

Couto, José Bernardo
1889 *Diálogo sobre la historia de la pintura en Mexico*. México, Secretaría de Fomento.
1947 ———— (2nd ed.). México, Edición crítica de Manuel Toussaint. México, Universidad Nacional Autónoma de México.

Covarrubias, Miguel
1940 "Modern Art," *Twenty Centuries of Mexican Art* (Catalogue), New York, Museum of Modern Art, pp. 137–145.

Delafosse, Jean Charles
1768 *Cronología historique* (San Carlos Library, México). Paris.

Farías y Alvarez del Castillo, Ixca
1940 *Biografía de pintores jaliscienses, 1882–1940*. Guadalajara, Editorial Ricardo Delgado.

Fernández, Justino
1937 *El arte moderno en Mexico: breve historia, siglos XIX y XX*. México, J. Porrua y Hijos.

1940 "De la crítica del arte en México: Ignacio Manuel Altamirando, 1880," *Letras de Mexico*, II, número 15, 9–11.
1945 "La crítica de Felipe López López a las pinturas de la cúpula del templo de la profesa, actualmente desaparecidas," *Anales del Instituto de Investigaciones Estéticas*, IV, número 13.
1952 *Arte moderno y contemporáneo de México*. México, Universidad Nacional Autónoma de Mexico, Instituto de Investigaciones Estéticas.

Fernández Villa, Agustín
1879 *Un folleto sobre la pintura en México*. Privately printed.

Flandrau, Charles Macomb
1909 *Viva México*. New York, D. Appleton and Company.
1951 New York, Harper.
(2nd ed.)

Flores Guerrero, Raul
1954 "Los muralistas del Siglo XIX," *Artes de Mexico*, No. 4, pp. 31–56.

Galinda y Villa, Jesús
1913 "Reseñe histórica de la academia nacional de bellas artes, antigua de San Carlos," *Anales de la Academia Nacional de Bellas Artes de México*, I, número 1 (julio), 9–32.

Gonzales, Agustín
1874 "Francisco Eduardo Tresguerras," *Hombres ilustres*, III, 105–112.

Gonzales Obregón, Luis
1911 *La vida en México en 1810*. México, Vda de C. Bouret.

Hammicken y Mexia, Jorge
1847 "El arte y el siglo," *La Revista Mensual*, I.

Humboldt, Alexander von
1810 *Vues des Cordilléres et Monuments des Peuples Indigénes de l'Amérique*. Paris.
1811 *Political Essay on the Kingdom of New Spain*. London, 4 volumes, John Black (trans.).

Keen, Benjamin
1955 *Readings in Latin-American Civilizations: 1492 to the Present* (Chaps. XXIII, XXIV), 250–276.

López López, Felipe
1868 *Juicio crítica sobre las pinturas de la cúpula del templo de la profesa, dirigidas por D. Pelegrín Clavé y ejecutadas en su mayor parte por los alumnos de la Academia de Bellas Artes de San Carlos*. México, Imprenta de "La Constitución Social."
1874 "Pintura al templo ejecutado por el distinguido artista Juan Cordero . . . ," *El federalista*, número 1347.
1874 ————. Reprinted as Appendix in *Poesías y discursos leidos en la festividad en que la Escuela Nacional Preparatoria laureado el eminente artista, Don Juán Cordero*.

Márquez, P. Pedro José
1801 *Discurso sobre el bello en general*. La estética indígena, Madrid.

Martí, José
1940 "Arte en México, 1875–1876," *Martí en Mexico*, III, 1–261.

Méndez Plancarte, Gabriel
1945 *Hidalgo, reformador intelectual*. México, Ediciones Letras de México.

Mexico y sus Alrededores. Colección de vistas, trajes, y monumentos.
1856– Litografías por Casimiro Castro, J. Campillo, L.
1857 Auda, y G. Rodríguez. Mexico, Establecimiento Litográfica Decaen.
1961 Second edition, Mexico, Editorial Centenaria.

Montenegro, Roberto
1933 *Mexican Painting, 1800–1860*. New York & London.

Revilla, Manuel G.
1893 *El arte en México en la época antigua y durante el govierno virreinal*. México, Oficina tipográfica de la Secretaría de Fomento.

Reyes Zavala, Ventura
1882 *Bellas artes en Jalisco.*

Romero de Terreros y Vinent, Manuel
1927 "El arquitecto Tresguerras, 1745–1783," *Anales del Museo Nacional*, V, número 1, 326–345.

Toscano, Salvador
1946 *Juan Cordero y la pintura mexicana en el siglo XIX*. Monterrey, Universidad de Nuevo Leon.

Toussaint, Manuel
1934 *La litográfia en México en el siglo XIX*. México, Estudios Neolitho.
1949 *Arte colonial en México: Parte V: 1781–1821*. México, Universidad Nacional Autónoma de Mexico, Instituto de Investigaciones Estéticas.

Valdés, Padre Octavio
194– *Biografía de Fray Francisco Templeque. La deca-*
(?) *dencia del arte religioso en México desde el tiempo de Tolsa y neo-clasisismo*. México.

Villela, Juan M.
1874 "La pintura mexicana," *El artista*, Tomo I. México, Zarco, Francisco.

Wolf, Eric R.
1959 *Sons of the Shaking Earth*. Chicago, University of Chicago Press.

PAINTING OF THE PEOPLE

Atl, Dr. See Murillo, Gerardo

Angel, Abraham
1924 *Mexico*. México, Talleres Gráficos de la Nación.

Barber, Edwin Atlee
1908 *The Majolica of Mexico*. Philadelphia, Pennsylvania Museum.

Brenner, Anita
1929 "Painted Miracles," *Arts*, XV (January), 11–18.
1929 "Street Murals in Mexico: *Pulquería* Decoration," XVI, número 3 (November), 163–166.

Cahill, Holger
1933 *American Sources of Modern Art*. New York, The Museum of Modern Art.

Caso, Alfonso
1942 "La protección de las artes populares," *América Indígena*, II, número 3, 25–29.
1950 "Prólogo," *Memorias del Instituto Nacional Indigenista*, I, número 2, 83–86.
1952 "El arte popular mexicano," *México en el arte*, número 12.
1958 "Arte mexicano ó arte en Mexico?" *Indigenismo* I.

Cervantes, Enrique A.
1939 *Loza blanca y azulejos de Puebla*. México.

Charlot, Jean
1923 "Manuel Martínez Pintao," *El Democrata* (agosto 5).
1925 "Un precursor del movimeinto de arte mexicano: el grabador Posada," *Revista de Revistas* (30 de agosto).
1926 "Manuel Manila, grabador mexicano," *Forma*, I, número 2 (noviembre-diciembre), 18–21.
1926 "Pinturas murales mexicanas," *Forma*, I, número 1 (octubre), 10–12.
1945 "José Guadalupe Posada," *Magazine of Art*, (January).

Cortés, Antonio
1935 *Hierros forjados*. México, Museo Nacional de Arqueología, Historia, y Etnografía.

Enciso, Jorge
1933 "Pintura sobre madera en Michoacán y Guerrero," *Mexican Folkways*, VIII, número I (January-March), 3–34.

Fernández Ledesma, Gabriel
1930 *Juguetes mexicanos*. México, Talleres Gráficos de la Nación.

Gamio, Manuel
1939 "Cultural Patterns in Modern Mexico," *Journal of Inter-American Relations*, I, número 2.
1945 "El resurgimiento del arte americano precolombino," *Boletín Indigenista*, V, número 2.

Instituto Nacional Indigenista
1950 *Bibliografía de los artes populares plásticos de Mexico*. México.

León, Francisco de P.
1939 "Los esmaltes de Uruapan," *D.A.P.P.* "Commentaries".

Mena, Ramón
1925 "El zarape." *Anales del Museo Nacional de Arqueología, Historia y Etnografía*, II, época 4.

Montenegro, Roberto
1929 *Máscaras mexicanas*. México, Secretaría de Educación.
1940 "Popular Art," *Twenty Centuries of Mexican Art*, pp. 109–112.

Murillo, Gerardo
1922 *Los artes populares en Mexico*. México, Secretaría de Industria y Comercio.
1923 *Mexican Folk Arts*. México.
1927 "Los retablos del señor del hospital," *Forma*, I, número 3, 17–20.

Nuñez y Dominguez, José de Jesús
1918 *El reboso*. Dir. de Bellas Artes.

Rivera, Diego
1926 "Retablos," *Mexican Folkways*. México, Talleres Gráficos de la Nación.
1926 "Popular Portraits," *Mexican Folkways*. México, Talleres Gráficos de la Nación.
1930 *Monografía; las obras de José Guadalupe Posada*. México, Talleres Gráficos de la Nación.

Romero de Terreros, Manuel
1923 *Las artes industriales en la Nueva España*. México, Editorial Pedro Robredo.

Secretaría de Educación Pública
1926 "Asimilando," *Forma*, I, número 2.

Toor, Frances
1928 "Guadalupe Posada," *Mexican Folkways*, IV, número 3.
1939 *Mexican Popular Arts*. México, F. Toor Studios.
1947 *Treasury of Mexican Folkways*. New York, Crown Publishers.

MURAL REVOLUTION

The Period

Beals, Carleton
1931 *Mexican Maze*. Philadelphia and London, J. B. Lippincott Company.
1932 *Porfirio Díaz, Dictator of Mexico*. Philadelphia and London, J. B. Lippincott Company.

Brenner, Anita, and George Leighton
1943 *The Wind That Swept Mexico*. New York, Harper and Brothers.

Chase, Stewart
1931 *Mexico: A Study of Two Americas*. New York, Macmillan.

Herring, Hubert
1942 *The Making of a Nation*. New York, The Foreign Policy Association.

Keen, Benjamin
1955 *Readings in Latin-American Civilization: 1492 to the Present*, Chapter XXIX, pp. 349–370.

Plenn, A. H.
1939 *Mexico Marches*. Indianapolis, Bobbs-Merrill.

Reyes, Alfonso
1964 *Mexico in a Nutshell* and *Other Essays*. Trans. Charles Ramsdell, University of California Press.

Strode, Hudson
1944 *Timeless Mexico*. New York, Harcourt, Brace and Company.

Tannenbaum, Frank
1929 *The Mexican Agrarian Revolution*. New York, The Macmillan Company.
1933 *Peace by Revolution*. New York, Columbia University Press.

The Paintings

Alba, Victor
1957 "Coloquios con Rufino Tamayo: el arte moderno y su porvenir," *Cuadernos*, XXII, 98–103.

Alfaro Siqueiros, David
1921 "Manifesto a los pintores de America," *Vida americana*, número 1.
1931 *Trece grabados en madera*. Text by W. Spratling. Taxco, Guerrero.
1949– *Crítica de la crítica del arte*. México, *Excelsior*.
1950
1950 "El muralismo de Mexico," *Enciclopedia mexicana de arte*, número 8.
1952 "Quelque Concepts Fundamentaux de Siqueiros sur l'Arte," *Mexico en el arte*, 235–248.
1954 "Retorno al arte mayor," *Artes de Mexico*, números 5 and 6, pp. 126–132.

Arenal, Angélica
1951 "La plástica ciudadena de Siqueiros," *Hoy*, número 741 (mayo 5), 55, 66.

Arriaga Ochoa, Antonio
1961 "Una lección de historia en el Castillo de Chapultepec," *Boletín del Instituto Nacional de Antropología e Historia*, número 3.

Best-Maugard, Adolfo
1923 *Método de dibujo: tradición, resurgimiento y evolución del arte mexicano*. México, Secretaría de Educación Pública.

Brenner, Anita
1926 "David Alfaro Siqueiros: un verdadero rebelde en arte," *Forma*, I, número 2 (noviembre), 23–25.
1929 *Idols Behind Altars*. New York, Payson.
1932 *Your Mexican Holiday*. New York and London, G. P. Putnam's Sons.

Cardoza y Aragon, Luis
1934 *Monografía de la obra de Rufino Tamayo*. México, Instituto Nacional de Bellas Artes.
1934 *Monografía: la obra de Carlos Mérida*. México, Instituto Nacional de Bellas Artes.
1937 *José Clemente Orozco: pinturas murales en la Universidad de Guadalajara*. México, Mundial.
1950 *Orozco*. Universidad Nacional Autónoma de México, Talleres Gráficos de Editorial Forimier.

1954   "Pintura mural contemporanea," *Artes de Mexico,* número 5, (diciembre).

Castellanos, Julio
1931   "Dibujos de Castellanos," *Contemporaneos,* II, números 40–41 (septiembre-octubre), 133–138.

Charlot, Jean
1924   "Las pinturas de la Escuela Nacional Preparatoria," *Eureka,* journal de los estudiantes de la Preparatoria.
1926   "Pinturas murales mexicanas," *Forma,* I, número 1 (octubre), 10–12.
1927   "Grabados en madera," *Forma,* I, número 5, 25–28.
1928   "José Clemente Orozco, su obra monumental," *Forma,* II, número 6 (junio), 32–51.
1931   "Obras de Jean Charlot," *Contemporáneos,* XI, número 37, 211–215.
1941   "Public Speaking in Paint," *American Scholar,* Autumn.
1945   "Rufino Tamayo," *Magazine of Art* (April).
1945   "Murals for Tomorrow," *Art News* (July 31).
1946   "Prehistoric Quota in Mexican Murals," *Kenyon Review,* VIII, number 1 (Winter), 3–13.
1946   "Renaissance Revisited," *Magazine of Art* (February).
1947   "An Aztec Artist, Xavier Guerrero," *Magazine of Art.*
1947   "José Clemente Orozco," *Magazine of Art* (November), 259–263.
1949–1950   "Orozco's Stylistic Evolution." *College Art Journal,* (Winter).
1950   *Art-Making from Mexico to China.* New York, Sheed and Ward.
1950   "Diego Rivera at the Academy of San Carlos," *College Art Journal.* Fall number.
1963   *The Mexican Mural Renaissance: 1920–1925.* New Haven, Yale University Press.

Charlot, Jean, and David Alfaro Siqueiros (Ing. Araujo)
1923   "El movimiento contemporaneo de la pintura de México," *El Demócrata,* July, August.

Chávez, Dr. Ignacio
1946   *Frescoes de Diego Rivera en Cardiología.* México.

Covarrubias, Miguel
1940   "Modern Art," *Twenty Centuries of Mexican Art,* pp. 137–145.

Crespo de la Serna, Jorge
1949   "Presencia inmortal de Orozco: las ideas y las formas," *Excelsior.*
1952   "Les Circonstances et L'Evolution des Arts Plastiques au Mexique, Pendant la Periode de 1900–1950," *México en el arte,* pp. 161–202.

Dickerson, Albert I.
1934   *The Orozco Frescoes at Dartmouth.* Hanover, New Hampshire, Dartmouth College.

Edwards, Emily
1932   *Frescoes of Diego Rivera in Cuernavaca.* México, Editorial Cultura.

1934   *Modern Mexican Frescoes: Guide and Map.* México, Central News Agency.

Evans, Ernestine
1929   *The Frescoes of Diego Rivera.* New York, Harcourt, Brace and Company.

Farías y Alvarez del Castillo, Ixca
1940   *Biografías de pintores jaliscienses, 1882–1940.* Guadalajara, Jalisco, Editorial Ricardo Delgado.

Faure, Elie
1934   "La Peinture Murale Mexicaine," *Art et Medicine* (April).

Fernández, Justino
1937   *El arte moderno en México: breve historia, siglos XIX y XX.* México, J. Porrúa y Hijos.
1942   "José Clemente Orozco," *Forma e Idea.*
1945   *Prometeo, ensayo sobre pintura contemporánea.* México, Editorial Porrúa.
1952   *Arte moderno y contemporáneo de Mexico.* México, Universidad Nacional Autónoma de México, Instituto de Investigaciones Estéticas.
1952   "Oeuvres Recentes d'Orozco," *México en el arte,* Edition Speciale en Francais, 203–220.

Gamboa, Fernando (Coordinator)
1951   *Diego Rivera: 50 años de su Labor Artística.* Exposición de Homenaje Nacional. Monograph: Symposium, Illustrated with photographs based on exposition in 1949. Museo Nacional de Artes Plásticas.

Gamio, Manuel
1916   *Forjando patria.* México, Porrúa Hermanos.
1929   La población del valle de México. 3 volumes.

García Maroto, Gabriel
1927   "La revolución artística mexicana: una lección," *Forma,* I, número 4, 8–16.
1928   "La obra de Diego Rivera," *Contemporáneos,* I (junio).

Greuning, Ernest
1924   "The Mexican Renaissance," *Century Magazine* (February).
1928   "Mexico and Its Heritage," *Century Magazine.*

Guzmán, Martín Luís
1916   *Diego Rivera y la filosofía del cubismo.* México.
1946   "Viñetas de Alfredo Zalce," Colección *Lunes,* número 25.

Hale, Gardner
1933   *Fresco Painting.* New York, W. E. Rudge.

Helm, MacKinley
1941   *Modern Mexican Painters.* New York, Harper & Bros.
1953   *Man of Fire: J. C. Orozco.* New York, Harcourt, Brace and Company.

Herring, Hubert C., and Herbert Weinstock
1935   *Renascent Mexico.* New York, Covici Friede.

Kirsten, Lincoln
1943   "Siqueiros in Chillán," *Magazine of Art,* XXXVI, No. 8, 283–287.

Koningsberger, Hans
1962 "Mexican Murals," *The New Yorker* (September 8), 114.

Lazo, Agustín
1926 "Máximo Pacheco," *Forma*, I, número 2 (noviembre), 3–6.

Leighton, Frederick W.
1923 "Pro-Proletarian Art in Mexico," *The Liberator* (December).
1924 "Rivera's Mural Paintings." *International Studio*, CXXVIII, número 321 (February 24).

Méndez, Leopoldo (ed.)
1960 *La pintura de la revolución mexicana, 1921–1960*. México, Fondo Editorial de la Plástica Mexicana.

Mérida, Carlos
1937 *Modern Mexican Artists*. México, F. Toor Studios.
1940 *Rivera Frescoes in Cuernavaca*. México, F. Toor Studios.
1940 *Ten Interpretive Guides to Mexican Frescoes*. México, F. Toor Studios.
1940 *Orozco's Frescoes in Guadalajara*. México, F. Toor Studios.

Miz de Sen
1960 "Biografía de un mural," *Novedades*, (29 de mayo).

Montenegro, Roberto
1930 *Veinte litografías de Taxco*. México, Murciélago.

Neumeyer, Alfred
1951 "Orozco," *College Art Journal*, X, número 2.

Norman, James
1953 "Juan O'Gorman's Mosaic Mural," *American Artist*, XVII, número 6 (summer), 62–67, 83–84.
1953 "Mexican Murals," *American Artist*, (February 24).
1956 "The Shouting Walls–Mexico's Outdoor Murals," *The Nation* (February 25), 159–160.
1956 "Shiny Showplace for Studies," *Life* (December 3), 102–105.

Novo, Salvador
1926 "Las escuelas al aire libre," *Forma*, I, número 1 (octubre), 16–17.

O'Gorman, Juan
1950 *Homenaje a Orozco*. (October 1).

Orozco, José Clemente
1940 *Orozco Explains*. New York, Museum of Modern Art.
1945 *Autobiografía*. México, Ediciones Occidente; Eng. tr., Austin: University of Texas Press, 1962.
1947 "Notas acerca de la técnica de la pintura mural en Mexico en los últimos 25 años," *Catálogo: José Clemente Orozco Exposición Nacional*. México, Instituto Nacional de Bellas Artes, Secretaría de Educación Pública.

Pach, Walter
1923 "Masters of Modern Art," *The Freeman*.

1927 "L'Art Au Mexique," *L'Amour de L'Art*, VIII (March), 85–89.
1929 "The Revolution in Painting: The Evolution of Diego Rivera," *Creative Art*.

Pellicer Cámara, Carlos
1961 Introducción, *La pintura de la Revolución Mexicana*. México, Fondo de Cultura Económica. Photographs by Manuel Alvarez Bravo.
1962 ———. English Edition. México.

Plenn, Abel
1934 "Fermín Revueltas," *Mexican Life*, X, número 3.

Plenn, Virginia y Jaime
1963 *The Guide to Modern Mexican Murals*. México, Ediciones Tolteca, S.A.

Ramos, Samuel
1935 *Diego Rivera*. México, Mundial.
1952 "L'Esthetique de Diego Rivera," *Mexico en el arte*, Edition Speciale en Francais, 221–234.

Reed, Alma
1932 *Orozco: A Book of Reproductions*. New York, Delphic Studios.

Rivera, Diego
1925 "From a Painter's Note Book," *The Arts* (January).
1926 "Autobiografía," *El arquitecto* (marzo-abril).
1926 "Projecto de Diego Rivera para un teatro," *Forma*, I, número 5 (octubre), 36–38.
1926 "El renacimiento del fresco en Mexico," *Forma*, I, número 6, 32–51.
1929 "The Revolution in Painting," *Creative Art*, (January).
1931 *Genius of America*. Commission on Cultural Relations with Latin America.
1933 *Frescoes of Diego Rivera*. New York, Museum of Modern Art.
1933 "What is Art For?" *Modern Monthly*, (June).
1933 "Art and the Worker," *Working Age* (June 15).
1934 "Architecture and Mural Painting," *Architectural Forum*, LX, No. 1 (January), 1–16.
1934 (with Bertram D. Wolfe) *Portrait of America*. New York, Govici-Friede.
1935 *Raices políticos y motivos personales de la controversía Siqueiros-Rivera*. México, Editorial Mundial.
1937 (with Bertram D. Wolfe) *Portrait of Mexico*. New York, Covici-Friede.
1938 (with André Breton) "Towards a Free Revolutionary Art," *Partisan Review* (Autumn).
1949 *Diego Rivera: cincuenta años de su labor artística: Exposición de homenaje nacional*. México, Museo Nacional de Artes Plásticas.

Rodríguez, Antonio
1954 "La pintura mural: eje del desarrollo artística de México en el siglo XX," *Artes de México*, 5 y 6, pp. 16–26.

Rodríguez-Lozano, Manuel
1927 "Reproductions," *Forma*, I, número 4, 1–15.

BIBLIOGRAPHY

Schmeckebier, Lawrence
 1924 "Orozco," *International Studio* (March).
 1929 "Arte y Revolución," *El universal* (marzo 7).
 1933 "The Frescoes of Orozco," *Mexican Life*, IX, número 3.
 1939 *Modern Mexican Art*, Minneapolis, University of Minneapolis Press.

Schmidt, James Norman (pseud.) see Norman, James

Sherwell, Guillermo
 1922 "Modern Tendencies in Mexican Art," *Bulletin of Pan-American Union*, CV, No. 4 (October).

Siqueiros, David. See Alfaro Siqueiros, David

Tablada, José Juan
 1927 *Historia del arte en México*. México, Aguiles.

Taller Gráfico Popular: Contemporary Lithographs. Liga de Escritores y Artistas Revolucionarios.

Toor, Frances
 1940 *Guide to Mexico*. New York, McBride.

Toscano, Salvador
 1950 "Julio Castellanos," *Mexico en el arte*, número 9, 69–74.

Velásquez Chávez, Agustín
 1935 *Indice de la pintura mexicana contemporanea*. México, Arte mexicano.
 1937 *Contemporary Mexican Artists*. New York, Covici-Friede.

Villaurrutia, Xavier
 1927 "Historia de Diego Rivera," *Forma*, I, número 5 (enero), 29–52.
 1952 "Rufino Tamayo," *Mexico en el arte*. Edition Speciale en Francais, 249–260.

Weston, Edward
 1961 *The Daybooks of Edward Weston. I*. Rochester, New York, George Eastman House.

Wolfe, Bertram D.
 1924 "Art and Revolution in Mexico," *Nation*, CXIX, No. 3086 (August 27), 207–208.
 1939 *Diego Rivera: His Life and Times*. New York and London, A. Knopf.

Wolfe, Bertram D. (with Diego Rivera)
 1937 *Portrait of Mexico*. New York, Covici-Friede.

Zalce, Alfredo
 1946 "Viñetas de Alfredo Zalce," (Guzman) Colección: *Lunes* 25. México.

INDEX

Note: Since many Mexican murals are not technically entitled, the author identified them by phrases indicating content. These subject terms appear in the text, and in this Index, bearing indication as names of murals by use of initial caps only, without italics.

Juárez, Benito: revival of Mexican Revolution by, 126: as President, 127, 264; rise of, 132; Reform Laws of, 145, 205, 260; mentioned 225, 255, 259, Plate 252

Juárez and Independent Mexico: 259, Plate 252

Judith (Old Testament woman): 134, 140

Justice and the Law: 183

Kahlo, Frida: 225
Kingsborough, Lord: 126
Kitagawa, Tamiji: 225
Knights of the Eagle: 38, 55, 75, 77, 106, 108, 205
Knights of the Jaguar (Tiger): 29, 75, 106, 107, 108, Plates 80, 83
Knights of the Sun: 38
Kubler, George: on Mexican murals, 65

La Asunción (parish church, near Tizatlan, Tlaxcala): 69
La Barca, Jalisco: murals in, 138, 164, Plates 105, 106, 107
Labor: depicted, 188
Laboratory of Microbiology and Bacteriology, Ministry of Health: 204
Lacandon Indians: 47
Lacanhá River: 47
La Collada, Oaxaca, Oaxaca: 92, Plate 63
Lake Patzcuaro: 110
Lake Region: 16th- and 17th-century art in, 110–112
Lake Yuriria: 112
La Merced, San Cristóbal las Casas, Chiapas: 96
Landlord Weighing the Grain: 187
Landscape with Airplane: 148, Plate 113
La Parroquia (parish church), Alpuyeca, Morelos: 156–158, Plates 129, 130, 131, 132
La Profesa (Parish Church), México, D.F.: 127, 132
La Purificación (Colonial Museum), Malinalco, México: 109, Plate 84
Lascurain, don Ramón: as director of Academy of San Carlos, 127
La Señora de la Encarnación, convent of: 184
Las Monjas, Chichén Itzá: 50, 54
Last Judgment: 78, 104, 134–136, Plate 101
Last Supper, the: 89, 161
Law and Justice: 183
Leaders of the Revolution: 274, Plate 263
Leal, Antonio: as Minister of Education, 227
Leal, Fernando: recruited as muralist, 171; work of, 175–178, 217, Plates 149, 202; painted by Charlot, 176, Plate 148
LEAR (Liga de Escritores y Artistas Revolucionarios): 216
Leaving the Mine: 187, Plate 164
Ledesma, Gabriel Fernández (painter): 256
Lenin: 227
Lenin as Leader: 225
LePlongeon, Augustus: 52

Lerma River: 261
Liberals: 126
Liberation of Children through Education: 220
"Liberators": 170
Liberators of Mexico: 271
Liberty Swinging: 183
Library, Secretaría de Educación Pública: 185
Lic. Sanitaria No. 3777, México, D.F.: 148, Plates 111, 112
Life: 204, Plate 188
Life and Conscience: 231
Life and Death: 220, 269
Life and Death of Christ: 114
Life and Earth: 196, Plate 179
Life of Simón Bolívar: 217
Life of St. Elias: 114
Life of St. Francis: 72, 110
Life of the Virgin: 77, 160
Liga de Escritores y Artistas Revolucionarios (Union of Revolutionary Writers and Artists): 216
Linati, Claudio (Italian artist): 126
Lincoln Library, Orientation High School: 194
Linné, Sigvald: 18, 104
Lions: 148, 158, 175, Plates 111, 136
Liquidation of Capitalist Power: 227
Liquidation of Revolution and Its Superstitions: 227
Litany of the Virgin: 136
lithography: 127
Little Red Riding Hood: 185
Little Tollan: 34
Little White Horse: 40
Loaves and Fishes, miracle of: 88
Logos, First Principle: 175
López, Pedro (provincial artist): 160
López Carmona, Armando: 257
López López, Felipe: 132, 133
López Mateos, Alfredo (President): 274
Lord of Tacuba: 256
Los Cuatro Grandes: 266
Los Doce ("The Twelve"): 64, 72, 81, 83, Plate 49
Los Dos Grandes: 227
Los Tres Grandes: 256
Lottery: 126
Lovers on Horseback: 164, Plate 145
Lower California: rock paintings in, 7
Lübeck Bible: 75
Lunch in the Rain: 190, Plate 171
Lunch Time: 200, Plate 185

"Machete, El": 172
Madelena, Querétaro: murals in, 163–164
Madero, Francisco (President): 170
Magdalen: 78
magic: sacred sites for, 7; instruments of, 9, 24
Main Reading Room, Library, Ministry of Public Education: 185
Majorca: 171
Making Pottery: 187
Maler, Teobert (explorer): 46, 50, 52, 58
Malinalco, México: murals in, 38, 109, Plate 84

Malinche (volcano): 13
Man at the Crossroads: 226, 228, Plates 212, 213, 214
Manifesto a los Plásticos de América: 171
Manila: 65
Man in Control of the Forces of Nature through Machinery: 219
Man of Our Epoch: 256
Mansion of the Sun above the Earth ("the divine land of war"): 38
Man Struggling with a Gorilla: 181
Man the Creator: 232
Manzanillo: 173
Margain, Carlos (archeologist): 47
Marina, Doña (Malinche): helper of Cortés, 63, 184
Marketing Tropical Fruit: 187
Markets, Industries, and Arts of the Aztecs: 249
Marquina, Ignacio: about Great Pyramid of Cholula, 13
Marriage Day of an Indian Girl: 275, Plate 267
Martínez, Fray José: 70
Martínez de Pocasangre, Miguel Antonio: 116
Martyrs of Mexican Independence: 188
Marx, Karl: 205, 227
Mary (mother of Jesus): 78, 86, 113, 130, Plate 90. SEE ALSO Virgin, the
Masques of Death: 190
Mass of St. Gregory: 72, 97
Mata, Philomino: as director of Painting, Academy of San Carlos, 126
Matamoras, Puebla: 89
Maternity: 181, 263, Plate 155
Matlatzinca Indians: 38, 109
Matos, Eduardo: 31
Maudsley, A. P.: on Chichén Itzá paintings, 50; and Temple of the Tigers, 54
Maximilian: fall of empire of, 145, 259; capture of, 163; mentioned, 46, 126, 132, 271, 272
Mayahuel, Goddess of the Maguey Plant: 33, 36, Plate 21
Mayan God of War: 48
Mayan Gods: 57, Plate 31
Mayan-Toltec culture: 50, 57, 58
Mayas: art of, 8, 45, 172, 200; civilization of, 8, 264; temples of, 9; language of, 12, 37, 63; land of the, 45, 158; agricultural Olympus of, 57; missionaries to, 64; ruins of, 126; motifs of, 185; mentioned, 96. SEE ALSO Southeastern Mexico
Mechanical Warriors: 234, Plate 225
Mechanics: 231
Medicine as Fruit of Earth: 269
Mediterranean culture: 64
Méndez, Leopoldo: 24, 225, 257, Plate 211
mendicant orders: SEE Augustinians; Barefoot Carmelites; Dominicans; Franciscans

Nagasaki: 86
Nahua: as culture of Toltecs, 32, 39
Nahuatl (language): 12, 32, 63, 75
Napoleon III: 126
Nacional, El: as organ of Revolutionary Government, 217
National Academy of San Carlos: becomes Imperial Academy, 126; director of Architecture of, 128; during Mural Revolution, 169, 170; strike against, 170; mentioned, 126, 127, 129, 134
National Conservatory of Music: 219, Plate 203
National Heritage: 276
National Institute of Anthropology and History: 8, 29, 33, 47, 275
National Institute of Fine Arts of Mexico: 47
Nationalist Revolution: 205
Nationalists: 126
Nationalization of the Poza Rica Properties: 271
National Mortgage Bank: 219
National Museum of Anthropology: 274–275, Plates, 265, 266, 267
National Museum of History: 259, 272–274; Plates 252, 262, 263
National Preparatory School: 113, 170, 172, 194, 217
National Stadium: 193
National Theatre: 169
National University: 263
Native Women in a Landscape: 185
Nativity: 97, 136
Negro Man: 262
Neri de Alfaro, Luis Felipe: 114, 116, 118
New Chichén, Yucatán: 50
New Fire of the Aztecs: 80
New Order Ascending: 256
New Redemption (Christ Destroys His Cross): 181
New School: 187
New Society: 268
New Spain: capitol of, 63; preaching friars in, 64; painting of, 87; amalgamation of races and cultures in, 123
New York, New York: 170
Nishizawa, Luis: 269
Noguchi, Isamu: 224
Noguera, Eduardo: on Xochicalco, 44
North America: 7
Northern Central Highlands: 16th- and 17th-century art in, 96–108; *arte popular* in, 160–162
Northern Mayan Empire: 46, 49
Northern Mexico: 8
Northwest Colonnade, Chichén Itzá: 51
Novo, J.: 163
Nuestra Señora de la Asunción (Cathedral), Cuernavaca, Morelos: 85–87, Plates 53, 54, 55
Nuevo Laredo: 265
Nun Practicing Abstinence: 136, Plate 104
Nutrition and Disease: 223

Oaxaca, Oaxaca: city of, 8, 39; art of, 12; Valley of, 40; 16th- and 17th-century art in, 89–94; mentioned, 39, 96, 225

Oaxtepec, Morelos: murals in, 87–88, Plates 56, 57, 58
Obregón, General Alvaro: Constitutional Army under, 170; as President, 171, 203; monument to, 219; mentioned, 205
Obregón Santacilla, Carlos (architect): 204
October Revolution: Tenth Anniversary of, 200
Officer, Banker, and Priest: 229
O'Gorman, Juan: as artist, 217, 220, 236, 241, 256–257, 272, Plates 229, 230; as architect, 263; mosaics by, 265; mentioned, 216
O'Higgins, Pablo: Rivera assisted by, 190; work of, 220, 224, 241, 257, 262, 271, 275, Plates 208, 210, 267
Old Order Descending: 256
Old Testament: as source for murals, 75; scenes from, 140
Old World: conception of beauty of, 9; art tradition of, 65, 145
Olmecs, Archeological: 12
Olmecs, Historic: 12, 36
Omniscience: 194
One Day in the Year: 148, Plate 109
On the Way to Heaven: 156, Plate 131
Open-Air School: 219, Plate 205
Open-Air Theatre of the National Normal School: 257, 261, Plates 248, 249
Orient, the: 145
Orientation High School: 194
Orizaba, Peak of: 13
Orizaba, Veracruz: murals in, 198–199, Plates 182, 183; mentioned, 170, 172
Orozco, José Clemente: on Dr. Atl, 169; some works of, 169, 194, 198, 272; 1916 exhibition of, 170; leaves Mexico, 170, 172, 200; returns to Mexico, 171, 227; as contributor to *El Machete*, 172; work of at Escuela Nacional Preparatoria, 178–184; on Jean Charlot, 189; goes to U.S., 200; in Europe, 216; work at Palacio de Bellas Artes, 227–228; in Guadalajara, 229, 231–235; in Jiquilpan, Michoacan, 236; work of, from 1941–1947, 243–245; death of, 245; last murals of, 257–261; on mural painting, 261; mentioned, 127, 256, 266, 274, 276, Plates 154, 155, 156, 157, 158, 159, 160, 161, 162, 215, 216, 221, 222, 224, 225, 226, 227, 228, 231, 232, 233, 234
Orozco Romero, Carlos: 170, 199
Otomis: language of, 12; Augustinians in country of, 64; as warriors, 108; mentioned, 96, 160, 163
Otumba: 80
Our Lady of the Assumption, Cuernavaca, Morelos: 85–87, Plates 53, 54, 55
Ozumba, México: 81–83

Pacheco, Máximo: as assistant to Fermín Revueltas, 179; as only muralist of Mexican government, 200; work of, 216–217, 223, Plate 185; mentioned, 171
Pachuca, Hidalgo: 97, 100
Paddock, John: on tomb at Zaachila: 45

Painter's Syndicate: 188
Palacio, El, Palenque: 46
Palacio de Bellas Artes (Palace of Fine Arts), México, D.F.: Rivera's and Orozco's work in, 227–228; Siqueiro's work in, 256; Tamayo's work in, 266; mentioned, 169; murals shown, Plates 212, 213, 214, 215, 245, 246, 247, 256, 257
Palacio de Cortés (state Capitol), Cuernavaca, Morelos: 209–215, Plates 196, 197, 198, 199, 200, 201
Palacio de Gobierno, Guadalajara, Jalisco: 199, 232, Plates 222, 223
Palacio de Gobierno, Morelia, Michoacan, 271
Palacio de Gobierno (State Capitol), Chilpancingo, Guerrero: 271
Palacio de Justicia de la Nación, S.E. of Zócalo (Supreme Court), México, D.F.: 243, Plates 231, 232
Palacio de Quetzalpapalotl, Teotihuacan: 30–31, Plate 16
Palacio de Xicotencatl, Tizatlan: 35–37, 69, Plates 34, 35, 36
Palacio en Plaza del Sol, Teotihuacan: 32
Palacio Municipal (City Hall), Poza Rica, Veracruz: 271
Palacio Nacional, Zócalo (National Palace), México, D.F.: 204–205, 228–229, 248–249, Plates 192, 193, 194, 217, 218, 219, 220, 237, 238, 239, 240, 241, 242
Palacio Real, México, D.F.: 83
Palenque, Chiapas: 46
Panel of the Hats: 274, Plate 264
Pani, Mario (architect): 257
Pantecatl, the Pulque God: 33
Pantocrator (All-Ruler): 175
Panuco River: 34
Papaloapan River: 13
Papantla, Veracruz: 32
Paradise: vision of, 112
Paris: 134, 169, 170, 171
Parra, Felix: 133
Parrás, Coahuila: murals near, 164
parrot: paintings of, 24, Plate 9
Passion of Christ: 87, 88, 100, 104, 109, 116, Plates 56, 91
Passion of Jesus: 98, Plates 69, 70, 71, 72, 73
Patio Chico, Escuela Nacional Preparatoria, México, D.F.: 179
Patio Grande, Escuela Nacional Preparatoria, México, D.F.: 175–184, Plates 147, 148, 149, 150, 151, 154, 155, 156, 157, 158, 159, 160, 161, 162
Patio of Festivals. SEE Second Patio, Ministry of Public Education
Patio of Work. SEE First Patio, Ministry of Public Education
Patzcuaro, Michoacan: murals in, 236–241, Plates 229, 230
Paz, Octavio (poet): about the Mexican Revolution, 146
Peabody Museum: 46, 50
Peace: 184
Peak of Orizaba (volcano): 39
Peak of Toluca: 33
Pedagogy Building: 269